THE WORLD'S WORST
CRiMiNALS

THE WORLD'S WORST CRIMINALS

Charlotte Greig with PAUL ROLAND,
NATHAN CONSTANTINE and JO DURDEN SMITH

ARCTURUS

Picture credits:

Corbis: 11, 12, 18, 20, 30, 36, 37, 47, 53, 67, 75, 79, 83, 87, 91, 100, 110, 125, 126, 128, 151, 152, 161, 185, 191, 200, 248, 251, 255, 264, 267, 268, 272, 275, 289, 301

Crime Library: 187

Empics: 163, 183, 220, 223, 224, 237, 238, 240, 242, 257, 259, 273, 280

Getty: 32, 54, 89, 90, 94, 103, 118, 164, 169, 189, 232, 246, 276, 296

Kobal: 150

PA Photos: 84

Rex: 48, 61, 76, 101, 131, 132, 134, 192, 195, 208, 215, 256, 263, 285

Shutterstock: 198, 283

Topfoto: 9, 16, 25, 27, 28, 41, 42, 43, 45, 51, 52, 65, 74, 81, 95, 96, 99, 104, 105, 108, 113, 117, 120, 136, 138, 143, 145, 147, 155, 156, 157, 165, 166, 173, 175, 204, 207, 211, 212, 217, 227, 243, 244, 253, 261, 265, 293, 294, 299, 300

With particular thanks to:

Pima County Sheriff Department, USA for their image on p. 33
The Sumner Item, Tennessee, USA for their image on p121
The Pantagraph, Illinois, USA for their images on pp139–140
Wichita County Sheriff Department USA for their image on p287

ARCTURUS

This edition published in 2012 by Arcturus Publishing Limited
26/27 Bickels Yard, 151–153 Bermondsey Street,
London SE1 3HA

ISBN: 978-1-84193-854-7
AD000487EN

Printed in China

CONTENTS

INTRODUCTION

Anyone who has been on the receiving end of a criminal's attentions will know that all criminals are bad. A pickpocket might be kind to his family, a burglar might be amusing company, a fraudster might be generous to charity. But there is nothing kind, amusing or generous about their crimes. When faced by a 'mark' or 'target', these criminals cast off any positive virtues they might have and behave with a singleminded ruthlessness that makes them a terror to encounter.

But some criminals are in a whole different league. Not for them the vicious pleasure of a broken window or graffitied wall. They have no time for the modest pickings of a household's goods or the payroll contents of a business. Such criminals are after bigger, more sadistic and infinitely more terrible prizes. Few who encounter them get off lightly, few get out alive.

These individuals are the world's worst criminals, and they are the subject of this book.

Some of these unsavoury characters are motivated by a simple greed for wealth. Bugsy Siegel pursued money with a single-minded brutality that left a string of bodies in his wake. As a mafia mastermind he had few equals in either innovative genius or vicious violence. In the end his own colleagues had enough of him and he died in a hail of bullets.

Money also motivated Bonnie and Clyde in their murderous tour of America. But there was something else too. They did not need to kill as often as they did to commit their robberies. Killing was just a simpler way to get what they wanted. Henri Landru, on the other hand, took killing for profit to a quite different degree of professionalism. He lured his many prey with cool efficiency and dispatched them just as calmly.

But not all of the criminals whose misdeeds are found in these pages operate so logically or cleanly. Many are motivated by lustful rages that turn them from outwardly normal humans into beings of unparalleled ferocity and bestial rage. Nobody who knew Ted Bundy in his normal life as a law student could possibly guess that when his urges took over he became a fiend driven by sexual urges to dominate, torture and kill a string of hapless women. Nor was there anything about electrician Dean Corll that tipped off his workmates about the delight he took in torturing teenage boys to death.

Other mass killers are more of a puzzle. Fred and Rosemary West murdered homeless, rootless teenagers in a quiet rural English town for years. Then, unaccountably, they stopped and lived an apparently normal life until the discovery of a body led to their crimes being unearthed. Gerard Schaefer claimed to have murdered dozens, even hundreds of times but investigating police could find no evidence to link him to more than two killings. Was he lying, telling the truth or lost in a manic world where he could no longer tell the difference between truth or lies?

Mad or sane, greedy or lustful, the world's worst criminals have but one thing in common. They are dangerous to meet. And some of them are still out there.

Alberto ANASTASIA

In 1957, nothing became Alberto Anastasia's life so much as his leaving of it. For he lived by violence – and he died by it. The boss of Murder Incorporated, New York's so-called 'Lord High Executioner,' was ultimately executed by those he'd once served. He had, to use a later expression, by then passed his sell-by date. The days of the gun-toting street-fighter were over.

Alberto Anastasia seems to have arrived in New York from Sicily as an illegal immigrant during the First World War.

▶ *Alberto Anastasia, the notorious boss of Murder Inc.*

But he was soon cutting his criminal teeth – like so many other future Mafia leaders – in the gang of Jacob 'Little Augie' Orgen, a New York labour-union racketeer. Orgen's assassination in 1927 split the gang into factions, and Anastasia soon threw in his lot with the three men who were to reshape and reorganize the Mafia on a national basis: Meyer Lansky, Vito Genovese and 'Lucky' Luciano. He became one of their strong-arms and hit-men, alongside 'Bugsy' Siegel; and when the New York Commission – or National Criminal Syndicate – was finally set up, he became the founding father of its enforcement arm, taking responsibility for long-distance contract killings.

In 1940, though, Abe Reles, one of Anastasia's killers-for-hire, turned stoolie and started giving detailed evidence about dozens of murders in which Anastasia was implicated. He went underground; and only re-emerged in November 1941 when Reles had an unfortunate 'accident', falling six floors to his death from the hotel in which the Brooklyn District Attorney had hidden him, under supposed police protection.

No one was ever charged in Reles' death. But the case against Anastasia, with him out of the way, collapsed; and he was free to play his part, after the war and the exile of 'Lucky' Luciano to Italy, in the vicious mob battles for control of

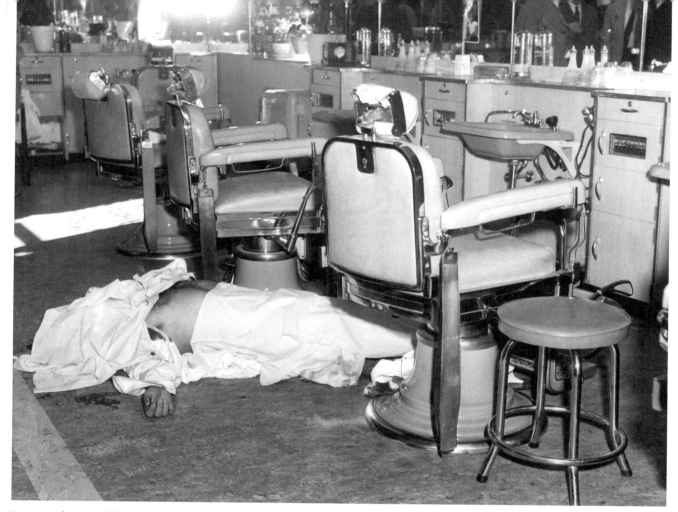

▲ *Last cut: Anastasia died as he had lived – violently*

Luciano's gambling, prostitution and drugs operations in the US. He emerged as head of the Mangano family. But his style of doing business – and his increasing ambition – didn't sit well with the bosses of the other clans. So on 25 October 1957, when Anastasia went down to the basement barber's shop in Manhattan's Park-Sheraton Hotel for his regular haircut, two men followed him and shot him to death with automatic pistols as he sat in the barber's chair. Then they threw down their weapons, went back up to street-level and disappeared.

Ten years later, a Mafia soldier called Joe Valachi claimed that the killing had been ordered by Anastasia's old associate, Vito Genovese, on the grounds that Anastasia had been invading his turf. The members of the Commission had agreed. In the old days, of course, at this point they would have got in touch with Murder Incorporated – and Alberto Anastasia himself.

ARELLANO-FELIX Brothers

Brothers Benjamin and Ramon Arellano-Felix jointly led one of the most successful and bloodthirsty criminal organizations of all time. During the 1990s, they came to dominate the enormously lucrative trade in smuggling drugs – primarily cocaine but also marijuana and amphetamines – into the United States.

Mexico has long been a crucial staging point for drug traffickers, and its proximity to the US meant it had a long history of small-scale smuggling operations. In the 1990s, however, these organizations came under centralized control, dominated by drug-smuggling cartels. The Arellano-Felix organization became the most brutal and feared of all these cartels.

EL MIN AND EL MON

The Arellano-Felix brothers grew up in the coastal province of Sinaloa, near Mazatlan. Their uncle, Miguel Angel Felix Gallardo, ran a drug-trafficking business out of Tijuana, further up the west coast, next to the US border. Before long, the four Arellano-Felix brothers – Benjamin, Ramon, Eduardo and Javier – headed north to work for their uncle. They began by smuggling electronic goods – televisions and so forth – and soon graduated to narcotics. In 1989, Gallardo was arrested and the brothers moved to take over the drug route.

Now that they were in charge, the brothers – in particular Benjamin, the oldest and the natural leader – saw the opportunity for all-out expansion. Their skills were a classic mix for Latin American drug barons – a lethal mixture of ingenuity and brutality. Benjamin was the brains of the operation, a mild-mannered man who could pass for an accountant. His youngest brother, Ramon, was unquestionably the leader when it came to brutality. The two brothers nicknamed each other El Min (Benjamin) and El Mon (Ramon).

The organization the Arellano-Felix brothers built up was known locally as the Tijuana cartel, after the dangerous border town in which they were based. However, the field of operation soon expanded to cover a hundred-mile stretch of the border between Tijuana and Mexicali. The brothers would send their drugs by boat or by car. They also used a secret tunnel. At one stage, the US authorities, acting on a tip-off, searched a farmhouse on the American side of the border. Inside they found an empty safe

that concealed the entrance to a wide, well-lit tunnel that ran for nearly a mile under the border – a literal pipeline for drugs trafficking.

MASSACRE AND MUTILATION

The Tijuana cartel's reputation grew to such a degree that the Drug Enforcement Administration in the US declared it 'one of the most powerful, violent and aggressive drug-trafficking organizations in the world'. Despite the cartel's increasing notoriety, however, the brothers were able to carry on without being arrested for thirteen years. To remain free, they spent an estimated million dollars a week on bribing politicians and policemen. Those who held out, or who were not important enough to need bribing in the first place, were killed. The brothers murdered hundreds – they killed witnesses,

bystanders, policemen, two police chiefs, several federal police commanders, judges and even a Roman Catholic cardinal, Juan Jesus Posadas Ocampo. He was gunned down at the airport in Guadalajara when members of the gang mistook his car for that of a rival drug baron. This misjudgement led them to lower their profile for a little while, but otherwise traffic and terror went on unabated.

Ramon, in particular, became a notorious figure around Tijuana, driving around in a red Porsche, sporting a mink jacket and heavy gold jewellery. He started to recruit a new type of gangster to the business. These were the so-called 'narco-juniors', rich kids who became hit men for fun rather than profit. Meanwhile, the brothers' brutality became ever more extreme. In 1998, they murdered the entire population of a small fishing village to set an example. Torture

▲ *The brains and the brawn behind the Tijuana cartel; 'El Min' (left) and 'El Mon' (right)*

▲ The ignoble end of one of Mexico's most notorious drug trafficers – Ramon Arellano-Felix lies dead on a curb in Sinaloa province

and mutilation became part of their way of working as well. A Tijuana prosecutor named Jose Patino Moreno was kidnapped along with two aides. When their bodies were found, they were unrecognizable. Almost every bone in their bodies had been broken and their heads had been crushed in a vice. Intimidated by the drug traffickers, local police claimed that the three men had died in 'a lamentable traffic incident'. Years later, two policemen would be convicted of involvement in the killings.

THE DAY OF RECKONING

Inevitably, the flamboyant Ramon was the first to die. He got caught up in a shoot-out with a rival drugs gang. After the gun battle the police found three corpses, one

of which carried ID in the name of Jorge Lopez. Soon afterwards, the body was removed from the undertakers by people claiming to be relatives of the late Mr Lopez. It was only afterwards that the police examined photos of the dead man and identified him as Ramon.

With Ramon's death, the gang's aura of invincibility was shattered. Soon afterwards, Benjamin was arrested at a house in the town of Puebla, his bags packed and ready for flight.

However, the younger brothers remain at large, and the rise of other drug lords like them has ensured that the multi-million dollar drug-trafficking industry has been barely affected by the fate of the Arellano-Felix brothers.

Ma BARKER

Ma Barker and her boys were a crime wave on the hoof, a close-knit and mobile Murder Incorporated. With their chief partner-in-crime Alvin Karpis, they executed anyone who was suspected of betraying them or selling them short; they did mail-robberies, held up banks, organized kidnaps, and shot down anyone in uniform who happened to cross their path, including, on one occasion, employees of Northwest Airways. There's no evidence that Ma herself had ever committed much in the way of crime before 1932 when the gang first hit the headlines. But with her sons along, she was a fast learner.

She was born Arizona Donnie Clark in the Ozarks, the wild mountainous backwoods of Missouri, of Scots, Irish and Indian blood; and all her sons, one way and another, went to the bad. By the beginning of the 30s, 'Doc' was in the Oklahoma State Penitentiary for killing a nightwatchman; Hermann was doing twenty-five years in Leavenworth for mail-robbery; and Fred was just coming to the end of a stint digging coal in the State Penitentiary in Kansas, where he'd

◀ *Ma Barker headed a family of criminals*

become friends with a killer called Alvin 'Creepy' Karpis.

It was Fred Barker and Alvin Karpis, when they came out of jail together, who first set the ball rolling. A few days after a robbery, they killed a sheriff who was inspecting the De Soto they'd used for it. So they took it on the lam from Ma's shack in Thayer, Missouri to a furnished house in St. Paul, taking Ma and her live-in lover, Arthur Dunlop, with them. Dunlop, though, wasn't to last long. For after living quietly for a while, they narrowly escaped a police-raid on their new headquarters. They must have decided that it was Dunlop who'd betrayed them. A day later his naked, bullet-riddled body was found by a lake near Webster, Wisconsin. There was a blood-stained woman's glove beside it.

From now on Ma seems only to have trusted ex-cons and escapers from one or other of her three boys' jails. Several of these now joined Fred, Alvin Karpis and her; and when the growing gang took a bank in Fort Scott, Kansas in June 1932, they used the proceeds to stage a Welcome Home party for one of Fred's ex-cell-mates. Three months later, with some of the $240,000 that they heisted from the Cloud County Bank in Concordia, Kansas, they bought 'Doc's' parole from the Oklahoma Pen — and even 'two years of absence' for his partner-in crime, Volney Davis. Leavenworth, though, proved a more difficult proposition. Hermann stayed behind bars.

December 1932: Minneapolis, Third Northwestern Bank — two policeman and a civilian killed. April, 1933: Fairbury, Nebraska, Fairbury National Bank — one gang member killed. June 1933: Minneapolis, Arthur Hamm Jr, of the Hamm Brewing Company kidnapped — yield, $100,000. The kidnappings, the bank-heists and the killings went on through 1933. In South St. Paul, one policeman was killed, another crippled for life. In Chicago, a traffic cop was gunned down while enquiring about an accident with the gang's car. The pressure on Ma's boys and the offers of rewards, though, began to pile up; and it was because of this that they decided in January 1934 to go for the big one.

They'd first decided simply to rob the Commercial State Bank in St. Paul. Then they decided to kidnap the Bank's president. After a month's negotiations about the ransom and conditions, they took the enormous sum of $200,000 — enough, they thought, to buy them new identities and new lives. Fred and 'Doc' Barker, Alvin Karpis and a few of the others had their fingerprints shaved off and their faces surgically altered. And then they all scattered to locations across the United States.

A year after the kidnapping, for all this, 'Doc' was picked up in the apartment of his Chicago girlfriend; and in it was found a map of Florida, with the area around Ocala and Lake Weir circled. This coincided with a tip the Feds had had: that Ma and Fred were hiding somewhere in the south, where there was a famous alligator known to locals as 'Old Joe.' Within days they raided a cottage on Lake Weir. Ma and Fred put up a fight, but by the time the shooting was over, they were both dead, Ma with a machine gun still in her hand. There were enough weapons in the cottage, J. Edgar Hoover later said,

'to keep a regiment at bay.'

The rest of the gang were soon picked up and finally Alvin Karpis was run to ground in New Orleans. Years later, in prison, Karpis, whose real name was Francis Albin Karpavicz, taught Charlie Manson the guitar.

Elizabeth BATHORY

A distant Hungarian relation of Vlad the Impaler, the Countess was married at fifteen to a castle-owning aristocrat named Count Ferencz Nadasy, and spent most of the succeeding twenty-eight years thinking up new forms of sadistic violence to try on the servants. Her husband and aunt helped provide the inspiration: he with his encyclopaedic knowledge of Turkish torture techniques, she with her penchant for using the flagellation of buxom peasant girls to turn herself on. Armed with a burning torch and her trusty pair of flesh-tearing pincers, the Countess killed and maimed more at less at will. As long as she stuck with peasant girls, the risk was minimal; the state was not there to restrain the aristocracy.

When her husband died in 1604, the Countess began looking for his replacement, but her age and – one would like to think – character made her a less than enviable proposition. How could she make herself more attractive? A servant girl unwittingly supplied the answer, spraying blood on the countess's face when slapped. Washing the blood off, the Countess noticed that the area of skin which had received the dousing looked more youthful than the rest. The lesson was clear. She needed blood, and lots of it.

The local peasant girls supplied the necessary. Daily baths in the red elixir required a lot of blood, and the castle servants must have spent most of their lives on wider and wider sweeps of the surrounding countryside. The unfortunate victims were drained, at first by conventional methods, and later with the aid of an iron maiden. This was a box moulded into human shape, its interior lined with sharp spikes. When closed, the spikes pierced the flesh, causing blood to flow from the still-living victim through a hole in the bottom. Once the victim was dead, the flesh was sometimes fed to local peasants – and future victims.

At least, this is how the legend goes. It has been pointed out that a human body only contains about a gallon of blood, hardly enough for a face-wash let alone a bath, and that blood is also highly prone to coagulation. So the Countess would have had severe logistical difficulties in arranging a decent bath.

If true, this was the least of her problems. Much more seriously, the

blood was not working – she still looked like a psychopathic old woman. Potential salvation only arrived after the Countess visited a local forest sorceress who pointed out the obvious – she needed noble blood for her noble skin.

The Countess duly arranged for twenty-five daughters of the minor nobility to attend her newly established charm school, and set about draining them. The bodies were tossed over the castle wall for the wolves.

Unfortunately for the Countess, the local peasants found them first. The bodies were reported to the authorities, who realized that a real crime – torturing and killing the nobility – had been committed. The military showed up at the castle, found blood and corpses everywhere, and arrested the indignant Countess.

Subsequent investigations revealed that she was responsible for the death of over 600 girls. She was tried and found guilty in 1611, but the worst punishment her fellow aristocrats could bring themselves to inflict was confinement in a single room of her own castle until her death a few years later. Her lower-class accomplices were publicly tortured and burned alive.

◀ *A myth or a murderess? The countess's civilized exterior belied a thoroughly uncivilized woman*

BECK and FERNANDEZ

The story of Martha Beck and Raymond Fernandez, dubbed the 'lonely hearts killers', was one of the most sensational ever to hit the headlines in the United States. It was a sleazy tale of two lovers who met through a lonely hearts column, and went on to rob and murder a series of gullible single women. The couple's actions marked them out as an unusually sick, vicious pair, but there was another aspect to the case that the public readily identified with: obsessive love.

Martha Beck was a lonely, overweight woman who had lived a relatively normal life as a single parent and a nurse, until she fell in love with Fernandez, a killer and conman. In the process, as she struggled to gain her lover's approval, she threw away any vestige of human decency that she might once have had. First she abandoned her own children and then helped to murder her lover's innocent victims, in one case a child of two. This sudden change in her personality fascinated commentators – at least until the full horror of her crimes was revealed – provoking a certain amount of sympathy from some members of the American public.

As well as this central theme of crazed passion, there were other features of the story that mesmerized the public: in court, evidence of the couple's bizarre sexual practices, which included Voodoo rites, came to light; and the press also made constant reference to Beck's size, to such a degree that it sometimes seemed she was on trial for being overweight, rather than for being a vicious murderer.

EXECUTION

The lurid details of the case emerged during a sizzling hot summer in 1949. During the trial, the court was packed with onlookers, mostly women, and police had to hold back the crowds. As the trial came to an end, both Beck and Fernandez were convicted of murder and sentenced to death. Even on death row, the dramas continued as the pair's constant feuds and reconciliations were reported in the press. On 8 March 1951, time finally ran out for both of them, and they were executed – first Beck and then Fernandez – by electric chair.

Raymond Fernandez was a Hawaiian-born Spaniard who had grown up in Connecticut and then, as a young man, had gone to Spain to work on a farm. There, he had married a local woman, Encarnacion Robles. During the Second

World War he had worked for British Intelligence, and then had gone back to the US to look for work, leaving his wife and baby in Spain. During the voyage, he had had an accident on board ship and had received a blow to the head. By the time he recovered from the injury, his manner had completely changed: instead of being friendly and outgoing, he had become aggressive and withdrawn.

Fernandez now began a career of theft and deception. He joined several lonely hearts clubs and corresponded with a number of women. After meeting them, he would steal their money, cheque books, jewellery and any other assets he could lay his hands on. Very few of the women he duped went to the police, ashamed as they were of their liaisons with a Latin lover.

In one case, Fernandez went further than robbery: he left a woman, Jane Thomas, dead in a hotel after an altercation. He then went to her apartment with a forged will and cleaned out her belongings so that he could sell them for cash, even though her elderly mother lived on the premises.

▶ *In thrall to Fernandez (centre) or a willing accomplice? Martha Beck (left) preyed on women who were very similar to herself*

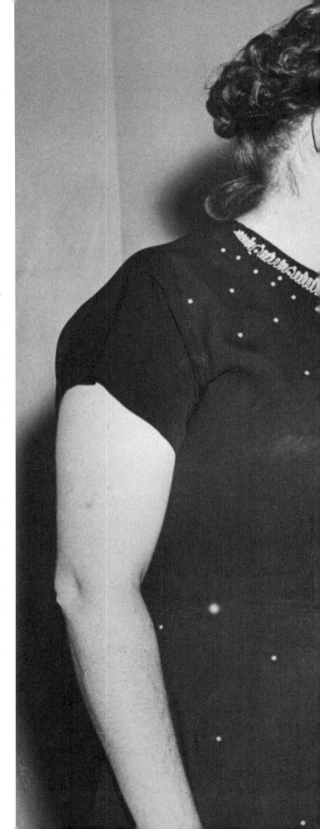

LONELY HEART

One of Fernandez' many correspondents was Martha Beck, a single mother of two. Beck later attested that she had suffered a difficult childhood. She claimed to have been sexually molested by her brother and blamed for the incident by her mother. At a young age she had become obese and had been the butt of cruel jokes at school. Although she went on to do well at nursing school, her size prejudiced her employers against her, and she ended up working in a morgue. Then she had become pregnant by a soldier who refused to marry her, even trying to commit suicide to avoid it – a circumstance that she had naturally found very depressing. However, Beck had gone on to find herself a husband and had became pregnant again, but, sadly, the couple soon divorced. As a single parent, she had worked hard and had eventually done well in her career as a nurse – until her fateful encounter with Raymond Fernandez.

When Martha Beck met Fernandez, she immediately became obsessed by him to the point of madness. She followed him to New York with her two children, and when he complained about them, she promptly took them to a Salvation Army hostel and left them there. Fernandez then told her of the way he made his living, preying off lonely women, and she decided to aid him in his chosen career. She would accompany Fernandez on his missions, often posing as his sister or sister-in-law, and helping to gain the victim's confidence.

Initially, Beck and Fernandez merely robbed and swindled women; eventually, they began to kill. Their victims were always lonely single women who had advertised for a companion or husband, and who were unlucky enough to contact Fernandez and his 'sister' Beck. They met their deaths in horrifying ways: Myrtle Young died of a massive drug overdose administered by Fernandez; Janet Fay was beaten to death by Beck; and Delphine Downing was shot in the head by Fernandez, in front of her two-year-old daughter Rainelle. When Rainelle would not stop crying for her mother, Beck drowned the child in a tub of dirty water.

As the details of the case emerged, the American public became increasingly horrified by the placid-seeming Beck. By the time the trial was over, there were very few who continued to sympathize with the overweight single mother who claimed that she had committed her crimes 'in the name of love'.

◀ *Serial killers who received the ultimate sentence: Beck and Fernandez both died by the electric chair*

David BERKOWITZ

On 17 April 1977, a letter was found on a Bronx street in New York from a postal worker called David Berkowitz. It was addressed to a police captain and read in part:

'I am deeply hurt by your calling me a woman-hater. I am not. But I am a monster. . . I am a little brat. . . I am the Son of Sam.'

Nearby was a parked car in which Berkowitz's latest victims, a young courting couple, had been arbitrarily gunned down. Valentina Suriani had died immediately; Alexander Esau died later in hospital, with three bullets in his head.

No one, of course, knew then that the Son of Sam was the pudgy twenty-four-year old Berkowitz. But for nine months he'd been terrorizing the late-night streets of Queens and the Bronx. He had killed three people and wounded four, seemingly without any motive at all. New York City Mayor Abe Beame had held a press conference to announce: 'We have a savage killer on the loose.'

The first attack had come out of the blue on 29 July 1976 at about one o'clock in the morning, when two young women, one a medical technician, the other a student nurse, were sitting chatting in the front seats of an Oldsmobile parked on a Bronx street. A man had walked up to them, pulled a gun out of a paper bag and fired five shots, killing one of them and wounding the other in the thigh. Four months later, the same gun had been used, again after midnight, against two girls walking home in the Queens district after seeing a movie. A man had walked up to them and asked directions; then he had simply opened fire. Both young women had been badly wounded, and one of them, with a bullet lodged in her spine, paralysed.

In between these two shootings, there had been yet another one – it turned out later from forensic evidence – using the same .44. Another young couple had been sitting in front of a tavern – again at night and once more in Queens – when someone had fired shots through the back window. The man had been rushed to hospital, but had recovered; the woman had not been hit.

The panic really began with the killer's fourth and fifth attacks. On 8 March 1977, a young student, Virginia Voskerichian, was shot in the face at close range only a few hundred yards from her home in Queens, and killed. Forty days later, with the deaths of Valentina Suriani and Alexander Esau and the discovery of

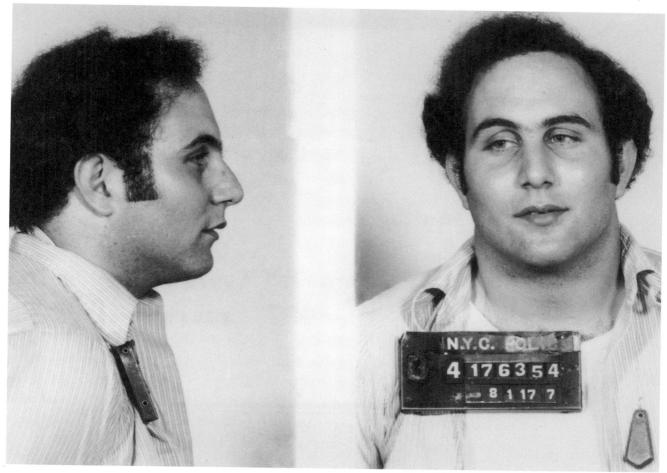

the letter, it became clear that the killings weren't going to stop. More than that, the killer now had a name – and it was a name to stir up nightmares.

'I love to hunt. Prowling the streets, looking for fair game – tasty meat,'

wrote 'Son of Sam.'

Restaurants, bars and discos in Queens and the Bronx were by now closing early for lack of business. People stayed home and kept off the streets at night, despite the deployment of 100 extra patrolmen and the setting-up of a special squad of detectives. For no one had any idea when 'the Son of Sam' might strike again, and the nearest description the police had been able to come up with was that he was a 'neurotic, schizophrenic and paranoid' male, who probably believed himself possessed by demons. . .

▲ *Berkowitz seemed to choose his victims at random*

He could, from that description, be any man at all — that was what was so frightening. He could even be a policeman himself — which might explain why he'd proved so elusive. This idea began to take hold when he struck yet again in the early hours of a late-June morning, shooting through the windscreen of a car in Queens and wounding another young couple. All the police could do in response to the gathering panic was once more to beef up foot-patrols in anticipation of the anniversary of his first murder a year before.

Nothing happened, though, on the night of 29 July 1977; and when he did strike again, it wasn't in his usual hunting-ground at all — but in Brooklyn.

In the early hours of the July 31st, he fired through the windshield of a parked automobile at a pair of young lovers sitting in their car near the sea-front at Coney Island. The woman died in hospital; the man later recovered, but was blinded.

This time, though, 'Son of Sam' had made a mistake. For a woman out walking her dog at about the same time not far away saw two policemen ticketing a car parked near a fire hydrant and then, a few minutes later, a young man jumping into the car and driving off. As it happened only one car, a Ford Galaxie, was ticketed that night for parking at a hydrant — and it was registered to a David Berkowitz in Yonkers.

When approached the next day by the police officer in charge of the search, Berkowitz instantly recognised him from the TV, and said:

'Inspector Dowd? You finally got me.'

As a figure of nightmare, Berkowitz was something of a let-down: an overweight loner with a moronic smile who lived in squalor, was pathologically shy of women and probably still a virgin. He later said he heard demons urging him to kill, among them a 6,000-year-old man who had taken over the body of a dog he had shot. On the walls of his apartment he'd scrawled a series of demonic slogans:

'In this hole lives the wicked king;'
'Kill for my Master;' and 'I turn children into killers.'

Berkowitz was judged sane, and was sentenced to a total of 365 years in prison. His apartment became a place of pilgrimage for a ghoulish fan-club; and he himself has since made a great deal of money from articles, a book and the film rights to his life.

Lizzie BORDEN

Lizzie Borden, so the old rhyme goes, took an axe and gave her mother forty whacks; when she saw what she had done, she gave her father forty-one. The truth is, though, that the number of whacks which despatched Abbey Borden and her rich husband Andrew in Fall River, Massachusetts in 1892, numbered nineteen and ten respectively – and daughter Lizzie, much to the delight of the courtroom which tried her, was finally acquitted.

But was she really guilty? She certainly had a motive. For Abbey was in fact thirty-two-year-old Lizzie's step-mother, and she resented her deeply, particularly after her father, usually very tight with his money, bought Abbey's sister a house and gave the deeds to his wife. Lizzie was also given to what her family had come to call 'funny turns.' One day, for example, she announced to her father that Abbey's bedroom had been ransacked by a burglar. He reported it to the police, who soon established that Lizzie had done the ransacking herself.

As for her father, whom she loved, the repressed spinster may even have had a motive for his murder too, apart from his meanness with money and the fact that, with both him and her step-mother dead, she would finally inherit it. For three months before his death in August, when outhouses in the garden were

▼ *Lizzie Borden 'gave her mother forty whacks'*

twice broken into, he'd convinced himself that whoever was responsible had been after Lizzie's pet pigeons. So he'd decapitated them – yes, with an axe.

Suffice it to say that at about 9.30 a.m. on 4 August, while dusting the spare room, Abbey Borden was struck from behind with an axe and then brutally hacked at even after she was dead. There were only two people in the house at the time, Lizzie and the maid Bridget who was cleaning the downstairs windows. Slightly less than an hour and a half later, Andrew Borden returned, to be told by his daughter that his wife was out. A few minutes later, after Bridget had gone upstairs to her room in the attic, he too was struck down while dozing on a settee in the living-room.

It was Lizzie who 'found' the body of her father, and the neighbours she immediately called in, found the body of his wife upstairs. They did their best to comfort her. But she seemed curiously calm, and she was happy enough to talk to the police as soon as they arrived. However, she began giving conflicting accounts of her whereabouts during the morning; and it wasn't long before the police, who found a recently cleaned axehead in the basement, came to regard her as the chief suspect. Only the day before the murders she'd tried to buy prussic acid in Fall River, they discovered; and when that had failed, she'd told a neighbour she was worried that her father had made many enemies, because of his brusque manner.

After the inquest she was arrested – and vilified as a murderess in the newspapers. But by the time her trial took place in New Bedford in 1893, the tide had begun to turn. Bridget and her sister played down her hatred of her step-mother; and though Bridget confessed that Lizzie had burned one of her dresses on the day after her parents' funeral, she said that there had been no bloodstains on it. Lizzie herself was demure and ladylike in the dock – she even fainted halfway through the proceedings. And in the end the jury agreed with her lawyer, an ex-governor of the State, that she could not be both a lady and a fiend.

After the trial, now rich, she returned to Fall River and bought a large house, in which she died alone in 1927. Bridget the maid returned to Ireland – with, it's said, a good deal of money. There's since been a suggestion that Lizzie became a killer during one of her 'funny turns' – caused by temporal-lobe epilepsy.

BRADY and HINDLEY

Britain has had other prolific serial killers than Ian Brady and Myra Hindley, but none has attracted so much attention or become so clearly the embodiment of evil as this couple, the so-called 'Moors Murderers' who brutally tortured and killed at least five children in the early 1960s. At the heart of the horror was the role of Myra Hindley, as, up to that time, only men were known to carry out serial sex murders of children. That a woman should have joined in seemed so utterly against nature that Hindley became Britain's number one hate figure, reviled even more than the principal agent of their crimes, Ian Brady.

Ian Brady was born in Glasgow, Scotland, on 2 January 1938. His mother, Peggy Stewart, was unmarried at the time and unable to support her child. She gave her baby, aged four months, over to the care of John and Mary Sloane, a couple with four children of their own. Peggy continued to visit her son for a while, though not revealing that she was actually his mother. The visits stopped when she moved to Manchester, England, with her new husband, Patrick Brady, when her son was twelve years old.

Ian was a difficult child, intelligent but a loner. In his teens, despite having passed the entrance examination to a good school, Shawlands Academy, he went completely off the rails. He became fascinated by Nazi Germany and by Adolf Hitler, missed school and committed burglaries. By the age of sixteen, he had been arrested three times. He was only saved from reform school when he agreed to leave Glasgow and go to live with his natural mother Peggy in Manchester.

When he arrived in Manchester, in late 1954, he made an effort to fit in, taking

◄ *Ian Brady was a bright, well-read man but he lacked the ability to work hard*

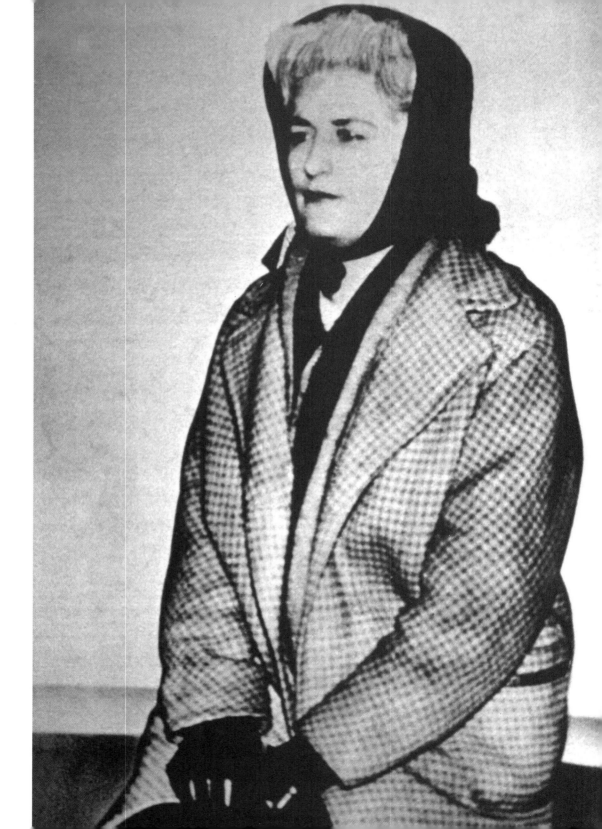

▶Myra Hindley in the clothes she wore to befriend and ultimately kidnap the children she and Brady murdered

his stepfather's name. He worked as a market porter, but within a year he was in trouble again. He was jailed for theft, and while imprisoned seems to have decided on his future career: professional criminal. With this in mind, he studied book-keeping. On his release, he found work as a labourer while looking for a suitable criminal enterprise. Unable to find anything, he put his new skill to more conventional use and got a job as a book-keeper with a company called Millwards Merchandising. A year later a new secretary arrived to work there: Myra Hindley.

BABY-SITTER

Myra Hindley had a slightly more conventional upbringing than Brady. She was born in Manchester on 23 July 1942, the oldest child of Nellie and Bob. During the war years, while Bob was in the army, the family lived with Myra's grandmother, Ellen Maybury. Later, when Bob and Nellie had trouble coping in the postwar years, Myra went back to live with her grandmother, who was devoted to her. Throughout her school years Myra was seen as a bright, though not overambitious, child with a love of swimming. In her teens, she was a popular baby-sitter.

Leaving school at sixteen, she took a job as a clerk in an engineering firm. Soon afterwards, she got engaged to a local boy, Ronnie Sinclair. However, she broke off the engagement, having apparently decided that she wanted more excitement in life. That wish was all too horribly granted when she took a new job and found herself working with Ian Brady.

Hindley soon fell for the sullen, brooding Brady. It took him a year to reciprocate her interest, but once they became lovers, he realized he had found the perfect foil for his increasingly dark fantasies. Brady had spent much of the previous few years obsessively reading. Particular favourites were Dostoyevsky's *Crime and Punishment*, Hitler's *Mein Kampf* and the Marquis de Sade's *Justine*, among other, less elevated books on sadomasochism. Brady increasingly saw himself as some kind of superman, beyond the bounds of good and evil. The devoted Myra lapped all this up. During their first years together she transformed herself with hair dye and make-up into the Aryan blonde of Brady's fantasies. She gave up seeing her friends and devoted herself utterly to her lover.

In 1964, Brady introduced Hindley to the next stage in their relationship: a life of crime. His first notion was a bank robbery. The dutiful Myra joined a gun club and obtained two weapons for him. However, before the robbery could be carried out, Brady changed his mind. It was not robbery he wanted to commit but murder of a particularly brutal and nasty kind.

FIRST VICTIM

The couple's first victim was sixteen-year-old Pauline Reade. The couple waylaid the teenager on the way to a dance on 12 July 1963. They lured her on to Saddleworth Moor, where Brady raped her and cut her throat. They then buried her there.

On 11 November Brady decided it was time to kill again. The victim this time was a twelve-year-old boy, John Kilbride, whom they abducted from Ashton-under-Lyme. Seven months later, in June 1964, another twelve-year-old, Keith Bennett, was abducted from near his home in Manchester. Both boys were raped, murdered and buried on the moors.

After six more months they struck again, on Boxing Day, 26 December 1964. This time they took a girl: ten-year-old Lesley Ann Downey. With Hindley's assistance, Brady took pornographic photographs of Downey, which he planned to sell to rich perverts. The couple, now entirely engrossed in their evil, even made an audio tape of their torture of the terrified little girl. Finally, Brady raped her and either he or

◀ *There was a huge police hunt of the moors, helped by the public. To this day at least one victim's body has not been found*

▲ *Victim Lesley Ann Downey's mother watches the search for her child's body*

Hindley – depending on whose account you believe – strangled her, before they buried her on the moors with the others.

Brady took to boasting about his exploits to Hindley's brother-in-law, David Smith. Angered when Smith did not believe him, Brady made Hindley bring Smith to their house on 6 October 1965, just as he was about to dispatch his latest victim, seventeen-year-old Edward Evans. Smith was not impressed but horrified and went to the police the next morning. They raided the house and found Evans' body there. Further investigation soon led them to start digging on the moors, where they discovered the bodies of Downey and Kilbride. Next, they found a box containing the photos and the tape documenting Downey's murder. At trial both Brady and Hindley tried to pin the blame on David Smith, but the sensational evidence of the tape led to them both being convicted of murder.

Brady and Hindley received a life sentence each. Hindley protested her innocence for a long time, but eventually came to accept partial responsibility. Brady accepted his guilt and later confessed to five other murders, which remain unproven. In 2002, he wrote a book on serial killers that caused controversy in Britain on its publication. That same year, Myra Hindley died in prison.

Troy BROWNLOW

The brutal murder of a teenage girl traumatized her community in Colorado, but despite the efforts of the police, it took 25 years to track down a suspect. In April 2005, 42-year-old Troy Brownlow was arrested at a convenience store in Tucson, Arizona, and taken into police custody.

At the time of his arrest, Brownlow was working as a personal trainer at a fitness

◄ Troy Brownlow had decided to 'go straight'; he had a new job and was about to become a father when a crime he committed 25 years earlier finally caught up with him

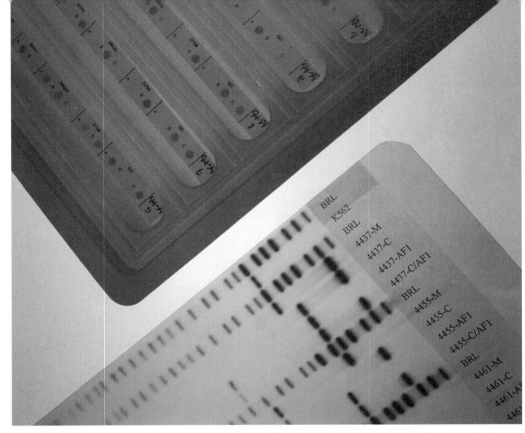

▶DNA mapping: forensic science is now sufficiently advanced that tiny pieces of evidence can be analysed for the presence of DNA many years after the crime has been committed

centre, but he had a history of brushes with the law, and his DNA profile had been put on a database after his release from an Arizona prison. Incredibly, Brownlow's DNA profile matched that of blood samples taken from the scene of the crime where Nanine Grimes was murdered in 1982.

DRUG AND ALCOHOL ABUSE

It turned out that Brownlow, now living in Tucson, had indeed been a neighbour of Nanine's in Adams County all those years ago. In fact, he had lived less than half a mile away from the Grimes' house. He had also

been an acquaintance of Nanine's sister, Deanna. When told that Brownlow had been picked up as a suspect, Deanna Grimes commented that she had known him since third grade, and that they had graduated from Thornton High School together in 1982.

Since his schooldays, Brownlow had been in trouble with the law on numerous occasions. He had a long history of drug and alcohol abuse, and had spent two years in prison in Arizona after being convicted of burglary. He had also spent time in jail in Arapahoe County for firing a bullet at the house of an ex-lover. His adult life had for many years been in chaos, but at the time of his arrest he insisted that he was trying to go straight. During his last spell in jail, he had spent his time quietly, reading, playing cards, and writing poetry. On being released, he had settled down in Tucson with his girlfriend, got a job as a personal trainer, and was looking forward to becoming a father.

WHITE HANDKERCHIEF
A 'CALLING CARD'

In April 2005, Brownlow was charged with the murder of Nanine Grimes. There was some controversy over this, since he had been a juvenile at the time of the murder, but as many pointed out, since then he had had plenty of time as an adult to come forward and declare himself. However, when he was charged, Brownlow argued that although he had been present at the murder, he had not committed it.

In his own version of the story Brownlow said that he had been at the house several times with two of his schoolmates who were 'smitten' with Deanna, although he himself was not. On the afternoon of Nanine's death, he was out walking near the Grimes' house, and somehow got 'sucked into' the events that took place, though he would not explain how. While he was at the house, a big man, unknown to him, appeared. Brownlow described the stranger as 'a rough and tumble kind of guy' and 'a good-sized dude'. He then told how he had become frightened and run out of the back door, jumping over the fence and cutting himself as he did.

Expressing his remorse Brownlow went on to say that he had felt guilty about not reporting the crime ever since it happened. On one occasion, he had mentioned it to a friend over the telephone when he was in jail. He claimed that he bitterly regretted not having contacted the police at the time, or since, to come forward as a witness, but said that he had been afraid to do so. He said that he wished he could have apologized to Deanna Grimes 'for being a coward'.

Brownlow pointed out several anomalies in the case, such as the fact that the mattress from the bed had gone missing since the murder. He also alluded to the fact that the murderer had placed a white handkerchief on the body as a 'calling card', and that later, a 'taunting letter' had been sent to police. This indicated, he said, that a cold-blooded murderer had done the deed, not an inexperienced, frightened high school boy such as he was at the time.

Nevertheless, Brownlow was convicted and sentenced to 25 years.

▶ *Ted Bundy did not show much remorse in court, and was always aware of the cameras on him*

Ted BUNDY

Ted Bundy is one of the most terrifying of all serial killers. Why? It is not simply because he was a sadist and necrophile who confessed to the murders of more than thirty women, and may conceivably have murdered as many as a hundred. It is also because, unlike most such monsters, he could actually pass for a regular guy – the good-looking young lawyer who lives down the street. Bundy was not a skid-row slasher who operated a safe distance away from respectable folk. He was a killer who spent time in ordinary places: the university campus, the mall, the park over the holiday weekend.

APPARENT NORMALITY

Perhaps the most deadly aspect of Bundy's modus operandi was that he played ruthlessly on his apparent normality. Typically, a victim – always a young woman with long dark hair in a centre parting – would be walking back to her student dorm, or out in the park. She would be approached by a personable, tousle-haired young man with his arm in a cast. He would explain that he needed help lifting something into his car. The nice young woman would offer to help the nice young man and she would follow him to his car. She would then disappear forever, or would be found in the woods, her body raped and sodomized, her head staved in by a furious assault with a blunt instrument.

Ted Bundy was born Theodore Robert Cowell in November 1946 in Vermont. However, he enjoyed little of the privilege typically credited to his generation. His mother, Louise Cowell, had become pregnant by a serviceman who had disappeared before Ted was born. She and her baby lived with her strict parents in Philadelphia, and in an effort to avoid scandal the family pretended that Ted was actually his grandparents' child, and that his mother was in fact his sister.

When Ted was four his mother moved to Tacoma, Washington, and married a man called John Bundy. About a year later, in 1951, Ted formally took his stepfather's name.

Bundy was a bright child who consistently achieved good grades in school. However, he was not an easy mixer. He was bullied when he was young and later, while becoming more apparently gregarious, he also acquired a reputation for petty theft and lying.

After high school he attended the University of Puget Sound in Washington. Around this time he met a

young, pretty woman called Stephanie Brooks, who had long dark hair worn in a centre parting. Stephanie was from a moneyed California family and she and Bundy went out together for a time. However, while Bundy became obsessed with her, she found him lacking in ambition and, when she left college, she broke off with him. Bundy was devastated.

MURDEROUS RAGE

He left college and moped for a while. Then he turned his disappointment into motivation to succeed. He re-enrolled in college, studied psychology and became active in the Republican Party. He worked for a suicide hot line, and received a commendation from the Seattle Police Department for catching a mugger. He found a new girlfriend, divorcee Meg Anders. He could scarcely have looked more like a model citizen.

Underneath, however, a murderous rage was building. First, he got back in touch with Stephanie Brooks, meeting up with her in California while on a business trip in 1973. She was impressed by the new go-ahead Ted, and – unbeknown to Anders – Stephanie and Ted began to talk of marriage.

In February 1974, Bundy broke off all

contact with Brooks. Just as suddenly as she had dumped him, he did the same to her. What she did not know was that, just beforehand, Bundy had committed his first murder. The victim was a young woman called Lynda Healy who he had abducted from her basement flat in Seattle. Over the next few months, five more young women would vanish in the surrounding area. Each one was last seen out walking, and each one had long dark hair with a centre parting.

REPEAT KILLINGS

It was clear that there was a serial killer on the loose, but at this stage the police had no bodies and no clues. Then came the events of 14 July. On that hot summer's day crowds had flocked to the shores of Lake Sammammish, but two of them – 23-year-old Janice Ott and nineteen-year-old Denise Naslund – had failed to make the journey back. Both had wandered off from their friends and vanished. When police investigated, several passers-by reported seeing Ott in conversation with a man whose arm was in a sling and was heard to say his name was Ted. After hearing this on the news, another witness then came forward and said that this Ted had asked her to help secure a sailboat to his car, a tan Volkswagen Beetle. When he told her the boat was somewhere up the road and

they would have to drive there, she had become suspicious and declined.

The police put out a description of the man called Ted and various calls came in. One of these was an anonymous call from Meg Anders, saying she thought the man might be her boyfriend Ted Bundy, who was starting to alarm her with his interest in violent sex and bondage. The police checked out Bundy, but the young Republican law student seemed too innocuous to worry about, and the lead was dropped.

Over the next three months bodies started to be discovered. Ott and Naslund were found buried in the woods, along with the skeleton of a third woman who could not be identified. Two more bodies were found the following month. Then Bundy moved his operations out of the state.

His next three victims were all abducted in Utah during the month of October. At this point, Bundy made his first mistake. On 8 November he attempted to abduct Carol DaRonch from a shopping mall in Salt Lake City. He pretended to be a police officer and lured her into his car, a VW Beetle, but she became suspicious and managed to escape, following a struggle. Later that night, seventeen-year-old Debbie Kent was not so lucky; Bundy abducted and murdered her.

ARRESTED

In the New Year, Bundy moved his hunting ground again, this time to Colorado. He abducted four more women there in the first half of 1975. Just before the fourth body was discovered, however, he was finally arrested. A policeman had stopped Bundy in Salt Lake City and looked inside the car, finding handcuffs and a stocking mask. Carol DaRonch was called in and picked Bundy out of a line-up as the man who had tried to abduct her. Her evidence was enough to have him convicted and sentenced to jail for attempted kidnapping.

Meanwhile other evidence linked Bundy to the killings in Colorado, and in January 1977 he was taken to Aspen to be tried for the murder of Caryn Campbell. The game was clearly up for Bundy. However respectable his exterior, it was all too plain that underneath was an appalling sexual sadist and murderer.

This should have been the end of the story but, waiting for trial, Bundy demonstrated new levels of resourcefulness. He escaped from custody during a court appearance and spent eight days hiding out in Aspen before being recaptured.

Incredibly, he then managed to escape again, cutting a hole in the roof of his cell, crawling along and cutting another hole down into a janitor's room, then walking unchallenged out of prison. This escape would last longer, and have far worse consequences.

AT LARGE

Bundy fled to Tallahassee, Florida, where he rented a room under an assumed name, close to the university. Two weeks after his escape, on 15 January 1978, he murdered again, giving up all subtlety in his approach. He broke into a sorority house and brutally raped and murdered two young women, leaving a third badly injured.

The following month, he failed in his attempt to abduct a schoolgirl. Three days later, he succeeded in abducting and murdering his final victim, twelve-year-old Kimberley Leach. After another three days, he was finally recaptured and this time he was convicted of first-degree murder: the evidence against him was the match of his teeth with the bite marks left on his victims. In July 1979 he was sentenced to death by electric chair.

Law student Ted Bundy launched several increasingly tenuous appeals. While in prison, he confessed to more than thirty murders. Women proposed marriage to him; one even succeeded in exchanging marriage vows with him when she appeared as a defence witness. Finally, however, on 24 January 1989, Ted Bundy was put to death.

AL CAPONE

Prohibition, which came into force in the United States in 1920, was a monumental act of political stupidity. For it was never backed by the ordinary man and woman in the street; and it was they, who by exercising what they saw as their right to go on drinking, handed power to the rum-runners and those who controlled them: men like Al Capone. They voted them, in effect, into office as a sort of underground government. Capone, at his height in the Chicago area, was known as the 'Mayor of Crook County.'

Alfonso Caponi was born in 1899 in New York; and grew up into a resourceful small-time hood, working in the rackets and as a bouncer in a Brooklyn brothel — where a knife-fight gave him his nickname: 'Scarface.' In New York, if he'd stayed there, he might never have amounted to much. But in 1920, when on the run from the police, he got an invitation from a distant relative of his family's to join him in Chicago.

The relative was Johnny Torrio, the ambitious chief lieutenant of an old-style Mafia boss called 'Diamond Jim' Colosimo, who controlled most of the brothels in the city. After the passing of the Volstead Act that brought in Prohibition, Torrio had tried to persuade Colosimo to go into the liquor business, but Colosimo'd wanted no part of it. So now Torrio made his move. He despatched Capone, his new personal bodyguard, to Colosimo's restaurant-headquarters one night, and Capone gunned him down.

Torrio, with Capone as his right hand, took over Colosimo's brothels and moved heavily into bootlegging. This brought them into direct competition with the mainly Irish gang of 'Deanie' O'Bannion, a genial ex-choirboy and ex-journalist

▼ *Capone was a ruthless and ambitious gangster*

▲ *Capone in jovial mood*

war for control of the liquor trade in Chicago, with Torrio and Capone pitted against O'Bannion's lieutenants and heirs, Hymie Weiss and 'Bugs' Moran, and also against the four brothers of the Sicilian Genna family. The going soon got too hot for Johnny Torrio, who in 1925 retired to Naples, taking $50 million, it's said, with him.

But Capone was made of sterner – and more cunning – stuff. He gradually eliminated the Genna family; and as he did so he bought politicians and judges, journalists and police brass, until he was in effect in control, not only of all enforcement agencies and public opinion, but also of City Hall. He made massive donations to the campaigns of Chicago Mayor 'Big Bill' Thompson; and he held court to all comers in fifty rooms on two floors of the downtown Metropole Hotel.

In 1929, having already got rid of Hymie Weiss, he was finally ready to move against his last surviving enemy, 'Bugs' Moran. Word was passed to Moran that a consignment of hijacked booze could be picked up at a garage on North Clark Street on St. Valentine's Day, but soon after his people arrived, so did Capone's torpedoes, two of them in police uniform. Six of Moran's men died in what became known as the St. Valentine's Massacre, along with an unfortunate optometrist who liked hanging out with

who served only the finest liquor and ran his business from the city's most fashionable flower-shop. But for a while both sides held their hand. Then in November 1924, in revenge for a trick which got Torrio a police record (and nine months in jail), O'Bannion was killed by Torrio's men in his shop, after they'd arrived asking for a funeral wreath.

The death of O'Bannion, who was buried in high style, triggered an all-out

hoods; and Moran himself only escaped because he was late for the appointment. As for Capone, he was on holiday that day in Biscayne Bay, Florida; and at the actual time of the slaughter at the SMC Cartage Company garage, was on the phone to the Miami DA.

In the end Capone was brought to book, not by the cops, but by the internal revenue service. In 1931, he was tried for tax evasion and sentenced to jail for eleven years. By the time he came out eight years later, the Mafia had moved on, had become more sophisticated; and he himself was not only old hat but half mad from tertiary syphilis. He died in his bed eight years later on his Florida estate. 'Bugs' Moran outlived him by ten years.

▼ *The St Valentine's Day Massacre, said to have been carried out on Capone's orders*

Butch CASSIDY and SUNDANCE

Butch Cassidy, whose parents were both British Mormons, was born George Leroy Parker in Beaver, Utah on 13 April 1866, the first of 13 children. In his early teens George left his parents' ranch to work on a dairy farm, where he met a cowboy cum rustler and horse thief called Mike Cassidy; George would start using the surname Cassidy after getting in trouble with the law aged 18. A few years later, after joining a cattle-drive, he robbed his first bank, netting around $21,000 at Telluride, Colorado on 24 June 1889. His accomplices were Thomas and William McCarty and perhaps 21-year-old Pennsylvanian Harry Longabaugh – already known to the law as The Sundance Kid.

At the age of about 18, looking for adventure, Longabaugh had travelled with relatives by covered wagon to Colorado; and his first nickname-cum-alias had been Kid Chicago. But in 1888, he had been arrested for rustling near Sundance, Wyoming; and forever after he was known as the Sundance Kid. As for Butch, he seems to have worked briefly as a butcher in Rock Springs between bank- and railroad-heists – and the name stuck.

Butch was a charmer; the Kid, more aloof; and both were accomplished escape artists. They each served just one prison stretch, the Kid after the 1888 rustling, and Butch in 1894 for – of all things – stealing a horse. For a while they went their separate ways. The Kid seems to have worked solo. But that was not Butch's way: when he came out of Laramie State Penitentiary after a two-year sentence, he formed a gang which soon became famous as the Wild Bunch. He and a shifting membership, which included Elzy Lay and Harry 'Kid Curry' Logan, went after banks and mine payrolls – and between jobs holed up, first in Robbers' Roost, Utah and then in the more celebrated Hole-in-the-Wall, Wyoming, a hideaway that had been used by Jesse and Frank James, among others.

It was at Hole-in-the-Wall that Butch and the Kid seem to have joined forces again; and in 1899 and 1900, with a series of brilliantly planned hold-ups – beginning with a train robbery at Wilcox, Wyoming which netted between thirty and sixty thousand dollars – they became both celebrities and very much wanted men. At some point Butch tried to make a deal with both the law and the Union Pacific Railroad – his freedom in return for future good conduct. But when negotiations broke down, the Wild Bunch promptly struck again: They held up another train in Tipton, Wyoming in August 1900, followed swiftly by a bank hold-up in Winnemucca, Nevada, which yielded another $32,000.

To celebrate, the Bunch went south, to Fort Worth, Texas – and made the big mistake of having a group photograph taken there. For detectives from the Wells Fargo Company and the Pinkerton Agency soon seized on it and had it published both all over the country and as far away, ultimately, as Britain and Tahiti. Bounty hunters pursued them; and to escape the heat, Butch, the Kid and the Kid's lover Etta Place, made their way, first to New York – where the Kid bought Etta a Tiffany watch – and then by steamer to Argentina.

They bought a ranch in Cholilo; and Etta and the Kid went back twice to the US on visits. But then they began to run out of money; and in March 1906 they started holding up banks again, first in San Luis Province and then in Bahia Blanca. In 1907, they robbed a train in Bolivia and then, swinging back into Argentina, another bank. Etta went back to the States and disappeared, and finally so did Butch and the Kid – either into death or oblivion.

The usual version of the story is that Butch and the Kid were cornered by the military in San Vicente, southern Bolivia, after holding up a mine payroll. There was a furious gun-battle; the Kid was fatally wounded and Butch, with his last two bullets, shot, first the Kid, then himself. Butch's sister, though, swore that he paid a visit to his family in Utah in 1925 and that he died twelve years later somewhere in the northwest of the United States. There are also rumours that the Kid joined Etta in Mexico City and died there in 1957. A mining boss, with whom they were friendly, had deliberately misidentified the bodies.

▼ *The Wild Bunch (L to R) Will Carver, Harvey 'Kid Curry' Logan, Harry 'Sundance Kid' Longabough, Ben 'Tall Texan' Kilpatrick and Butch Cassidy*

Mark CHAPMAN

Mark David Chapman was a drifter; a nobody. No one took any notice of him, nobody loved him and it is likely that nobody would ever had heard of him were it not for the bloody killing he carried out on 8 December 1980. For Mark Chapman was the man who shot and killed John Lennon.

On Saturday 6 December 1980, a young man named Mark Chapman checked into the YMCA on 63rd Street, just off Central Park West in New York City. Chapman had been born in Texas on 10 May 1955. He had grown up in Georgia, an overweight child who was unpopular at school. In his teens he became a committed Christian and youth worker. In despair after a failed relationship, he moved to Hawaii where he planned to kill himself. When his suicide attempt failed, he found a renewed appetite for life.

He met and married his Japanese American wife, Gloria, and things went well for a couple of years. Gradually, however, his behaviour became increasingly eccentric and he developed an obsession with John Lennon. Strangely, he was also obsessed with the J. D. Salinger novel, *The Catcher in the Rye*. When Chapman heard that John Lennon had a new record out he felt compelled to meet his idol.

That Saturday, Chapman spent several hours outside the Dakota building, clutching a copy of *Double Fantasy*, waiting for Lennon to appear. When he did not, Chapman retreated to the YMCA for the night. Next day, he moved to the nearby Sheraton Hotel and returned to his vigil. Once again Lennon failed to show, and Chapman contented himself with buying a copy of *Playboy* featuring a John Lennon interview. That night he called an escort agency, but when the call girl arrived told her he merely wanted to talk to her, just as Holden Caulfield, the hero of *The Catcher In The Rye*, had done in a similar situation.

Next morning at 10.30 a.m. he woke up, took out the hotel Bible, opened it to the beginning of the St. John Gospel, and wrote in the word 'Lennon' after 'John'. Then he picked up his copy of *Double Fantasy* and his gun, and headed off to the Dakota building, picking up a copy of *The Catcher In The Rye* from a bookstore on the way.

AUTOGRAPH

Once at the Dakota building he became so engrossed in the book that he didn't notice Lennon entering the building. He

continued to wait and chatted with other Lennon fans. Soon after lunchtime a fellow fan spotted five-year-old Sean Lennon coming out with his nanny. Chapman shook the child's hand. During the course of the afternoon he saw other celebrities including Lauren Bacall and Paul Simon coming and going. Finally, around six o'clock, John Lennon came out with Yoko Ono, heading for a recording studio. Chapman offered him

the record to sign and Lennon did so graciously, asking him, 'Is that all you want?'

Part of him, Chapman said later, was satisfied with this, wanted to take his autograph and go home to Hawaii and get on with his life. Another part of him, however, had a much darker purpose in mind, and that part won out.

Chapman continued to wait outside the Dakota building. At around 10.50 p.m.

▲ *The iconic image of John Lennon and his wife, Yoko Ono, during their famous 'make love not war' protest in 1969*

John and Yoko returned from the recording studio. Yoko Ono got out of the white limousine first.

This is what happened next, by Chapman's own account, as given to the police a few hours later: 'He walked past me, and then a voice in my head said, "Do it, do it, do it," over and over again, saying "Do it, do it, do it, do it," like that. I pulled the gun out of my pocket. I handed it over to my left hand. I don't remember aiming. I must have done it, but I don't remember drawing the bead or

whatever you call it. And I just pulled the trigger steady five times.'

Lennon tried to get away from the gun, but four of the five bullets hit him. Even so he managed to run up six steps into the concierge's station. There he said the words, 'I'm shot', then fell face down.

'BIGGER THAN JESUS'

Born in Liverpool on 9 October 1940, John Lennon was the son of a merchant seaman and grew up in a working-class area of Liverpool, England. His parents,

Julia and Alf, split up when he was five, his father abandoning the family. Julia was left to cope on her own, and found herself unable to, so John was sent to live with his aunt Mimi. He continued to see his mother Julia, with whom he had a troubled relationship. She taught him to play the banjo, which gave him a distinctive style when he later picked up the guitar.

When Lennon was seventeen, Julia was killed in a car accident and he was obliged to go to the morgue to identify her body, an incident which scarred him emotionally for life. As a young man, Lennon went to art school but dropped out, instead forming a band called *The Silver Beetles* with Paul McCartney and George Harrison. In 1962, Lennon married his girlfriend Cynthia Powell and became the father of a son, Julian.

The band, whose name was soon shortened to 'The Beatles' went on to tour Germany, and eventually achieved worldwide success. Crucial to their popularity were the songs of Lennon and McCartney, which developed from the bright, melodic pop of the early sixties to the introspective psychedelia of their later period. The Beatles became one of the most influential bands of their time, not only musically but in terms of the new 1960s counterculture in general, and their opinions were asked on every question under the sun. Lennon took the opportunities offered to him by his fame to express his often controversial beliefs, sometimes adding ironic comments that people took seriously, such as that The Beatles were 'more popular than Jesus'. This particular remark infuriated the Christian church, and Lennon was roundly condemned by many members of the establishment.

Lennon's personal life also became the subject of controversy after he divorced his wife Cynthia and married artist Yoko Ono. Together, the pair recorded experimental albums and conducted a series of attention-grabbing public protests, including lying in bed surrounded by posters for peace and receiving members of the press for interviews. Because of stunts such as these, certain sections of the media presented Lennon and Yoko as laughably eccentric, but in retrospect, there is no doubt that they drew attention to several important political causes at the time, such as the war in Vietnam.

ACRIMONIOUS DISPUTES

As well as the establishment and the media, there were many fans of the Beatles who felt that Ono's influence on Lennon was a negative one. Lennon began to include his wife in every aspect of the band's recording work, and she became a constant presence everywhere he went. Ono's influence, and other issues to do with leadership of the group, eventually caused Lennon's relationship with The Beatles to break down. There followed a series of acrimonious disputes with Paul McCartney and the other Beatles, after which Lennon recorded as a solo artist and with Ono, until his retirement in 1975 following the birth of his second son, Sean. In 1980, Lennon returned to the studio, recording an album, Double Fantasy. At this time, shortly before his murder, he appeared to have come out of a fallow creative period in his life, to the delight of his fans.

During the 1960s, Lennon had once been asked how he thought he would die, and had replied that he expected to be 'popped off by some loony'. He had also expressed anxiety, in later years, that he was being stalked. As it turned out, these words, delivered in his humorous, offhand way, proved prophetic.

Lennon's sudden death shocked his many fans worldwide, and turned the former Beatle into an icon — or even a saint — almost overnight. Despite the fact that, by the time he was murdered, the reclusive star had undergone long periods of creative inactivity, and was reported at various times to have been violent, drug-addicted, alcoholic and mentally unbalanced, after his death his reputation grew until he became, not only one of the seminal figures of popular music during the twentieth century, but a figurehead for peace and love, attracting a loyal following among rising generations of new fans — which he continues to do to this day.

DEAD ON ARRIVAL

While Lennon was dying, Chapman just stayed where he was. He got out his copy of The Catcher in The Rye and started reading, waiting for the police to arrive. When they did, he put his hands in the air and surrendered, saying 'I acted alone.' Lennon was rushed in a police car to St Luke's Roosevelt Hospital, but died soon after his arrival.

Within hours there was a crowd of thousands of people outside the hospital. The following day the whole world seemed to be united in mourning of a kind not seen since the Kennedy assassination.

Mark Chapman was arrested, brought to trial, and pleaded guilty to murder. He was convicted and sentenced to a term of life imprisonment. He is still serving his sentence, despite several parole hearings, at least in part because the authorities firmly believe it to be highly likely that Chapman would be himself murdered were he ever to be released.

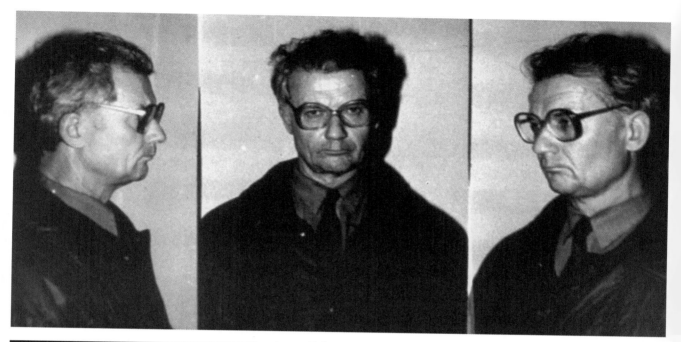

Andrei CHIKATILO

Between 1978 and 1990, a serial sex murderer who became known as 'the Forest Strip Killer' terrorised the region around Rostov in southern Russia. When he was finally caught, he turned out to be a mild-mannered schoolteacher and Communist Party member called Andrei Chikatilo.

In all he had committed at least fifty-three murders – of women, children and drifters – over a period of twelve years. Chikatilo, though – who'd confessed to them all – was found guilty of only fifty-

two of them. For another man had been executed for the first of his murders, that of a nine-year-old he'd lured into a rented shack at the age of 42.

That first killing of Chikatilo's, however, set the pattern for all the rest. For Chikatilo was impotent; and after choking the nine-year-old and attempting unsuccessfully to rape her, he ended up violating her with his fingers.

It was the sight of the blood from her ruptured hymen that seems to have set him off. For he stabbed her repeatedly in what became a prolonged frenzy of intense sexual excitement; and from then on power, blood, sex, torture and death became inseparably interlinked in his mind.

▲ *Andrei Chikatilo – Russia's most notorious murderer*

▲ *Chikatilo always professed his guilt once he was captured*

It was two years before he struck again – his victim this time a seventeen-year-old girl playing hookey from school who was willing to have sex for the price of a meal. He took her into the woods and beat her to death. Then he bit off one of her nipples and masturbated over her corpse.

From then on, the number of tortured and mutilated bodies began to pile up: older women, children and teenagers of both sexes. In 1984, Chikatilo was actually arrested by an investigating detective who noticed him behaving strangely on a bus. But though a rope, a long coil of wire and a knife were found in his briefcase, he was eventually released because his blood-type didn't match that of the killer's. As it turned out, the bespectacled Chikatilo, fortunately for him, was a medical anomaly for his semen- and blood-type were different, AB and A. He was struck off the list of suspects.

He was finally caught, many brutal murders later, only in October 1990, when the last of his victims was found in woods near a remote country station. A policeman remembered asking a man he'd seen emerging nearby, dressed in a grey suit and with cuts to his finger and ear, for his identity. It was Chikatilo. He was first put under surveillance, and then pulled in. After several days' grilling, he confessed.

Put on trial in April 1992, he had no excuses – though he did mention that he'd seen his elder brother eaten by his neighbours in the Ukraine during the famine of the 1930s. He said:

'When I used my knife, it brought psychological relief. I know I have to be destroyed. I understand. I was a mistake of nature.'

He was executed, by firing squad, in February 1994.

Reginald CHRISTIE

England may have given the world the definitive serial killer in Jack the Ripper but, after that Victorian monster vanished from view, relatively few serial murderers followed in his footsteps. Perhaps that is why the sordid life and crimes of Reginald Christie gained such a hold on the public imagination in the 1950s, even inspiring a feature film named, like Ludovic Kennedy's classic book on the case, *10 Rillington Place*.

Reginald Christie lived for fifteen years at the west London address of 10 Rillington Place, until his sudden departure in March 1953 – a departure that was explained when the new tenant found three dead bodies in a boarded-up wardrobe, one more under the floorboards and another two in the garden. The neighbours were reportedly stunned. Christie was not a well-liked man, being a snobbish type, but he was no one's idea of a mass murderer.

WRONGLY HANGED?

The address was already notorious. Just three years previously, another tenant named Timothy Evans – who had rented the top-floor flat while Christie and his wife had the ground floor – had been convicted of murdering his infant child and had been suspected of murdering his wife. Surely the same shabby little house could not have been home to two separate

▼ *Christie's crimes came to light when a hapless builder stumbled on the bodies*

53

murderers? Or could it have been that Timothy Evans was wrongly hanged and that the real murderer was actually John Reginald Christie?

Reginald Christie was born near Halifax in Yorkshire on 8 April 1898. He had an authoritarian father and a mother inclined to overprotection. It was a combination that turned Reginald into an attention-seeking hypochondriac; he was to remain so throughout his life. One of his formative experiences was unexpectedly seeing his grandfather's dead body when he was eight years old (a very similar experience that also had a profound influence on serial killer Dennis Nilsen).

LONER

Christie did not mix easily with other children and became something of a loner. In his teens he had a disastrous first sexual experience with a girl who laughed at him when he failed to gain an erection. This was the start of his lifelong problem with impotence – one to which he was eventually to find a rather drastic solution.

Christie left school in 1913 and worked at various jobs before enlisting in the army in 1916, during the First World War. He served as a signalman and was sent to the front in 1918, when he suffered from the effects of a mustard gas attack.

Following his wartime experiences, he had a nervous reaction that led to him claiming to be blind for several months, and being unable to speak for a longer period. Nevertheless, in 1919 he met Ethel Simpson, and married her the following year.

He found a job as a postman but was soon sacked and sent to prison for three months for stealing letters. Not long after his release, unable to get a job locally, he moved to London. Ethel remained with her family in Sheffield; their marriage had failed sexually, and she knew that Christie had been visiting prostitutes.

Over the next decade Christie disappeared into a lowlife London world of petty criminality and prostitution. He lived with a prostitute for a while and, in 1929, was sentenced to six months in prison after assaulting her with a cricket bat. He received another prison sentence in 1933 after he stole a car belonging to a priest he knew. While in prison this time, he wrote to Ethel and, evidently being very lonely, she agreed to come to London and live with him once he was released.

Christie reinvented himself as a sober, respectable citizen, becoming a Special Constable during the war – however, he

▶ *Bodies found in the garden of 10 Rillington Place are brought out*

continued to frequent prostitutes behind Ethel's back. In 1938, the couple moved into Rillington Place in Notting Hill.

RESPECTABLE INDIVIDUAL

Unbeknown to anyone, this now respectable individual committed his first two murders during the war years. His first victim was an Austrian immigrant called Ruth Fuerst. He strangled her to death while raping her, an act that he found uniquely satisfying and was to practise several times more. His next victim was Muriel Eddy, a woman he met through work. He tricked her into inhaling carbon monoxide, and then, when she lost consciousness, he raped and strangled her. Both women were eventually buried in the back garden.

The end of the war seemed to halt Christie's killing spree for a while. The next murder with which he is associated did not occur until 1949. This time, the victim was Beryl Evans, the wife of the upstairs tenant Timothy Evans. There are several conflicting accounts of her death. The most likely one is that Christie pretended to be able to give her an abortion. He attempted to sedate her with gas and, when that failed, he knocked her unconscious and strangled her to death, before also murdering her baby daughter Geraldine, and then deliberately incriminating Timothy.

At the ensuing trial in 1953, the jury believed the apparently respectable Christie, rather than the illiterate Evans. Evans was found guilty and hung; Christie was left to carry on his career of murder.

It was three more years before he struck again.In December 1952 he told neighbours that his wife Ethel had gone back to Yorkshire. In fact he had strangled her and put her under the floorboards.

Over the next six weeks he lured three prostitutes to his house – Rita Nelson, Kathleen Maloney and Haroldina McLennan. He gassed, raped and strangled them, boarding them up in a cupboard. Then, with no money left for the rent, he simply walked out and began sleeping rough.

Meanwhile, a builder working for the new tenant at Rillingon Place made a ghastly discovery. Christie's face was pictured in all the national newspapers as England's most wanted criminal.

It was not long before a policeman recognized and arrested him. In custody, Christie confessed to his crimes, though he never admitted to the murder of the infant Geraldine. His defence team had no alternative but to plead insanity. However, the jury were not persuaded and Christie was duly found guilty. On 15 July 1953 he was hanged.

Joe CLARK

Nobody wants to dig up a body — especially the body of someone who has died as the result of a tragic accident, and whom relatives feel should be left to rest in peace. Yet in some cases, after such an accident — sometimes years later – doubts begin to be raised as to how exactly the victim met their death.

In these cases, the body must be dug up and looked at once again, this time more carefully. This is what happened in the dramatic case of Chris Steiner, a fourteen-year-old boy who was presumed drowned simply through a tragic accident, and who lay in his grave for a year before the authorities learned that his death may have been a violent one, and decided to investigate further.

MANNER OF DEATH: UNDETERMINED

Chris Steiner lived in Baraboo, Wisconsin, and on the night of 4 July 1994, disappeared from his home. It was a mystery as to why he had disappeared; his parents could give no reason for it, and could not believe that he had simply run away from home. When the police were called in, they noticed sinister indications at the scene of the crime. It was clear that Chris' bedroom window had been wrenched open, and there were muddy footprints on the carpet of the room, which suggested that someone had come in from outside and abducted the boy. Downstairs, a patio door was found to be unlocked, and it was thought that the intruder had entered the house through this door. A search was launched, but it was only six days later that the teenager's body was found. It was lying over a tree beside a sandbar on the Wisconsin River.

The quiet, peaceful community of Baraboo was shocked by this horrific, unexpected discovery. An autopsy on the body was performed, but the coroner could not say what had caused the boy's death. There was no sign that Steiner had been attacked or wounded. He had not been strangled. His body was bloated from being in the water, and thus his cause of death was listed as drowning. However, the coroner could not ascertain the manner of his death which meant that this could not be classified and his death was listed as undetermined.

Despite the circumstances of Steiner's disappearance, and the signs that he had been abducted from his home, the police were unable to make any headway in the subsequent investigation. Without any clear leads to follow, the case soon went cold.

LIKED TO HEAR BONES BREAK

It was only when the murderer struck again, and this time the victim escaped, that Chris Steiner's death was re-investigated. A year had passed when, on 29 July 1995, another boy from the area,

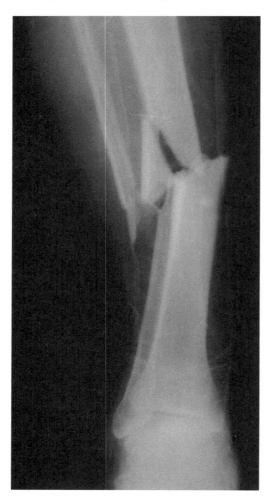

▶ *What was the draw of broken bones?*

thirteen-year-old Thad Phillips, was abducted from his home, this time in the early hours of the morning.

The abductor was Joe Clark, a seventeen-year-old young man who lived in the area and who was known to the police as a troublemaker. Joe carried Thad to a deserted house a mile away, Thad still confused as to what was going on. It was only once they were there that Thad realized he had made a big mistake. Clark took him to a filthy upstairs room, laid him on the bed, and began to torture him by twisting his ankles until one of them broke. In extreme pain, Thad got up and struggled downstairs, but Clark followed him and pinned him down again, this time breaking his leg at the thigh. Clark then told Thad how much he liked to hear bones break, and continued to torture the boy for hours. In a sick parody of caring for the boy, Clark then fashioned crude bandages for his victim's legs from socks and braces, before leaving him alone.

A short while afterwards, Clark returned, this time with a girl, who sat with him in the living room and then left the house. Clark then discovered, to his surprise, that Thad had now dragged himself all the way to the kitchen. To punish him, Clark took him upstairs again and tortured him once more.

That evening, Clark went out again. Before he went, he made sure that his victim could not escape by locking him in a bedroom closet. Alone in the closet, Thad must have felt his time was running out, but he was determined not to give in to despair. He summoned all his willpower, and told himself that he would survive. He found an old electric guitar in the closet and managed to batter the door down with it. Somehow, he managed to drag himself downstairs again, and although he kept fainting with pain, was able to reach the telephone. He dialled 911 and told the operator where he was and what had happened.

BOASTED ABOUT MURDER

The police came quickly to the house. There they found Thad with fractures to both of his legs, dehydrated and suffering enormous pain and fatigue. Thad told them the story of his ordeal, describing his tormentor, and saying that he had boasted about other victims he had injured, one of whom was Chris Steiner. The police immediately suspected local troublemaker Joe Clark. In Clark's bedroom, they found a chilling piece of paper with a list of boys' names on it. There were eighteen names under three separate headings: 'Get To Now'; 'Can Wait'; and 'The Leg Thing'. The names on the list all were local boys.

Clark was charged with attempted homicide, and was convicted. He was sentenced to a prison term of a hundred years. However, after this conviction, he chose to plead not guilty to the murder of Chris Steiner.

In order to find out what had happened to Steiner, his body had been exhumed. With the knowledge of what had happened to Thad Phillips, Steiner's body was checked for bone breakages, and X-rays were taken. Sure enough, the X-rays revealed that his legs had been broken in four separate places, in the same way that Thad's were. It seemed that Clark had broken the legs, then thrown the boy in the river, where he drowned.

Clark's parents tried to protect their son by claiming that he had been at home on the night of Steiner's murder, but it was known that Clark often left the house while his mother was sleeping. An inmate of the juvenile detention institution in which Clark had spent time also testified that Clark had boasted to him about killing a boy and afterwards draping his body over a tree in the river.

There was not much doubt that Clark was guilty as charged, and on 7 November 1997, Clark was convicted of the murder of Chris Steiner. He was sentenced to life imprisonment plus a further term of fifty years. To this day, Clark maintains that he was innocent of Steiner's murder, but – not surprisingly – there are few that believe him.

Mickey COHEN

Mickey Cohen, like his mentor Bugsy Siegel, was a strange mixture of charm and menace. Together these two men, both New York Jews from working-class backgrounds, carved out a place for organized crime in Hollywood. Unlike Siegel, Mickey Cohen survived well enough in the Mafia jungle to make it past sixty years old, and to die in his own bed, two rare achievements in the underworld of crime.

MOONSHINE MADNESS

Meyer Harris 'Mickey' Cohen was born in New York City on 4 September 1913. He spent his early years in the sprawling slum that was Brownsville, Brooklyn, before his family moved out west to Boyle Heights, Los Angeles when he was six years old. His family ran a drugstore there, in the midst of what was a largely Orthodox Jewish neighbourhood. This was during the years immediately following Prohibition, and the drugstore soon became a front for a moonshine liquor operation. By age nine young Mickey was happily involved in this family business, and was arrested making a delivery of his brother's moonshine. His brother, however, had enough local connections for the police to let Mickey go. Mickey had had his first taste for the gangster lifestyle and he liked it.

FIGHTING AND GAMBLING

Another thing he liked was boxing. Though small of stature, Mickey Cohen had plenty of aggression and power. He fought as a featherweight and won an amateur championship, aged fifteen. At that point he left home, determined to turn pro. He headed for New York where his boxing reputation grew and - the sport being a big favourite with mobsters – he made the acquaintance of a number of leading figures in organised crime, including Owney Madden, the man behind such mob-run operations as the Cotton Club and the Mafia's very own resort in Hot Springs, Arkansas.

Mickey Cohen's fight career peaked with a bout against the featherweight World Champion, Tommy Paul. This resulted in a bad beating for Cohen, whereupon he promptly quit the ring and moved straight back into crime. He started by holding up gambling joints. This was a risky business, as many of these places were run by the mob. Cohen was lucky that, rather than kill him the local mob realized he had a talent that could be exploited. He moved from New York to Cleveland to Chicago, graduating

from holding up card games to running them. Along the way he gained the personal approval of top Chicago boss Al Capone.

When things got a little too hot in Chicago, Cohen moved back to Cleveland for a while, working with Lou Rothkopf. Cleveland didn't have enough action for Cohen, so Rothkopf suggested Mickey take a trip to California where his associates Meyer Lansky and Bugsy Siegel were staking out their turf in Hollywood.

Mickey took the advice and made his way up the ranks of the organization to become Siegel's right-hand man. He was soon embroiled in fighting between the Siegel and Lansky outfit and a rival outfit, led by Jack Dragna, the previous LA mob boss. This was a conflict between old and new, Italian and Jewish. The conflict

▲ *Mickey Cohen (right) next to his right-hand man, Johnny Stompanato, during a trial in 1950. Eight years later Stompanato was murdered by Hollywood actress Lana Turner's 14-year-old daughter*

frequently became bloody, and Mickey Cohen was lucky to escape unscathed from several attempts on his life. Once, members of Dragna's gang opened up with machine guns as Cohen sat in his car. Ducking down, he managed to drive his car to safety, shaking off his pursuers.

HOLLYWOOD BECKONS

Increasingly, Siegel's attention became taken up with establishing a giant casino, The Flamingo, in Las Vegas. Siegel was the front man for this project, but when the Flamingo made an initial huge loss, he was suspected of skimming off money from the project and his fellow mobsters ordered his death. The hit was carried out with clinical efficiency in 1947. Mickey Cohen must have suspected he would be tainted by his boss' misdeeds but instead he was promoted to become the number one boss on the West Coast.

Now Cohen started to move in elevated circles. He became friendly with Harry Cohn, boss of Columbia Pictures and assorted movie stars, including Frank Sinatra and Sammy Davis Jr. At one stage he was caught in a dispute between two of his friends. Cohn was furious that the black Sammy Davis Jr should have an open affair with white actress Kim Novak, and wanted Mickey Cohen to have Davis killed. Cohen managed to talk him out of it.

Mickey's right-hand man, the notorious gunman Johnny Stompanato, also got involved with the Hollywood elite. He had affairs with Ava Gardner and then Lana Turner. This relationship led to a scandal when Lana Turner's fourteen-year-old daughter, Cheryl Crane, shot Stompanato dead on 4 April 1958.

LIFE IN ALCATRAZ

The scandal once again drew unwanted publicity towards Cohen. Matters got worse following the 1960 election of John F. Kennedy. His brother Robert Kennedy became Attorney General and was determined to stamp out Mafia activity. Soon Cohen was arrested for tax evasion for the second time in his life (he had already served a brief sentence in the early 1950s). This time he was looking at a much longer sentence, but given the chance to walk free if he informed on other major organised crime figures.

Cohen refused and was sentenced to fifteen years in prison. He spent the first part of his sentence in the notorious Alcatraz prison and, when he was finally released in the early 1970s, went into semi-retirement. He wrote a book, In My Own Words, about his criminal career. However, it was not long before he succumbed to the ravages of stomach cancer. He died on 29 July 1976 at home in California.

Carroll COLE

One of the few serial killers known to have the IQ level of a genius is Carroll Edward Cole. Paradoxically, however, he turned out to be the absolute model of the disorganized killer. When Cole killed, there was no pattern or logic to his crimes; there were no cryptic clues left behind, or crosswords puzzles sent to the police. Most of the times Eddie Cole murdered, he was too drunk to remember anything about it. The fact that he was allowed to roam free for so long and kill so many people is sad testament to the incompetence of the legal and medical authorities.

Carroll Edward 'Eddie' Cole was born on 9 May 1938 in Sioux City, Iowa, the second son of LaVerne and Vesta Cole. His sister was born in 1939, and soon afterwards the family moved to California, where LaVerne found work in a shipyard. Not long after that LaVerne was drafted to fight in the Second World War.

BULLYING MOTHER

While his father was away, Eddie Cole's mother started having affairs. Sometimes she would take her son with her, and afterwards threaten and beat him to ensure that he did not tell his father. Vesta was a cruel bully, especially in her treatment of her son. She dressed him as a girl and made fun of him. When Carroll went to school, he was teased about his name by his schoolmates, and became increasingly angry and withdrawn. He claimed (in an autobiography he wrote while in prison) that when he was nine years old he drowned one of his tormentors, a fellow nine-year-old called Duane, but at the time the police regarded the incident as an accident.

In his teens, Carroll drifted into petty crime. He was regularly arrested for drunkenness and minor thefts. After high school he joined the army but was soon discharged after stealing some pistols. By this time, he was showing signs of mental deterioration. In 1960, he attacked two couples parked in cars in a lovers lane. Soon afterwards, he called the police in Richmond, California, where he was living, and told them that he was plagued by violent fantasies involving strangling women.

PSYCHIATRIC HELP

The policeman he spoke to advised him to get psychiatric help; Cole spent the next three years in and out of mental institutions. At the last of these, Stockton State Hospital, a Dr Weiss wrote: 'He seems to be afraid of the female figure and cannot have intercourse with her first but must kill her before he can do it.' Despite this apparently damning diagnosis, Weiss approved Cole's release in April 1963.

On release, Cole drifted east to Dallas, Texas, where his brother Richard was living. There he met and married Billie Whitworth, an alcoholic stripper. Not surprisingly, this relationship failed to cure him of his violent feelings towards women. After two acrimonious years, the marriage ended when Cole burnt down a motel after convincing himself that Whitworth was having sex with men there. He was imprisoned for arson.

On release, Cole attempted to strangle an eleven-year-old girl in Missouri. He was arrested for the crime and sentenced to five years in prison. After serving his sentence, he was released again and ended up in Nevada, where he attempted to strangle two more women. Once again, he turned himself in to the psychiatric services. There, the doctors noted his murderous fantasies but still saw no reason to detain him and he was given a ticket back to San Diego, California.

FIRST THREE VICTIMS
In San Diego he murdered for the first time as an adult. He killed three women there, each of whom he had picked up in a bar, had sex with and then strangled. He later claimed that they had all proved themselves unfaithful to their husbands, and so reminded him of his adulterous mother.

These killings set the template for the next ten years. Cole drifted: in each new place he strangled women, generally in a drunken stupor. In the case of a woman he murdered in Oklahoma City, he claims he came out of an alcoholic blackout to find slices of his victim's buttocks cooking on a skillet.

By 1979, Cole was back in San Diego, married again to another heavy-drinking woman. While there, he murdered a woman called Bonnie Sue O'Neill and left her body outside his workplace. Still the police failed to interview him. Soon after that, he murdered his wife.

This time, there was a documented history of how he had threatened to kill her. A neighbour found him drunk, digging a grave underneath the house. The neighbour called the police, who found Cole's wife's body in a closet in his house. Extraordinarily, they decided that she had probably died of alcohol poisoning and pressed no charges against Cole.

Cole then left San Diego and went back on the road. He killed another woman in Las Vegas, and then returned to Dallas, where he strangled three more women during November 1980.

Cole was a suspect in the second of these killings and was actually found on the scene of the third murder. He was arrested and held in custody. The police then came to the conclusion – once again – that the victim had probably died of natural causes, and were about to let him go. However, before they could do so, Cole confessed – not just to this murder but to his whole history of killing.

On 9 April 1981, Cole was convicted of three of the murders committed in Texas. He was sentenced to life imprisonment in Huntsville Prison.

In 1984, his mother died, and his attitude seems to have changed. Soon afterwards, rather than serve out his sentence, and look forward to a possible parole, he agreed to face further murder charges filed in Nevada, even though he knew these could involve the death penalty.

In October 1984, Cole was indeed sentenced to death in Nevada. Anti-death penalty campaigners tried to have his sentence commuted but Cole wanted none of it. When the sentence was passed, he said the words 'Thanks, Judge'. In December 1985, he was executed.

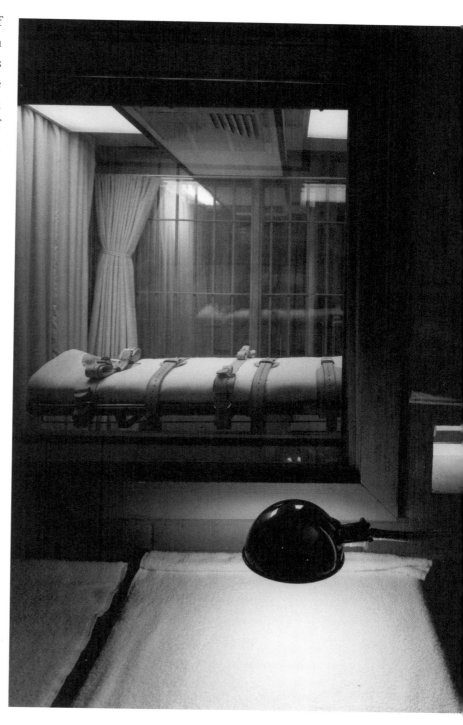

▶ *Cole's last moments: finally the authorities took notice of him, and took his life for the ones he had in turn taken*

Ray and Faye COPELAND

Ray and Faye Copeland were perhaps the most unlikely team of serial killers in American history. An elderly married couple, they were old-fashioned farming people living an apparently simple life that revolved around the daily chores on their farm in Nebraska. As it turned out, however, their life was anything but simple; together they were hiring a series of young men to work as farmhands and then murdering them as part of a scam to make themselves rich. For a long time they went undetected – after all, they were both senior citizens, on the face of it living quietly in the countryside. But finally, the law caught up with them and revealed the horrifying truth about life – and death – on the Copeland farm.

DEPRESSION

Ray Copeland was born in Oklahoma in 1914. While Ray was growing up, his family moved around, struggling to survive during the Depression. As a young man, he began a life of petty crime, stealing livestock and forging cheques, until he was caught and served a year in jail. After his release, he met his future wife, Faye; a loyal accomplice to his crimes during their long marriage.

The couple quickly had several children and money became tight. Ray continued to steal livestock and to forge cheques; his increasingly bad reputation meant that the family had to keep moving around. During this time Ray served several jail sentences, until he finally came up with a new plan: not to go straight, but to improve his illegal money-making methods so that he would go undetected.

FRAUDSTER

Since he was well known by now as a fraudster, Copeland could not buy and sell cattle himself. To circumvent this problem, he began to pick up drifters and hobos, employing them as farmhands. He would go to market with his employees, who would buy cattle for him and pay for them with bad cheques. After the transactions, Copeland would sell the cattle quickly, and the farmhands would disappear without trace. For a while the scam worked, but then police caught up with them. Once again, Ray Copeland went to jail.

On his release, Copeland resumed his criminal activities, but this time he made sure his farm hands operated more independently from him. This went on until a previous employee, Jack McCormick, phoned the Nebraska Crime Stoppers hotline in August 1989 to tell them about the Copelands. He had been employed on the farm, and claimed that he had seen human bones there. He also said that Ray Copeland had tried to kill him.

Police were initially sceptical of the claims, but once they checked Copeland's record, they decided to investigate them thoroughly. In October 1989, they visited the Copeland farm armed with a search warrant, dozens of officers and a team of bloodhounds. However, they initially failed to find any incriminating evidence. Then, just as they were beginning to give up hope, the remains of three bodies were found in a nearby barn. They were the bodies of three young men. All had died from a bullet shot to the head from behind. As the search went on more bodies were discovered, all killed by the same weapon, a .22 Marlin rifle that was later found in the Copeland home.

It was by now clear that Copeland was a cold-blooded murderer who had callously killed his employees in the pursuit of his money-scam. But what of his wife Faye? During the investigation, a piece of evidence came to light that was not only incriminating, but also deeply sinister: a quilt that Faye had fashioned out of the clothing of the dead men.

When she came to trial, Faye's defence mounted a picture of her as a dutiful wife and mother who had endured beatings and general ill-treatment from her bully of a husband. However, the quilt remained a macabre reminder that whatever her involvement, Faye Copeland knew perfectly well that her husband was a serial murderer and did nothing to stop him.

Faye Copeland was sentenced to death by lethal injection. On hearing the news, Ray Copeland showed no emotion. Ray was also sentenced to death by lethal injection. Aged 69 and 76, Faye and Ray Copeland became the oldest couple in the United States ever to receive the death sentence. However, neither of the executions took place: Ray died while awaiting execution, and Faye's sentence was commuted to life imprisonment. She later died, aged 82, of natural causes.

▼ *There was more money to be had in murder than there was in farming*

Dean CORLL

Some crime investigations go backwards, not forwards – and this was the case with Dean Corll. For by the time Houston police found him, on the morning of 8 August 1973, Corll was already dead, with three frightened teenagers on the scene. What the police had to do was find out why, to look back into the past that had brought the thirty-four-year-old Corll and the teenagers together – and the past proved very scary indeed.

At first it seemed like a glue-sniffing-and-sex party that had got seriously out of hand, mostly because one of the teenagers, Wayne Hedley, had brought along a girl – and Dean Corll, a homosexual, didn't like girls one bit. When Hedley recovered consciousness after their first big hit of glue, he'd found himself handcuffed, with Corll standing over him with a gun and threatening to kill them all. After pleading for his life, Hedley was released on condition: that he now rape and kill the girl while Corll did the same with the other boy.

The boy was stripped naked and handcuffed to a specially made plywood board. Corll then repeatedly sodomised him. Hedley, though, lying on top of the girl, couldn't get an erection – and he soon wanted out. He begged to be allowed to go, but Corll refused. So he picked up the gun as Corll continued to taunt him, and finally pulled the trigger.

Not nice, but not very complicated, it seemed – until that is, Hedley admitted under questioning not only that he'd often procured boys for Corll, but also that Corll had boasted that morning of killing a number of them and 'burying them in the boatshed.'

The boatshed turned out to be a boathouse-stall in southwest Houston; and when the police started digging, they turned up the first of what proved to be seventeen corpses. Later Hedley took them to two other sites, and a further ten were found – but not even that was the real total of victims, Hedley said four were still out there, missing.

It was clear enough by now that Hedley was deeply involved; and so was another kid, David Brooks, who'd introduced Hedley to Corll. They'd both procured victims for Corll and had both taken part in their murders. The pattern, first set in 1970, seemed to have remained the same from the start: Either Hedley or Brooks – or both – would bring back children or teenagers to Corll's house for glue-sniffing. Then,

when they were unconscious, they'd be tied to the board, sometimes two at a time, and used, first for sex, then for torture, then for murder. One of the bodies found had bite-marks on the genitals; another had had them cut off altogether. The youngest victim was nine.

Who exactly Dean Corll was was at first something of a mystery. He worked for the Houston Lighting and Power Company; and on the evidence of photographs, which often showed him holding toy animals, he looked like a man who had never completely grown up. This turned out to more or less true: raised in Indiana and Vidor, Texas, he was a mummy's boy. Because of illness,

he spent much of his youth at home; and her succession of bad marriages meant that she was his only constant as he was being raised.

He even helped her out when she started a candy-making business at home for extra money. Candy is, of course, dandy, as Dorothy Parker wrote: it makes you popular with other children — and it's interesting that Corll picked up his first procurer, David Brooks, outside a school with an offer of candy.

Both Brooks and Hedley were sentenced to life imprisonment The telephone call that Hedley made to the police on that morning in August had done him no good at all.

Juan CORONA

Juan Corona arrived in the United States from Mexico as a migrant labourer some time in the 1950s. By the beginning of the 70s, married and with four little girls, he was a labour contractor in California's Sacramento Valley, organizing gangs of drifters and casual workers to pick peaches in the area around Yuba City. He was a religious man and well-liked. But he was also — if the juries at his two trials were right — a homosexual multiple murderer.

▶Juan Corona was a well liked family man

The first body was found by the police on 19 May 1971, when a Japanese-American farmer complained that a trench had been dug in his orchard without his permission and then, later, filled in. When the police investigated the scene, they found buried in it the body of a hobo who had been stabbed in the chest and slashed about the head with a machete. There was evidence that he'd had homosexual intercourse some time before his death.

Three days later, a tractor driver on the nearby Sullivan ranch, where Corona housed his crews in a dormitory, found another patch of disturbed earth; and again the police were called. This time they found the body of an elderly man — and not far away, seven more graves, each of them containing a body. The victims, all male, had been stabbed and slashed about the head, and had died at some time over the previous two months. Their shirts had been yanked up to cover their faces; their trousers were either missing or had been pulled down round their ankles. There were clear signs, the police said, of 'homosexual activity.'

In one of the graves, there were also two scraps of paper: receipts for meat signed 'Juan V. Corona.' Furthermore, one of the victims had been last seen getting into Corona's pick-up truck. As the police searched the ranch, the thirty-seven-year-old was arrested on suspicion of murder.

◀ *Corona was alleged to have murdered 25 men*

In all, over a seventeen-day period, twenty-five bodies were found – and in the grave of the last one was further evidence of Corona's involvement, in the shape of two of his bank-deposit slips. He was tried for the murder of all twenty-five, and found guilty, despite the fact that the evidence was entirely circumstantial – and despite the fact, too, that the only man in Corona's family who was both homosexual and had a record for assault with a machete was his half-brother Natividad. In 1970, Natividad had been sued for $250,000 in damages by a young Mexican found in his café slashed about the head in a way similar to the dead men – and he'd lost.

Corona appealed for a retrial, and in 1978 he was granted it, on the grounds that his attorney had given him an inadequate defence. (He had not even raised, for example, the issue of insanity, though Corona, in the 1960s, had suffered from a mental illness, diagnosed at the time as schizophrenia.) The second trial, in 1982, ended the same way as the first, upholding the guilty verdicts, largely because of the evidence of a Mexican consular official who'd visited Corona in prison in 1978. He reported that Corona had told him:

'Yes, I did it. But I'm a sick man and can't be judged by the standards of other men.'

Doctor CRIPPIN

Dr. Hawley Harvey, later Peter, Crippen is one of the most famous — and most reviled — murderers of the 20th century. Yet he was a small, slight man, intelligent, dignified, eternally polite and anxious for the welfare of those around him. With his gold-rimmed spectacles, sandy whiskers and shy expression, he was, in fact, more mouse than monster. His problem was his wife.

Crippen was born in Coldwater, Michigan in 1862, and studied for medical degrees in Cleveland, London and New York. Around 1890, his first wife died, leaving him a widower; and three years later, when working in a practice in Brooklyn, he fell in love with one of his patients, a 17-year-old with ambitions to be an opera singer, called Cora Turner. She was overweight; her real name was Kunigunde Mackamotzki — she was the boisterous, loose daughter of a Russian-Polish immigrant. But none of this mattered to Crippen. He first paid for her singing lessons, and then he married her.

In 1900, by now consultant physician to a mail-order medicine company, Crippen was transferred to London to become manager of the firm's head office; and Cora came to join him. On arrival in London, though, she decided to change her name once again — this time to Belle Elmore — and to try out her voice in the city's music halls. She soon became a success and acquired many friends and admirers. She bleached her hair; became a leading light in the Music Hall Ladies Guild; and entertained the first of what were to be many lovers. Increasingly contemptuous of her husband, whom she regarded as an embarrassment, she forced him first to move to a grand house in north London that he could ill afford, and then to act as a general dogsbody to the 'lodgers' she soon moved in.

Crippen took such consolation as he could with a shy secretary at his company called Ethel La Neve. But in 1909, he lost his job, and his wife threatened to leave him, taking their life savings with her. By the beginning of the following year, he'd had enough. On January 19th, he acquired five grains of a powerful narcotic called hyoscine from a chemist's in New Oxford Street; and the last time his wife was seen was twelve days later, at a dinner for two retired music-hall friends at the Crippens' home. Two days after that, as it turned out, Crippen began pawning her jewellery, and sent a letter to the Music Hall Ladies Guild, saying that she'd had to leave for America, where a

◄ Dr Crippen is one of the most infamous murderers of the 20th century

relative was seriously ill. Later he announced that she'd gone to the wilds of California; that she had contracted pneumonia; and, in March – after Ethel had moved into his house – that she had died there.

Two actors, though, who'd been touring in California returned to England and, when told, said they'd heard nothing at all about Cora's death. Scotland Yard took an interest; and Crippen was forced to concede that he'd made up the story: his wife had in fact left for America with one of her lovers. Though this seemed to satisfy the detectives, he then made his first big mistake: he panicked, settled his affairs overnight and left with Ethel the next day for Europe, after persuading her to start a new life with him in America. When the police called again, it was to

▲ *An artist's impression of Crippen's capture*

wireless telegraph to send a message to his employers. Each day from then on, in fact, he sent via the same medium daily reports on the doings of the couple which were published in the British newspapers. Meanwhile, Chief Inspector Dew of Scotland Yard took a faster ship and arrested Dr. Crippen and 'son' Ethel when they reached Canadian waters.

Huge, angry crowds greeted them when they arrived back a month later, under arrest, in England. The newspapers had done their job of transforming the pair of them into vicious killers. But Crippen always maintained that Ethel had had absolutely no knowledge of the murder; and when they were tried separately, she was acquitted. Crippen, though, was found guilty and was hanged in Pentonville Prison on November 23rd 1910. Before he died, he described Ethel as

'. . .my only comfort for the past three years. As I face eternity, I say that Ethel Le Neve has loved me as few women love men. . . Surely such love as hers for me will be rewarded.'

It is not known whether she was rewarded, or indeed what became of her, though one story recounts that she ran a tea-shop in Bournemouth, under an assumed name, for forty-five years.

find them gone. They began a thorough search of the house. What remained of his wife – rotting flesh, skin and hair – was found buried under the coal cellar.

Unaware of the furore of horror created by this discovery in the British press, Crippen – his moustache shaved off, under an assumed name, and accompanied by Ethel, disguised as his son – took a ship from Antwerp to Quebec in Canada. But they were soon recognized by the captain who, aware of a reward, used the new invention of the

Andrew CUNANAN

Andrew Cunanan was a gay man whose apparent frustrations with his lack of success erupted in a killing spree that was as violent as it was senseless. After killing a string of men, both friends and strangers, Cunanan travelled to Miami and lay in wait for Gianni Versace, the fashion designer, shooting him in the head on the front steps of his palatial home, Casa Casuarina, at South Beach. Afterwards, Cunanan fled and went into hiding. He was found eight days later, and chose to kill himself rather than go into custody.

The murder of Gianni Versace horrified the media when it took place on 15 July 1997. At the time, Versace was at the height of his success as one of the foremost fashion designers in the world, having designed glamorous, flamboyant clothes for rock stars such as Elton John. With his trademark T-shirts and unstructured suits, designed for the TV series *Miami Vice*, Versace had pioneered a relaxed look for men that had become synonymous with 1980s style.

Andrew Cunanan, by contrast, was a good-looking, personable young man who became part of the gay scene but who – unlike Gianni Versace – never had the talent or application to do more than drift on its more treacherous currents. Cunanan was born on 31 August 1969. His father, Modesto, was Filipino, a fact that Andrew later often disguised, pretending that he came from a Latino background instead.

His mother, Mary Ann, was a strict Catholic, and was not happy with her husband, who was something of an authoritarian. Modesto's job in the hospital corps of the navy often took him away from home, and when he returned he often became paranoid that his wife had been having affairs, even accusing her of giving birth to a child that was not his.

◀ *Gianni Versace at the height of his career in 1994*

▶ *A couple look on in shock at the blood-stained steps of Versace's Miami Beach villa on Ocean Drive*

The couple had four children, the youngest of whom was Andrew. When Andrew was born, his mother suffered a bout of depression, and he was mainly cared for by his father. Andrew grew up to be extremely bright with a high IQ but often played the fool, finding it difficult to settle down to work at school. The tensions of his home life were evident in his behaviour, but people found him entertaining and fun, and on the whole accepted his obvious homosexuality from a young age.

SELLING SEX

From the age of about fifteen, Andrew began to frequent gay bars and clubs, often changing his name and appearance and making up stories about his life. Before long, he was selling his body as a male prostitute to rich, older men and spending the money on flashy new designer clothes.

His parents had no idea what was going on, but they were having troubles of their own. Modesto had changed his employment and become a stockbroker, but had lost money and the couple split up. Modesto returned to the Philippines. Andrew quarrelled with his mother and followed his father there, but was horrified to find him living in squalor, and soon returned – after prostituting himself once again to earn the fare home.

NEW LIFE

Once back in America, Andrew carved out a new life for himself in San Francisco, often posing as a young naval officer. There, he began to lead the high life, and once actually met and chatted briefly to Gianni Versace at a party. At the same time, his life was beginning to spin out of control. He was acting in gay porn videos, some of them very violent, and his self-destructive mood was beginning to sour. He was drinking excessively, and became angry and unpredictable with friends; he was paranoid that he had AIDS, but was afraid to seek medical help; and he was also broke, having been abandoned by his rich lovers. For reasons that are still unclear, Cunanan's anger suddenly spilled over into violence, and he accused two ex-boyfriends, Jeff Trail and David Madson, of having an affair with each other. The men were both well-to-do, which also fuelled Cunanan's jealousy. Cunanan's behaviour became abusive and he telephoned Trail, threatening to kill him. He then went to visit Madson in Minneapolis, who tried to reassure him by inviting Trail over to his house, but a bitter argument broke out. Cunanan found a hammer in the kitchen and clubbed Trail over the head with it repeatedly, smashing his skull and killing him. Madson panicked, and helped Cunanan roll the body up in a rug; and a couple of days later, the pair took off together in Madson's jeep. Later, Cunanan inexplicably pulled a gun on Madson and shot him, killing him as well.

The next two victims were complete strangers. The first was an elderly man named Lee Miglin who was standing outside his house when Cunanan approached for directions. He took Miglin into the garage, bound, tortured and killed him before spending the night in the house and taking off in Miglin's car the next day. The second was 45-year-old William Reese, the caretaker of a cemetery, whom he held up and shot.

SUCCESSFUL DESIGNER

Gianni Versace was to be next. He had been born on 2 December 1946 in Calabria, Italy. His father sold electrical goods and his mother owned a dress-making store. As a boy, Gianni learned the tailoring trade, both sewing and designing clothes. In 1972, he began receiving commissions to design for clothing companies and later opened his own store. During the 1980s, his own collections became hugely popular, and he became known as the designer who dispensed with the old-fashioned tie, yet still managed to make his men look stylish and well-groomed. He also began to dress some of the most famous names of the day, in the world of film, pop and even

royalty – Princess Diana was one of his close friends.

By the 1990s, along with Ralph Lauren and Giorgio Armani, he had become a world-famous designer with a huge clothing empire to his name.

GLAMOROUS LIFESTYLE

By the time he reached fifty, Versace had about as much success as any man could want, and was talking about leading a more relaxed life with more time for entertaining. He had bought a large property on Ocean Drive, overlooking the sea at Miami Beach, and transformed it into an Italianate palace for himself and his friends. At the time, Miami Beach was the hub of a fashionable gay social life, and there was an array of ever-changing restaurants and clubs to see and be seen in. However, there was also a darker side to this sophisticated world of money, glamour and power; AIDS was terrifying the gay community, and there was a constant undertow of drug abuse and violent sex lurking below the glittering surface of the Californian gay lifestyle.

SHOT TWICE IN THE HEAD

Amazingly, Cunanan managed to escape the police after his killing spree, though they were now on his trail. He holed up in Miami Beach. There, he checked into a

◄ Frustrated with his life, Andrew Cunanan (left) went on a killing spree which included gunning down Gianni Versace

hotel, dined in restaurants and wandered the streets for two months without anybody noticing him – a fact that caused much criticism of the local police force when it came to light after Versace's killing. During this time, he followed Versace's movements, and noted that the designer often went to a café on his own in the mornings. On the morning of 15 July 1997, he followed Versace home from the café and shot him twice in the head as he was opening the gate of his house.

The fact that Versace was so famous prompted the FBI to launch a huge search for the killer, who was found eight days later, hiding out on a private houseboat. A caretaker discovered Cunanan there and alerted the police, who surrounded the houseboat. A dramatic standoff took place, with Cunanan refusing to come out and give himself up. When the police finally moved in, they found Cunanan dead on the floor. He had shot himself with his murdered friend Jeff Trail's pistol.

POST-MORTEM

A post-mortem revealed that Cunanan was not suffering from AIDS, despite the rumours that this was what had sent him over the edge. It still remains unclear exactly what motivated Cunanan, beyond a generalized sense of jealousy and anger at the world. Because of this, since Versace's death, there have been conspiracy theories to explain what happened, including the theory that his assassination was masterminded by the Mafia. However, it seems that, to date, no one has a clear answer as to exactly why Versace met his death that day, and the murder will continue to puzzle commentators for many years to come.

Jeffrey DAHMER

Jeffrey Dahmer is among the most troubling of all serial killers – an apparently regular guy who turned into a psychopathic murderer, necrophile and cannibal.

Dahmer was born on 21 May 1960, the son of Lionel, a chemist, and Joyce, a homemaker. Joyce was highly strung, while Lionel worked long hours; the pair argued a great deal but to all appearances this was still a normal family household. However, at an early age, Jeffrey developed a fascination with dead animals. Then, aged six, following a hernia operation and the birth of his younger brother David, he became withdrawn. He remained solitary and friendless throughout his childhood. In his teens, his fascination with dead creatures intensified. He would cycle around looking for road kill, which he would carefully dismember. By the time of his high-school graduation, he had also become a heavy drinker.

Jeffrey's parents did not appear to notice his troubles, as by this time they were locked in an acrimonious divorce. During the summer of 1978, just as Jeffrey was due to graduate, they both moved out of the house, leaving Jeffrey there alone. His response was to pick up a hitchhiker, Stephen Hicks, take him home, have sex with him and then, when Hicks tried to leave, to hit him on the head with a bar bell, strangle him, dismember his corpse and bury it nearby.

ALCOHOLIC

Jeffrey's father Lionel had by this time moved in with his second wife Shari, who pointed out to her new husband that his son was an alcoholic. Lionel responded by giving Jeffrey an ultimatum: to stop drinking or to join the army. Jeffrey refused to stop drinking, so his father saw to it that he enlisted in January 1979, aged eighteen. Dahmer appeared to enjoy army life, but he was soon discharged for drunkenness. He then moved into his grandmother's basement and his life continued its downward spiral.

In 1982, Dahmer was arrested for indecent exposure, and then again in 1986. Each time his father paid for lawyers, and for his second offence Dahmer was given a suspended sentence and counselling. The counselling clearly had little effect, however, as he went on to kill three times during the next year.

FIRST VICTIM

His first victim that year was Steven Tuomi, whom he met in a gay bar. He murdered Tuomi in a hotel, put the body in a suitcase, took it home, had sex with it and then dismembered it. Next, Dahmer murdered a fourteen-year-old Native American boy called James Doxtator, who hung around the Milwaukee gay scene. After Doxtator came a Mexican youth named Richard Guerrero. (Dahmer's career of savagery categorically disproved a previously held theory that serial killers only murder within their own race.)

At this point Dahmer's grandmother, bothered by his drunkenness and the terrible smells coming from his apartment, evicted him. Dahmer moved into his own flat in Milwaukee in September 1988. The next day, he lured a thirteen-year-old Laotian boy there, offering to pay him for a nude modelling session. He drugged the boy and fondled him but did not become violent. The boy's parents reported Dahmer to the police. He was sentenced to a year in prison for sexual assault. While waiting for sentence, however, he killed his next victim, Anthony Sears.

Dahmer served ten months in prison before beginning his final killing spree. Between June 1990 and July 1991, he murdered another twelve men. In the end he was committing a murder almost every week, and his treatment of his victims was becoming ever more bizarre. He was obsessed with the notion of creating zombies – half-humans who would be his playthings. To this end he drilled holes in his victims' skulls while they were still alive, and dripped acid into their heads. (Unsurprisingly, none of his victims survived.) In at least one case, he also

▲ *Jeffrey Dahmer photographed at his trial*

▶ *In prison, Dahmer refused to be placed in solitary confinement. On 28 November 1994, a fellow inmate took an iron bar and smashed it down on Dahmer's skull. The blow killed him*

tried cannibalism. He kept his victims' body parts in his refrigerator, and placed their skulls on an altar in his bedroom.

Most disturbing of all was the case of Konerak Sinthasomphone, the brother of the Laotian teenager he had previously molested. Dahmer drugged Konerak, but the boy managed to escape from the apartment. Two young black women found Konerak and called the police, but when they arrived on the scene, Dahmer persuaded the police that the drugged and bleeding Konerak was his boyfriend. Incredibly, the police returned the boy to Dahmer, who promptly took him home and murdered him.

In the next few weeks, a frenzied Dahmer went on to kill his last four victims. On 22 July 1991, his final intended victim, an adult black man, Tracy Edwards, escaped from the apartment, a pair of handcuffs trailing from his wrist. Edwards managed to flag down a police car and then led the police back to the apartment, where they were horrified to find a human head in the refrigerator.

Dahmer's killing spree was finally over. As details of the story emerged in the press, the full picture of Dahmer's horrific crimes shocked an America that had become wearily accustomed to tales of murder and perversion.

By 22 August 1991 Dahmer had been charged with a total of fifteen counts of murder. His trial began on 30 January 1992. He pleaded guilty but insane. The jury found him sane and he was sentenced to fifteen consecutive life sentences.

The FRITZL CASE

Josef Fritzl told conflicting stories about his mother Maria. In some, she was 'the best woman in the world', in others she had been a cold, brutal being – almost inhuman.

'She used to beat me, hit me until I was lying in a pool of blood on the floor,' he once claimed. 'I never had a kiss from her.'

Later on, Fritzl claimed, his mother did not mellow with age. Instead, her harsh nature stayed with her, even into old age. When Fritzl was a senior citizen himself, he revealed that Maria's last years were spent in a locked room with a bricked-up window. Fritzl told concerned neighbours that his mother had died, when in reality she had been his captive. In ordinary circumstances, Fritzl's behaviour towards his mother would be shocking, but in the context of his other crimes the incident ranks as little more than a footnote.

EMERGENCY CALL

The world knew nothing of Fritzl's crimes until the morning of Saturday 19 April 2008, when he telephoned for an ambulance. Seventeen-year-old Kerstin Fritzl was seriously ill at his home, number 40 Ybbsstrasse in the Austrian town of Amstetten.

The ambulance attendants were puzzled by the condition of their unconscious patient. Her symptoms were like nothing they had ever encountered. Deathly pale and missing many of her teeth, Kerstin was close to death. She was transported immediately to the local hospital. A few hours later, Josef Fritzl turned up. Describing himself as her grandfather, he presented a letter from Kerstin's mother, Elisabeth.

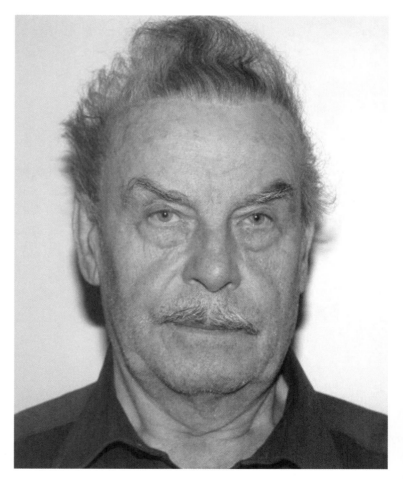

▼ *Josef Fritzl locked up his mother for the last few years of her life; it gave him ideas...*

'Please help her. Kerstin is very scared of strangers. She has never been in a hospital before. I've asked my father for help because he is the only person she knows.'

Josef Fritzl explained Elisabeth had run off to join a religious cult many years before, leaving the child with him. The police were called in as Kerstin lay close to death and a team of investigators began a search for Elisabeth Fritzl. The authorities wanted to question the mother about what they thought might be criminal neglect. Enquiries were made all over Austria and all sorts of databases were checked, yet nothing could be found on Elisabeth that was not at least a few decades old.

▼ *40 Ybbsstrasse, Amstetten – the house looked ordinary, but revelation of its secrets would rock Austria*

TELEVISED APPEAL

At the end of Kerstin's second day in hospital, the doctors made a televised appeal. They were struggling to diagnose Kerstin's condition and they thought that her mother might be able to help them. When Elisabeth failed to contact the hospital the police showed up at 40 Ybbsstrasse. They wanted to take DNA samples from the Fritzls. Josef's wife Rosemarie provided a sample, as did the other children Elisabeth had 'abandoned'. However, Josef himself was far too busy to give the authorities any of his time.

One week after Kerstin had been taken to hospital, Rosemarie was surprised to see Elisabeth in her house. Her daughter had been away for nearly 24 years. Elisabeth was accompanied by two children, Stefan and Felix. Rosemarie had not been aware of their existence. Josef explained that their daughter had heard the doctors' appeals and had left the cult she had been with, so that she could see her seriously ill daughter.

When Elisabeth visited the hospital, the police were waiting. They wanted to know where the young woman had been during the previous two decades, and how it was that she had abandoned her children. Elisabeth was taken to the police station where she was questioned for hours. As midnight approached, Elisabeth revealed that she had not joined a cult and she had not abandoned her children. Instead, she had been imprisoned by her father in the cellar at 40 Ybbsstrasse.

Having broken her silence, Elisabeth told the police that she would reveal everything about the last 24 years of her life on condition that she never had to see her father again. After the stunned investigators had acceded to her wishes, Elisabeth began a two-hour monologue in which she described in considerable detail the ordeal she had endured.

She told the police that her father had lured her into the cellar on 29 August 1984, where she had been sedated with ether and placed in a hidden bunker. It seemed that the foundations of number 40 Ybbsstrasse were something of a maze. The oldest part of the house dated back to 1890 and numerous modifications had been made in the years that followed, including a 1978 addition that had been constructed by a builder.

For reasons of secrecy, however, Fritzl had built the bunker himself. It could only be reached by going down the cellar stairs, passing through a number of rooms and unlocking a series of eight doors. The final door was hidden behind a large shelving unit.

The bunker itself consisted of a kitchen, a bathroom, a living area and two bedrooms. There was no source of natural light, and the air was stale and stagnant. The ceiling was very low – it was less than 2 m (6 ft) high at best. It had not been difficult for Fritzl to construct the bunker. As an electrical engineer, he had always been good with his hands.

GOOD PROVIDER

Born in Amstetten on 9 April 1935, Fritzl had been raised alone by his mother after his father had deserted his small family. Josef Fritzl Snr went on to fight as a Nazi stormtrooper and was killed during the Second World War. The younger Josef had been a good student with a notable aptitude for technical matters. He had just begun his career with a Linz steel company when he married 17-year-old Rosemarie at the age of 21. The couple had two sons and five daughters together, including the beautiful Elisabeth.

Fritzl was a very good provider, but he was also an unpleasant husband and father. In 1967 he was sentenced to 18 months in prison after having confessed to the rape of a 24-year-old woman. After his release he was employed by a construction firm and later on he travelled throughout Austria as a technical equipment salesman. Until April 2008, the electrical engineer had no further brushes with the law. That is not to say that he led an exemplary life. Among his neighbours he had a reputation as an unfriendly man, one who kept himself to himself and his family away from others. There was talk that he was very firm with his children and that absolute obedience was expected.

No matter how much Fritzl's neighbours gossiped about him, none of them had the faintest conception of what was taking place in his household. In 1977, Fritzl began sexually abusing Elisabeth. She was 11 years old at the time. Although she told no one, not even her close friend Christa Woldrich, it is easy to imagine what a devastating effect it must have had on her.

'I did get the impression that she felt more comfortable at school than at home,' Woldrich told one reporter. 'Sometimes she went quiet when it was time to go home again.'

In January 1983, Elisabeth ran away from home, ending up in Vienna. She was then 16 years old. Even though she tried her best to hide, she only managed to remain free for three weeks before the police found her and returned her to her parents. The authorities calculate that Fritzl was well into the construction of the bunker at this point. Eighteen months after the police had brought the girl back to number 40 Ybbsstrasse, Elisabeth's incarceration began.

Fritzl appeared to be very open about what had happened to his 18-year-old daughter. He told everyone that she had been a drug-taking problem child who had gone off to join a religious cult. But there was no cult, of course. Fritzl backed up his story by forcing Elisabeth to write a letter in which she told everyone not to search for her because she was now happy.

Elisabeth was alone in the bunker until the birth of her first child. Her only visitor was her father, who would arrive every few days to bring her food. He would then rape her. The nightmare became greater still during Elisabeth's fourth year underground when she became pregnant for the first time, suffering a miscarriage. Elisabeth's second pregnancy led to the birth of Kerstin and Stefan arrived in the following year. There would be seven children in all, including Michael, who died when he

▼ Elisabeth Fritzl who now lives under an assumed name in an Austrian village known as 'Village X'

was three days old. While Kerstin, Stefan and Felix, the youngest, lived in captivity, Fritzl arranged for the others to be taken care of by Rosemarie.

It had been difficult to explain the babies away. After all, Rosemarie knew nothing of the bunker. Like everyone else, she believed the troubled Elisabeth had achieved some sort of happiness as a member of a fictitious cult. However, Fritzl had already laid the groundwork by portraying Elisabeth as an unstable and irresponsible daughter. All that remained was to smuggle the babies upstairs in the middle of the night and then leave them on the front doorstep with a note from Elisabeth.

In May 1993, 9-month-old Lisa became the first of the grandchildren who would be cared for by Rosemarie. When Monika appeared in the following year, the press took note. 'What kind of mother would do such a thing?' asked one newspaper. After having raised seven of her own children, the neighbours took pity on Rosemarie. However, the senior citizen made no complaints and she proved to be devoted to her grandchildren. All three did well at school and they seemed happy and healthy despite their incestuous background.

Even the unfriendly Fritzl received a certain amount of grudging respect and admiration for helping to raise three young children during the years in which one

▲ *A police van stands outside the house in Amstetten as officers begin to untangle Fritzl's web of incest*

might rightly expect to take things easy.

For the children in the bunker, life could not have been more different. Kerstin, Stefan and Felix knew they had siblings living in the house above their heads. Indeed, Kerstin and Stefan could remember the babies being taken away. To add insult to injury, Josef would bring videos that showed Lisa, Monika and Alexander enjoying a lifestyle that was vastly superior to their own.

Despite her suffering, Elisabeth did her best to provide Kerstin, Stefan and Felix with some semblance of a normal upbringing. She gave them regular lessons, in which they learned reading, writing and mathematics. All of the children, whether they were raised in the bunker by Elisabeth or upstairs by

Rosemarie, ended up being intelligent, articulate and polite.

IN THE BUNKER

Fritzl has never explained why he took Lisa, Monika and Alexander upstairs, while keeping their siblings captive below. One possible explanation might have been lack of space. With a total area of around 35 square metres (380 square feet), the bunker was becoming increasingly cramped, particularly when the children grew bigger.

After the birth of Monika in 1993, Fritzl alleviated the problem somewhat by expanding the size of the bunker to 55 square metres (600 square feet).

On 27 April 2008, nine days after Fritzl had telephoned for an ambulance, a number of police officers arrived at the house of Josef and Rosemarie Fritzl. Josef Fritzl was taken into custody while Rosemarie and her grandchildren were taken to a psychiatric hospital, where they were reunited with Elisabeth.

On the day after his arrest, Fritzl confessed to keeping Elisabeth captive and fathering her children. He defended his actions by claiming that the sex had been consensual and that Elisabeth's incarceration had been necessary in order to rescue her from 'persons of questionable moral standards'. Elisabeth had refused to obey his rules ever since she had entered puberty, he said.

As Fritzl awaited trial for his crimes he became more and more enraged by the media coverage. Eventually, the electrical engineer released a letter through his lawyer in which he spoke of the kindness he had shown his family. Fritzl pointed out that he could have killed them, but chose not to.

On 16 March 2009, the first day of his trial, Fritzl was charged with rape, incest, kidnapping, false imprisonment, slavery, grievous assault and the murder of baby Michael. He pleaded guilty to all of the charges with the exception of grievous assault and murder.

In keeping with the agreement she struck with the police on the day she finally emerged from the bunker, Elisabeth did not appear in court. Instead, the 42-year-old woman's testimony was presented in the form of an 11-hour video recording. The prosecution later revealed that Elisabeth had been watching the proceedings from the visitors' gallery. She had been heavily disguised to avoid being recognized.

The news caused Fritzl to break down. He changed his plea to guilty on all charges, thereby ending the court case. That same day he was sentenced to life imprisonment, with no possibility of parole for 15 years.

Albert DeSALVO

The case of the 'Boston Strangler' is one of the most enduringly mysterious in the annals of serial murder.

What is known for sure is that between June 1962 and July 1964 eleven women were murdered in the Boston area – all raped and strangled. Most people at the time assumed there was a single serial killer on the loose, and dubbed him the Boston Strangler. Others, including many on the police investigation, thought that there were two killers, because one set of victims were all older women between the ages of fifty-five and seventy-five, while five of the last six to die were women in their late teens

▼ *DeSalvo proved to be an enigmatic killer. The extent of his crimes remains a mystery*

▶*DNA evidence taken from Mary Sullivan, one of the victims of Albert DeSalvo, did not match that of the killer, leading to the theories about Nassar*

PHYSICALLY ABUSED

Albert DeSalvo was born in Chelsea, Massachusetts, on 3 September 1931. He was one of six children born to Frank and Charlotte DeSalvo. Frank DeSalvo was a violent man who dealt out regular physical abuse to his family, and was jailed twice before Charlotte eventually divorced him in 1944. Albert became a troubled teenager, repeatedly arrested for breaking and entering, assault and other minor offences.

In 1948, aged seventeen, Albert joined the army and was stationed in Germany. While living there he met and married a German woman, Irmgard Beck, who came with him when he was transferred back to the States, to Fort Dix in New Jersey. At Fort Dix, DeSalvo was accused of molesting a nine-year-old girl but the matter was dropped when the mother declined to press charges. However, the affair resulted in him being discharged from the army in 1956.

SEXUAL DEMANDS

At this point Albert and Irmgard, plus their baby daughter Judy, moved back to Massachusetts. Over the next few years DeSalvo worked a series of jobs, and was regarded as a likeable man by his fellow workers. Not all was well, though: he was arrested several times for burglary and there was sexual tension

and early twenties. These latter murders were also significantly more violent than the others. For this reason, some concluded that there was a first murderer fixated on older women (perhaps motivated by a hatred of his mother), followed by a copycat killer using the same modus operandi but preying on younger women.

However, all this speculation was quelled when, in early 1965, a man named Albert DeSalvo, who had recently been arrested for a series of rapes, confessed to all eleven murders, as well as some other killings that had not previously been attributed to the Strangler.

between him and his wife. Irmgard was very unenthusiastic sexually after their daughter had been born with a hereditary disease and she was terrified of having another handicapped child. Albert, meanwhile, demanded sex from his wife five or six times a day.

This manic sexual behaviour soon led DeSalvo into trouble. During the late 1950s reports began to come in from Massachusetts women about the 'Measuring Man': a man who claimed to be from a modelling agency and would persuade women to let him run his

▼ *Attorney F. Lee Bailey, here holding a photograph of DeSalvo in custody, became famous for taking on high-profile cases such as the Boston Strangler's*

measuring tape all over their bodies. When DeSalvo was once more arrested for burglary, on 17 March 1960, he surprised police by confessing that he was the Measuring Man.

Due to the lack of violence involved in his crime, DeSalvo received a relatively lenient two-year sentence. With time off for good behaviour, he was released after eleven months. Far from teaching him a lesson, however, his time in prison seemed to have turned him into a more aggressive predator. Over the next two years he raped hundreds of women (300 by police estimates, 2,000 by his own exaggerated account), often carrying out more than one rape on the same day. He was known as the 'Green Man' rapist, since he often made his assaults while wearing green work clothes. These rapes were carried out during the same time period as the Boston Strangler killings, but the police made no connection between them at the time.

On 3 November 1964, DeSalvo was arrested on suspicion of being the Green Man rapist, after a witness gave the police a description that reminded them of the Measuring Man. DeSalvo promptly confessed and was sent to Bridgewater State Hospital for psychiatric observation. While he was there he confessed first to a fellow inmate, George Nassar, and

subsequently to the police, that he was also the Boston Strangler.

The police were delighted to have the Strangler presented to them on a plate in this way. However, various problems remained. In particular, none of the witnesses who had seen the Boston Strangler, including his one surviving victim, were able to pick DeSalvo out of a police line-up. In the end DeSalvo, represented by the infamous lawyer F. Lee Bailey, made a deal with police that led to him receiving a life sentence for the Green Man rapes, but never being formally charged with the Strangler murders.

In November 1973, DeSalvo was stabbed to death by a fellow prisoner. However, his death failed to bring speculation to an end. Many people believe that DeSalvo only confessed to the killings as part of a deal with George Nassar, whereby Nassar would claim the reward for finding the Boston Strangler and would give half the money to DeSalvo's family to provide for them while he was in jail.

Today, however, the consensus from experts who spent a substantial amount of time with DeSalvo, is that the man imprisoned as the Green Man rapist was indeed the legendary Boston Strangler responsible for all the crimes attributed to him.

John DILLINGER

The bank robber John Dillinger was the original 'Public Enemy Number One', the first man to be branded by the FBI as America's most dangerous criminal. However, while the state regarded him as a menace, there were many who saw him as a hero, a latter-day Robin Hood. This dual status was a result of the times in which he lived. In the early 1930s, America was going through the Depression. Many banks had gone bust, taking people's savings with them. Others were busy foreclosing on small debtors and taking their houses. The public no longer trusted the banking system and when outlaws robbed the banks, many people found it hard to condemn them.

Furthermore, the golden age of mass communications had dawned. Radio and newsreels transported stories around America in a flash. One side effect of this was the beginning of the culture of celebrity. John Dillinger was among the first of the celebrity criminals, his exploits were followed by the American public as keenly as those of any Hollywood film star.

John Herbert Dillinger was born in Indianapolis on 22 June 1903. He grew up in the middle-class Oak Hill neighbourhood. His father, John Wilson Dillinger, was a hard-working grocer. His mother died of a stroke when he was only three years old. His sixteen-year-old sister Audrey took over the running of the family for a while, and later John Sr remarried. Much of John's upbringing, however, was left to his father, who would alternate between being a strict disciplinarian and spoiling his son with expensive toys.

GANG RAPE

This confusing combination may well have been a factor in John Jr growing up to be a difficult, rebellious child. He formed his own gang of local kids, known as the Dirty Dozen. They stole coal from passing freight trains and got into trouble. A more dangerous side to the young Dillinger's nature emerged when he and another boy tied a friend down in a nearby wood mill and turned on the circular saw. Dillinger stopped the saw only when it was inches from cutting into his friend's body. Aged thirteen, Dillinger and some friends gang-raped a local girl.

Dillinger left school aged sixteen and got a job as a mechanic, leading a wild lifestyle when he was not in work. His father had tried hard to make him toe the line. Now he thought it was time for drastic action: he sold up and moved the whole family to a farm near Mooresville, Indiana. However, John reacted no better to rural life than he had to the city and soon got into trouble again.

Dillinger was arrested for stealing a car and decided to avoid prosecution by joining the navy. This only lasted a matter of months, however, before he deserted his ship when it docked in Boston. Returning to Mooresville, he married sixteen-year-old Beryl Hovius in 1924. He then became friends with a man named Ed Singleton, the town pool shark. Together they tried to rob a Mooresville grocer, but were caught in the act. Singleton pleaded not guilty, stood trial

▶ Dillinger's court case was followed by millions of Americans as it was reported on the new and immensely popular technology of radio

and was sentenced to two years. Dillinger, following his father's advice, confessed and ended up being sentenced to ten to twenty years in the Indiana State Prison. The harshness of the sentence seems to have turned Dillinger against society once and for all.

ESCAPE AND CAPTURE

While inside, Dillinger made repeated attempts to escape. He also met up with several more experienced criminals who would have a big influence on his subsequent career. Chief among them were two bank robbers, Harry Pierpoint and Homer Van Meter. Much of their time was spent discussing means of escape. They found a corrupt guard: all they needed was for someone on the outside to bribe the guard to bring some guns into the prison.

The chance came when Dillinger was suddenly paroled ahead of time on 10 May 1933, the reason being that his stepmother was desperately ill. On the outside, Dillinger laid plans to spring his friends from jail.

Then, a few days before the planned jailbreak, Dillinger robbed a bank in the small town of Bluffton, Ohio. He was arrested and sent back to jail in Lima, Ohio, to await trial.

While he was in jail the police searched him and found a document that seemed to

be a plan for a prison break. Dillinger denied it and, before the police could get to the bottom of it, eight of Dillinger's friends escaped from the Indiana State Prison, using the guns that had been smuggled into their cells. During their escape, they shot two guards. On 12 October, three of the escaped prisoners repaid the favour and busted Dillinger out of prison, shooting a sheriff in the process.

▲ *John Dillinger, under heavy escort, en route to Indiana by air to answer charges of murdering a policeman in a hold-up*

▶ *A relaxed Dillinger in prison, surrounded by people eager to get a photograph with him. His celebrity was never in doubt*

Now the Dillinger gang swung into action with a vengeance. They pulled several bank robberies. They raided the police arsenals at Auburn, Indiana, and Peru, Indiana, stealing several machine guns, rifles, ammunition and bulletproof vests. Their robberies became ever more high profile. Then, during a raid on a Chicago bank that December, a police officer was killed. Every cop in the country was on the lookout for the gang, but they now had plenty of money and headed to Florida.

WEAPONS ARSENAL

Next, they decided to head west to Tucson, Arizona. On the way, however, Dillinger could not resist robbing a bank in Gary, Indiana. This time Dillinger himself shot and killed a policeman as he made his getaway. When they arrived in Tucson, the gang found that they were not as anonymous as they had hoped. A local fireman identified them and soon they were arrested. They were found in possession of three Thompson submachine guns, two Winchester rifles mounted as machine guns, five bulletproof vests and the vast sum of more than twenty-five thousand dollars in cash, part of it from the Chicago robbery.

Dillinger was taken back east to the county jail in Crown Point, Indiana, to await trial for the murder of the police officer. The jail was said to be 'escape proof'. However, on 3 March 1934, Dillinger demonstrated that, as long as it has human beings running it, no jail is truly escape proof. He made a replica gun out of wood, then coloured it black with boot polish. He used the replica gun to force a prison officer to give him a real gun. With the help of another inmate, he took several hostages and drove out of the prison in the governor's own car.

This sensational sting made Dillinger an even bigger hero in the public eye. It also made J. Edgar Hoover's newly formed FBI ever more determined to catch him. A nationwide manhunt began. Pierpoint had been arrested in Tucson and subsequently executed. However, Van Meter was still on the loose and Dillinger teamed up with him. He formed a new gang featuring the murderous talents of Lester Gillis a.k.a. Baby Face Nelson, a man never happier than with a machine gun in his hand. They continued where the old gang had left off, robbing a series of banks, and engaging in another shoot-out with the FBI, this time in St Paul, Minnesota.

THE GAME IS UP

Following the shoot-out, in which Dillinger was wounded, the gang went on the run again. They robbed a police station of guns and bulletproof vests before heading to a resort lodge called Little Bohemia, near Rhinelander, Wisconsin, where they planned to hide out for a while. However, the FBI received a tip-off and arrived en masse at Little Bohemia. Once again, it looked as if the game was up for Dillinger. However, the attempted arrest went disastrously wrong. The FBI killed an innocent bystander, Baby Face Nelson killed an FBI agent and all the gangsters got away.

Dillinger's fame was now at its zenith. Perhaps beginning to believe his own publicity, he returned to Chicago, had some minor plastic surgery and began to thumb his nose at the law, appearing in public to watch the Chicago Cubs play baseball, or to visit nightclubs. Finally, however, he fell victim not to FBI ingenuity but to the greed of his fellow criminal. A brothel-keeper named Anna Sage, a friend of Dillinger's new girlfriend Polly Hamilton, sold him out.

On the night of Sunday 22 July, FBI agents were waiting as Dillinger, with Sage and Hamilton on either side, walked out of a theatre. Dillinger quickly realized what was happening and grabbed a pistol from his right trouser pocket as he ran towards the alley. Five shots were fired from the guns of three FBI agents. Three of the shots hit Dillinger and he fell face down on the pavement, dead at last.

Nannie DOSS

Many serial killers have been driven by perverted ideas of sex. Nannie Doss may be one to have been driven by a perverted notion of romance. When investigators asked this mild-looking grandmother about the four husbands she had murdered (among at least ten victims in all), she explained her actions by saying: 'I was looking for the perfect mate, the real romance of life.'

Nancy 'Nannie' Doss was born in the rural town of Blue Mountain in the hill country of north-west Alabama in 1905. She had a tough childhood. Her father James Hazle was an authoritarian farmer who worked his children as if they were hired farmhands and beat them if they failed to keep up with his demanding pace of work. Despite, if not because, of her father's strictness, Nannie became a wilful teenager, known for her promiscuity. In 1921, aged sixteen, she married a co-worker at the Linen Thread Company, Charles Braggs, and they had four children in quick succession. Nannie jumped into the relationship to escape her domineering father but found herself living with her new husband's equally domineering mother. When Charles himself turned out to be a drunk and a womanizer, Nannie responded by going back to her wild ways.

The marriage clearly was not built to last and it came to an end with what appeared to be a double tragedy. In 1927 the couple's two middle children both died in separate episodes of suspected food poisoning. At the time no one suspected foul play, but soon afterwards Charles Bragg ran off, taking their eldest daughter with him. He later claimed that he was frightened of his wife and had made a point of not eating anything she prepared.

ANOTHER 'TRAGEDY'

With her husband gone, Nannie took a job at a cotton mill to support herself and her remaining daughter, Florine. In due course she moved across the state line to Georgia and remarried, to a man named Frank Harrelson. Harrelson turned out to be another alcoholic ne'er-do-well, although the relationship persisted until 1945 when another apparent tragedy struck. Once again a child died. This time it was Florine's daughter, Nannie's granddaughter. Florine had left her infant son with her mother while she visited her father. Three days later the baby was dead. The suggestion was that he might accidentally have swallowed rat poison.

Three months later, Nannie claimed her first adult victim. Frank Harrelson came home drunk and abused her one time too many. The next day, she put rat poison in his corn liquor. Several agonised days later he was dead, and, once more, no one suspected a thing.

Fortunately for Nannie, she had recently insured Frank's life and she now used the payment to buy a house in Jackson, Mississippi, where she lived until 1947. At this point, Nannie answered a lonely hearts advertisement – romance magazines and lonely hearts columns were Nannie's favoured reading matter – placed by a man named Arlie Lanning from Lexington, North Carolina. Two days after they met, they were married. However, once again Nannie's new husband proved to be a disappointment. Arlie was another drunk, and after three years Nannie had had enough of him.

In February 1950 Nannie served Arlie a meal of stewed prunes and coffee. He had terrible stomach pains for two days, and then died. Nannie told the neighbours that his last words were: 'Nannie, it must have been the coffee.' Of course, he may have been wrong: it may have been the arsenic in the coffee, but then again it could have been the prunes, that had been stewed in rat poison. The doctor, needless to say, did not suspect murder,

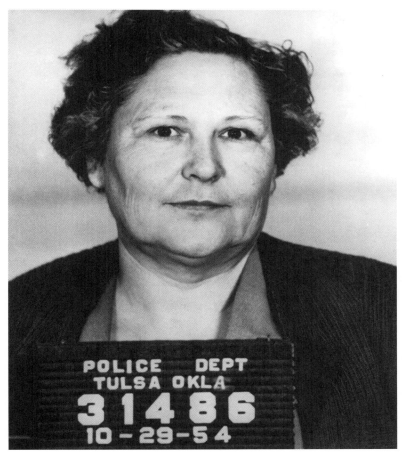

▲ *The official photo of Nannie Doss taken on her arrest*

not even when their house – which would have gone to Arlie's sister in his will – mysteriously burnt down, leaving Nannie with the insurance payment.

As soon as the insurance cheque cleared, Nannie left town. She visited her sister Dovie – who promptly keeled over. In 1952 Nannie signed up to a new innovation, a dating agency called the Diamond Circle Club. Through the agency Nannie met Richard Morton from Emporia, Kansas. Yet again he proved a

▲ *Nannie's unsuspecting victims did not stand a chance against her lethal doses of poison, which were easily dissolved in other substances*

one of Nannie's prune cakes, Samuel was admitted to hospital with stomach pains. He survived and was released from hospital twenty-three days later.

That evening, Nannie served him a perfectly innocent pork roast, which he washed down with a rather more dangerous cup of coffee that she had laced with arsenic. He died immediately, and this time the physician ordered an autopsy.

They found enough arsenic to kill twenty men in Samuel's stomach. The police confronted Nannie, unable to believe that this fifty-year-old grandmother could be the killer. She unnerved them by giggling at their questions; then, when they refused to let her continue reading her romance magazine, she confessed to killing not just Samuel but her previous three husbands as well.

The news was an immediate sensation. The press dubbed Nannie the 'Giggling Granny' and she was put on trial for murder. She was duly sentenced to life in prison and, after serving ten years of her sentence, died in 1965, aged sixty. Further investigation revealed that Nannie's four husbands, two children and granddaughter were not the only victims; Nannie's mother, two sisters, a nephew and a grandson had also died of arsenic poisoning.

disappointment, not a drunk this time, but a fraud and a womanizer. He was not to be her next victim, however: that was her mother Louise, who came to stay in January 1953, fell ill with chronic stomach pains and died. Three months later, Richard Morton went the same way. Yet again the doctors failed to ask for an autopsy.

During her brief marriage to Morton, Nannie had continued corresponding with her lonely hearts, and immediately after the funeral she went to Tulsa, Oklahoma, to meet the likeliest new prospect, Samuel Doss.

They were married in June 1953. Doss was not a drinker or womanizer: he was a puritanical Christian and a miser. Once again, and despite these advantages, Nannie's new husband failed to meet her romantic ideal. A little over a year later, in September 1954, shortly after eating

John DUFFY

In real life, crime detection is rarely as simple as the fictional cases portrayed on TV. Fictional detectives invariably have a single suspect in their sights and have only to prove the case against them, while the dilemma facing real detectives is often to identify a guilty, faceless individual from among a million or more inhabitants of a major city. It is a process of painstaking elimination known as the 'needle in the haystack' method and it hasn't changed significantly in 200 years, only now we have computers to speed up the sifting process.

▲ *Railway Rapist John Duffy was jailed at the Old Bailey in London*

In 1986 the British police were working their way through a list of nearly 5,000 known sex offenders in the hope of catching a brutal serial killer known as the 'Railway Rapist', who had raped 27 women and murdered two more in London and Surrey, all near railway lines.

All the police knew for certain was that he was short, with a pockmarked face and fair hair and that, in the latest case, he had made crude attempts to destroy the evidence of rape by drowning his victim. They also knew that he had attempted to get rid of the evidence in the case of another of his victims by inserting paper into her vagina and setting it alight. Clearly he was a supremely callous and calculating individual.

After the second murder a man answering the vague description was seen running for the 6.07 train from East Horsley to London, prompting a frantic manual search through two million tickets, but no incriminating fingerprints were found.

By this time the police were getting desperate. They had a number of significant clues, including a length of string used to bind the victims' hands, and they had identified the attacker's blood group from semen stains. Analysis of the stains revealed the presence of an uncommon enzyme known as phosphoglucomutase which would eliminate a large number of suspects, but there was no time to interview every man on the list. The killer was likely to strike again at any moment and the police were stretched to breaking point trying to cover all the regional railway stations, which were unmanned by British Rail staff at weekends.

WORKING AGAINST THE CLOCK

After Detective Chief Superintendent Vincent McFadden made the decision to pool the resources of all the various investigating teams in the Home Counties, the list was whittled down to a more manageable 2,000 suspects. Each was invited to give a blood sample, but one declined. His name was John Duffy, an ex-railway worker who fitted the description and had a record for rape and assault with a knife. But while the police were debating whether or not to risk arresting him without conclusive evidence he admitted himself to hospital after suffering what he claimed was a mugging, which had also conveniently robbed him of his memory. On his

release he raped another woman, but the police still did not automatically link this to Duffy.

At this point in the investigation, McFadden turned to Dr David Canter, a professor of psychology at the University of Surrey, and requested a psychological profile in an attempt to identify the killer. Canter read the case reports and concluded that the so-called 'centre of gravity' connecting these crimes was a 5km (3 mile) area around the Finchley Road in north London and that the killer most likely lived in that neighbourhood. Among a further 16 points Dr Canter highlighted was the likelihood that he would be a semi-skilled worker who had experienced a volatile marriage and now had two close male friends. The data was duly fed into the computer and the name John Duffy was highlighted as a positive match.

A search of Duffy's home unearthed the unusual string used in the attacks and then one of the two friends admitted beating Duffy to give the appearance that he had been mugged so that he could claim to be suffering from amnesia. But the evidence which clinched the case was the discovery of 13 fibres on various items of Duffy's clothes which had come from the sheepskin coat of a victim he had tossed into the river and left to drown.

The sign reads:

MURDER ENQUIRY

BETWEEN 4 pm 17/4/86 AND 8 AM 18/4/86 A MURDER TOOK PLACE ON FOOT

▲ *Train travellers were asked if they had seen anything out of the ordinary*

In the end, the DNA evidence was not decisive; Duffy was jailed for 30 years on the physical evidence and the testimony of three of his surviving victims, and with his conviction the era of this ever-elusive random sex murderer was ended. Since the days of Jack the Ripper sex killers had been notoriously difficult to catch and convict for the simple reason that their behaviour was impulsive and unpredictable. But a combination of computers, psychological profiling and genetic fingerprinting means that sex crimes are now as solvable as other crimes of violence.

Ruth ELLIS

Ruth Ellis, born in Rhyl, Wales in 1927, has the distinction of being the last woman in Britain to be hanged. Twenty-eight years old when she went to the scaffold, she was as much victim as killer.

▼ *Ruth Ellis, the last woman to be hanged in Britain*

Men, from the beginning, were Ruth Ellis's problem – and she theirs. Raised in Manchester – a waitress and for a while a dance-band singer – she'd fallen in love at the age of 17 with an American flyer, only for him to be killed in action in 1944. Soon after his death she bore him a son; and six years later she married a dentist and had a baby daughter by him – only for him to divorce her shortly afterwards on the grounds of mental cruelty. Now with two small children to take care of, and with no qualifications except her looks, she did what she had to. She became a club-hostess and hooker. She migrated to London; and there, in Carrolls Club in 1953, she met a man called David Blakely.

Blakely was a racing driver, a sophisticated, debonair man, but he soon became obsessed with Ruth. He offered to marry her, but she refused; and while she played him along, she also took up with one of his friends. For a year or so she managed to keep both men happy. But by 1954 Blakely had become almost insanely jealous. He started to beat her. He gave her a black eye; he broke her ankle; he also started seeing other women. But when Ruth finally threw him out as a result, he came back like a whipped dog, once more begging her to marry him. Again Ruth refused, but by now, it seemed, they were doomed to each other.

They set up house together in Egerton Gardens in Kensington. But by now Blakely had a taste for infidelity. At the

◀ *Ellis with Blakely in happier times*

beginning of April 1955, Ruth Ellis had a miscarriage; and a few days later Blakely said he had to go and see a mechanic who was building him a new car. She followed him to an apartment in Hampstead, and when she heard a woman's laughter inside, she knocked on the door and demanded to be let in to see him. He refused, and when she began to shout, the police were called.

The next day she returned; and this time she saw Blakely coming down the steps arm-in-arm with a pretty young girl. She made up her mind. On the evening of 10 April, Easter Sunday, when she found him coming out of a

Hampstead pub called the Magdala, she took a gun out of her handbag and shot him six times. There was no real doubt that she was guilty. She later told the police:

> 'I am guilty.'

— and added:

> 'I am rather confused.'

At her trial in June of the same year, she confessed:

> 'I intended to kill him.'

It took the jury just fourteen minutes to find her guilty. She was sentenced to death, and a month later, despite widespread protests, she was hanged. Her son, the child of the American pilot, committed suicide in 1982, following years of depression. Her daughter, in a newspaper interview a year later, said she couldn't get out of her mind the image of the hangman —

> 'peering through the peephole into her cell, trying to work out how much rope he should use to make sure that frail little neck was broken.'

◀ *It took the jury just 14 minutes to find Ellis guilty of murder*

Albert FISH

Albert Fish – the model, at least in part, for Thomas Harris's fictional killer Hannibal Lecter – is perhaps the most bewildering of all serial killers. At the time of his arrest in 1934 he was sixty-four years old, a slightly built, mild-mannered old man with grey hair and a shabby suit, as innocuous-looking an individual as one could hope to meet. However, under the placid exterior there lurked a man of extraordinary violence; according to psychiatrists, Fish had tried and enjoyed every perversion known to humanity, including eating the flesh of the young children he had savagely tortured and murdered.

BRAGGART

Just how many children this seemingly benevolent old man killed we will never know. There are no more than four whose deaths can certainly be attributed to Fish, though at least a dozen killings, plus a large number of rapes, seem probable. Fish himself – an early example of the serial killer as braggart – claimed to have killed hundreds, with at least one murder in every state. The psychiatrist who examined him most closely believed that Fish probably committed at least a hundred rapes.

So what kind of background produced this monster? Albert Fish was born on 19 May 1870. His father Randall Fish was a boat captain, operating on the Potomac River. Albert's given name was Hamilton Fish, apparently in honour of a family link with Washington's eminent Hamilton family. So this was a respectable, relatively well-off world that Albert Fish was born into. All this changed, however, when his father died in 1875. His mother had to find a job and put Albert, aged five, into an orphanage. It was there, in response to teasing from the other boys, that he started to call himself Albert. More seriously, it was here that he acquired a lifelong taste for sadomasochism, after the regular bare-bottom whippings he received. He became a persistent bedwetter who regularly ran away from the orphanage. When he was nine, his mother removed him.

DRIFTER

Albert left school at fifteen. He soon found he was a very able painter and decorator and he followed this trade for the rest of his life, drifting from town to town as he did so. By 1898 he had married, settled in New York, and

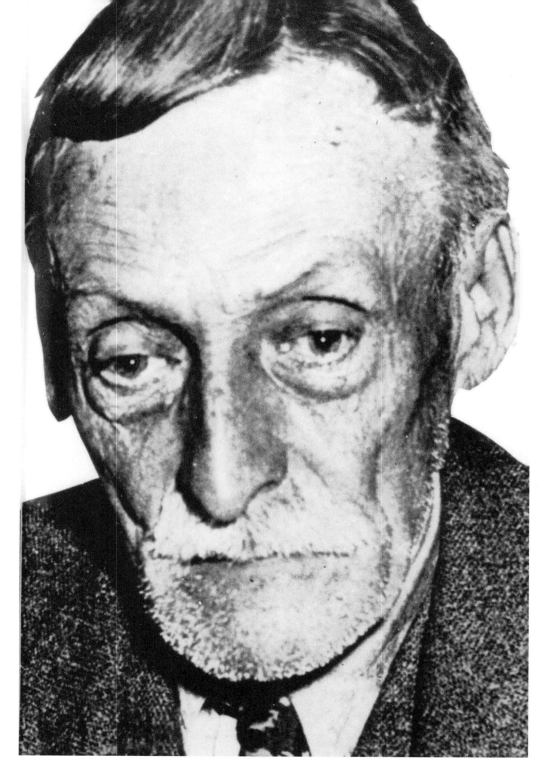

▶Albert Fish appeared to be a harmless old man, but his looks hid a terrible secret

fathered six children. Fish himself claimed that he committed his first murder during this period, killing a man in Delaware in 1910. However, most people, including his children, dated his descent into madness from the time his wife left him, running off with a boarder in 1917. Thereafter he appeared to suffer from hallucinations: he would take the children to a summer house in Westchester where he would climb a hill, shake his fist at the sky and declare himself to be Christ, before asking his children to beat him on the buttocks. He became obsessed with pain, driving needles into his groin and inserting fabric into his anus before setting it on fire. Eventually his oldest son had had enough of his father's demented behaviour and threw him out of the family house.

Fish was regularly arrested, sometimes for vagrancy, sometimes for petty theft and sometimes for indulging in one of his favourite perversions, sending obscene letters to women. Each time he would be examined, pronounced peculiar but harmless and tossed back into the community. Exactly how many murders and rapes he committed during the 1920s and early 1930s we will never know.

However, it was one case in particular that ensured both his notoriety and his downfall. At the beginning of June 1928 he noticed an advertisement in the newspaper from one Edward Budd, an eighteen-year-old looking for a job in the countryside. Fish answered the advert, arriving at the impoverished Budd household in the guise of Frank Howard, a farmer from Long Island who was looking for a willing worker. Despite 'Mr Howard's' rather shabby appearance, he was a well-spoken man and the Budd family were happy to believe in him as a benefactor, especially when he handed out dollar bills to the other children. On meeting the rest of the family, Fish decided against abducting the burly Edward and instead focused his attention on twelve-year-old Grace. He persuaded the family to let him take her to a children's party that his sister was holding.

That was the last the family saw of her. Fish took Grace to the deserted summer house in Westchester. There he strangled her, dismembered her body and over a period of nine days ate as much of her body as he could, before burying her bones behind the house.

A huge manhunt was launched but without success. It was only the determination of one man, Detective Will King, that kept the case alive. Even so, he might never have got his man if Fish had not succumbed to the urge to brag about his crime. In 1934 he sent the Budds a letter telling them exactly what had happened to their daughter. This vile act led to his downfall. The envelope Fish used had a distinctive logo that eventually led Detective King to a New York flophouse. There he finally came face to face with Albert Fish. On being challenged, Fish lunged at King with a straight razor but King overpowered and arrested him.

On arrest, Fish began a rambling, obscene confession. As well as the Grace Budd murder, he was also responsible for the killings of four- year-old Billy Gaffney in 1929 and five-year-old Francis McDonnell in 1934.

The only question was whether his defence of not guilty by reason of insanity would be accepted. Fish was, as several psychiatrists pronounced, fairly obviously mad.

The jury, eager for his heinous crimes to be punished, rejected the insanity defence and found Fish guilty. He was sentenced to death by electrocution, a fate he positively relished. He was executed at Sing Sing Prison on 16 January 1936. The electric chair short-circuited the first time they pulled the lever, apparently due to the pins and nails Fish had embedded in his body.

▶ *A police officer, with an electromagnetic metal detector, looks for a buried kitchen knife as evidence against Albert Fish. The case was a very public affair, and rapidly became infamous*

'Pretty Boy' FLOYD

Oklahoma's 'Pretty Boy' Floyd provides the link between the semi-legendary outlaws of the Old West – Jesse James, Wild Bill Hickok to name but a few – and the gangsters of the early twentieth century; Al Capone and Dutch Schulz, for example. Essentially, Pretty Boy Floyd was an outlaw who simply found cars more efficient than horses when it came to running from the law.

Charles Arthur Floyd was born in Bartow County, Georgia, on 3 February 1904, the fourth of eight children born to Walter Lee and Minnie Floyd, hard-working rural Baptists. In 1911, when Charles was seven, Walter Lee decided to move the family to Oklahoma, where he heard there was work in the cotton fields.

The family settled in the Cookson Hills and became tenant farmers. Through immense hard work they prospered. Walter eventually opened a general store in the town of Akins. At first Charles seemed to be one more hard-working member of the family, leaving school after the sixth grade to help out with the business.

A CHANGED MAN

All this changed in 1919, when Charles set off to the harvest fields of Kansas and Oklahoma to make some money. Working in the fields, he fell in with a rough crowd of drifters and vagabonds. When he returned he was a changed man. He started getting into fights and hanging around the local pool hall. He then met his wife, Ruby, and appeared to go straight for a while, but it was not to last. The two set up home and had a baby, Charles Dempsey Floyd and Charles Sr went back to working in the fields, but with an increasing sense of dissatisfaction. He met a petty criminal called John Hilderbrand, who told him how he had robbed a manufacturing company in St Louis of $1,900. Hilderbrand encouraged Charles to join him in carrying out future raids. In August 1925, Charles decided to give it a try. He left home and carried out several successful robberies.

Unfortunately, the duo then made the classic mistake of inexperienced crooks. They bought an expensive car, a new Studebaker, and cruised around the streets of Fort Smith, Arkansas. This soon attracted the suspicion of the police and, before long, Charles was arrested, found guilty for a variety of robberies and sentenced to three years in prison. At his trial the clerk to the court described Charles as 'a mere boy – a pretty boy with apple cheeks' – and a nickname was born, no matter that Charles himself absolutely hated it.

RESTROOM ESCAPE

In prison Charles met many, more experienced, criminals, who urged him to come in with them when he was released. At first Charles wavered, but when he learned that his wife had divorced him, his mind was made up. On release he headed straight for Kansas City, then a Mecca for criminals of all sorts. He stayed in a boarding house popular with criminals, and there met Beulah 'Juanita' Baird, who became his girlfriend. Before long he had hooked up with the Jim Bradley Gang and joined them in a series of raids on banks across Ohio.

At first they were successful, but on 8 March 1930, their luck ran out and they were arrested in Akron, Ohio, following a gun battle. This time Floyd was sentenced to fifteen years . However, en route to the penitentiary at Columbus, he performed one of the stunts that was to make his name. During the journey, Floyd talked his guards into uncuffing him so that he could use the restroom. He smashed the window, jumped out and escaped, making it all the way back to Kansas City.

There he found a new partner, William Miller (a.k.a. Billy the Baby Face Killer).

The two of them, along with Juanita, set off to rob banks across the east and south. Once again, though, Floyd almost met his comeuppance in Ohio. The forces of the law caught up with them and there was a shoot-out. Miller was killed and Juanita injured, but Floyd himself managed to escape.

▲ *Pretty Boy Floyd's apple cheeks belied a criminal mind, but his destruction of banks' paperwork did mean he had more of a claim to the Robin Hood legend than most*

FOLK HERO

He returned to the Cookson Hills where folk had little love for the law and would protect him. Over the next year or so, Floyd carried out an enormous number of bank robberies – over fifty in 1931 alone. These were the exploits that made him a folk hero, because when he robbed banks, he would also make a point of destroying any mortgage documents he could find. This made him very popular with local farmers as, during these Depression years, the banks were busily foreclosing on mortgages.

During this time, Floyd also reunited himself with his wife and son. She had remarried but fell in love with Floyd once more, and left her husband to live as a family with Floyd in Fort Smith, Arkansas, where they adopted the alias of Mr and Mrs Charles Douglas.

This was an unusually happy and contented period in Floyd's life. However, after six months, Ruby suggested that they move to Tulsa, Oklahoma, and there they were turned over to the police by informants eager for the reward money. Once again, though, Floyd managed to escape the law by the narrowest of margins. He returned to the hills and soon became confident enough to give an interview to a reporter, one that helped to ensure that he became a legend.

FBI PURSUIT

In 1933, Floyd decided to make his way back into big time crime and headed for Kansas City with his new partner, Adam Richetti.

While he was there, on 17 June 1933, an incident known as the Kansas City Massacre took place. This was a gun battle between mobsters and the FBI, in which several FBI agents were shot dead. It is very doubtful that Floyd was actually there, but FBI chief J. Edgar Hoover claimed that he had been, and from this point on Floyd was a major target for the FBI.

He fled to Buffalo, New York. In October 1934, following the death of John Dillinger, Floyd was officially named Public Enemy Number One. The FBI agent who shot Dillinger, Melvin Purvis, was set on his trail.

Floyd decided to flee to Mexico. On the way there, passing through Ohio on 18 October, his car crashed into a ditch. The police stumbled on the car and Floyd fled on foot into a nearby forest. Purvis was notified immediately and FBI agents combed the area.

After four days on the run, Purvis finally tracked Floyd down and shot him dead as he tried to escape. After his death, Floyd's body was shipped to Cookson Hills where more than twenty thousand people attended his funeral.

John Wayne GACY

Even by comparison with his fellow serial killers, John Wayne Gacy, 'the killer clown' has become something of an icon of pure evil. This is partly to do with the way he dressed up as a clown to entertain children at parties near his suburban Chicago home – what more sinister notion could there be than that beneath the clown's make-up lies a sex killer? And partly it is because of the sheer enormity of his crime: thirty-three young men raped and murdered, almost all of them buried beneath his suburban house.

John Wayne Gacy was born on 17 March 1942, St Patrick's Day, the second of three children born to Elaine Robinson Gacy and John Wayne Gacy Sr. He grew up in a middle-class district of northern Chicago, and was raised as a Catholic. His childhood was largely uneventful. Look a little closer, though, and there were troubles. John Gacy Sr was a misanthropic man who frequently took out his anger on his son through physical beatings and verbal abuse. John Gacy Jr in turn became very close to his mother. Aged eleven, he sustained a nasty accident when he was struck on the head by a swing. It caused him to have regular blackouts during his teens. During his teenage years he also complained of heart problems, though this seems likely to be just a symptom of a lifelong tendency to hypochondria – whenever he was under pressure he would claim to be on the brink of a heart attack.

Gacy did poorly in high school, left without graduating and headed for Las Vegas in a bid to make his fortune. Instead, he ended up working in a mortuary, where he showed an unhealthy interest in the corpses. He then returned to Chicago and began attending business college. While there, he discovered his considerable ability as a salesman; he was able to talk people into anything.

MODEL CITIZEN

In 1964, Gacy married Marlyn Myers, a woman he had met through work and whose father had a string of Kentucky Fried Chicken franchises. Gacy decided to join the family business and became a restaurant manager. The couple had a child and Gacy became extremely active on the local charity and community group circuit around their new home in Waterloo, Iowa.

All this came to an end in May 1968, when Gacy was charged with raping a young employee named Mark Miller.

Gacy was sentenced to ten years for sodomy and his wife promptly divorced him.

GOOD BEHAVIOUR

He was released from prison after just eighteen months, thanks to his good behaviour while inside. His father had died while he was in prison, but now his mother – to whom he had always been close – stood by him and helped him to set up in business again. He bought a new house in the Chicago suburbs and established himself as a building contractor. In June 1972 he remarried, this time to divorcee Carole Hoff. Carole and her two daughters moved into Gacy's house and the family soon became popular in their neighbourhood. Gacy would give parties with Western or Hawaiian themes and was active in local Democratic politics.

COURT CASE

Carole Hoff was aware of Gacy's past but under the impression that he had put it all behind him. This was far from true. In fact, just before they married, Gacy had been charged with sexually assaulting a minor, but the case had collapsed when his accuser failed to come to court. However, rumours soon began to circulate about Gacy's conduct with the teenage boys he liked to employ in his business. By 1975, his marriage was definitely deteriorating. Carole was disturbed to find homosexual pornography around the house. Gacy refused to apologize and even told her he preferred men to women. The couple divorced in 1976. It emerged that throughout their marriage Gacy had been picking up strangers in Chicago's gay bars and had carried out several murders, burying the bodies under the house. Neighbours had even complained about the terrible smell.

Now that his marriage was over, Gacy gave full vent to his lust for killing. He developed a modus operandi. Victims, either picked up on the streets or chosen from his work force, would be lured back to the house and given alcohol and marijuana. Gacy would then offer to show them a magic trick. The victim would be asked to put on a pair of handcuffs, and would then find out that this was no trick: the handcuffs were all too real and they were now in Gacy's power. Gacy would proceed to torture his victims before finally killing them by strangling them to death while raping them.

CLOWN VISITS

Time and again, Gacy got away with it. His neighbours suspected nothing, although they persistently complained about the smells coming from his house. He carried on giving parties and started dressing up as 'Pogo the Clown' to visit sick children in hospitals. He became such a valued member of the local Democratic Party that he had his photograph taken shaking hands with the then First Lady, Roslyn Carter.

Finally, in 1978, his secret life began to catch up with him. In February of that year he abducted a young man called Jeffrey Rignall, chloroformed him, raped and tortured him and then, oddly, dumped him in a park rather than killing him. Rignall went to the police who showed little interest, but, acting alone, he managed to track down his abductor and made an official complaint that was just starting to be investigated late that summer.

HOUSE SEARCH

Gacy had still not been charged with anything when, on 16 October, a fifteen-year-old boy called Robert Piest went missing. His parents discovered that he had been going to meet John Wayne Gacy about a job. Gacy pleaded ignorance but the investigating officer decided to press ahead with a search of Gacy's house. They discovered an array of suspicious objects: handcuffs, pornography, drugs and so forth. They also noted the terrible smell. Gacy was confronted with this evidence

▲ *Popular and jovial, Gacy made a strange suspect*

and eventually confessed to having carried out a single murder. The police returned to the house and began to dig. Soon they realized there was not one victim but dozens. In all, twenty-eight bodies were found around the house; the five most recent victims had been dumped in nearby rivers, as Gacy had run out of burial space.

Charged with thirty-three counts of murder, Gacy entered a plea of insanity. However, the jury found it hard to

▲ Protesters were able to express a little of how they felt about the killer as they threw Gacy's belongings onto a bonfire

believe that a man who dug graves for his victims in advance was the victim of uncontrollable violent impulses, so he was duly sentenced to death. While in prison he became a grotesque celebrity: credulous admirers were able to call a premium-rate number to hear his refutation of the charges against him. He gave frequent interviews and showed admirers his paintings. Towards the end of his time on death row, he began to claim that he had not killed after all, but had been the victim of a mysterious conspiracy. All to no avail, however. On 10 May 1994 he was put to death by lethal injection.

Carlton GARY

Serial killers are conventionally motivated by sexual perversion or, occasionally, by money. It is perhaps surprising that, even in as divided a society as the United States, racial hatred has rarely been a motive for serial murder. In fact, for a long while, profilers maintained that serial killers only murdered within their own racial group. This may generally be true, but there are exceptions. One of them is Carlton Gary, the 'Stocking Strangler' (also known as the 'Chattahoochee Choker'), a black man who killed seven elderly white women during a nine-month reign of terror in his hometown of Columbus, Georgia. He is also thought to be the killer of two other elderly white women in Albany, New York, though this remains unproven.

Carlton Gary was born on 15 December 1952 in Columbus, Georgia. His father was a construction worker who wanted nothing to do with his son, and would accept no financial responsibility for the child. Gary only met his father once, when he was twelve years old.

HATRED

His mother was desperately poor and led a nomadic life. As a result, Gary was malnourished as a child, and was often left with his aunt or great aunt. Both women worked as maids for elderly, wealthy, white women. It has been conjectured that this may have led Gary towards the pathological hatred of older white women that manifested itself later. During his childhood, Gary suffered a serious head trauma in elementary school, when he was knocked unconscious in a playground accident. Head injuries are well known to be a common factor in the backgrounds of many serial killers.

In his teens, Gary became a heavy drug user, and between the ages of fourteen and eighteen he gathered a string of arrests for offences including robbery, arson and assault. He also acquired a wife, Sheila, and had two children. In 1970, he moved to Albany, New York, where he had plans to carve out a career as a singer, for which he showed some talent. In the meantime, he carried on with his criminal activities.

THE ASSAULTS

In May of that year, an elderly woman named Marion Brewer was robbed and attacked in her Albany hotel room. Two months later 85-year-old Nellie Farmer

▲ *Carlton Gary waits out his time on death row*

69-year-old Martha Thurmond, murdered on 23 October. Five days later, the killer now known to a terrified public as the Stocking Strangler struck again, raping and killing 74-year-old Kathleen Woodruff. This time, no stocking was left at the scene.

WRONG MAN

Four months later, the Strangler struck again. On the night of 12 February 1978, the killer attacked Ruth Schwob, but she triggered a bedside alarm and her assailant fled. He went just two blocks down the road, before breaking into another house and raping and strangling 78-year-old Mildred Borom.

Police announced that they suspected a black man of the murders. Eight months later, following a robbery in Gaffney, Georgia, Carlton Gary was arrested and sentenced to twenty-one years in prison for armed robbery. He escaped from custody in 1983 and remained at large for over a year before being rearrested. New evidence came to light, including a gun that was traced back to Gary and a possible fingerprint match that led the police to believe that this armed robber was also the Stocking Strangler.

Gary was eventually arrested and charged with three murders. In August 1986, he was convicted of the crimes and sentenced to death.

was robbed in her nearby apartment, and strangled to death. Following a third assault on an elderly woman, Gary was arrested. It was discovered that his fingerprints matched one left at the scene of the Farmer murder.

Gary admitted having taken part in a robbery but claimed that an accomplice, John Lee Mitchell, was responsible for the actual murder. Mitchell was released on appeal; Gary meanwhile was jailed for robbery. He escaped from custody on 22 August 1977, and headed back home.

On 16 September, 60-year-old Ferne Jackson was raped, beaten and strangled to death with a nylon stocking at her home in the Wynnton district of Columbus. Nine days later 71-year-old Jean Dimenstein was killed in a similar fashion, as were 89-year-old Florence Scheible, murdered on 21 October, and

Pee Wee GASKINS

Five foot two inches of vicious cruelty, Pee Wee Gaskins has a claim to being the United State's most prolific serial killer – that is, if his own account, which has him killing well over a hundred victims, is to be believed. What is certain is that Pee Wee Gaskins was as cold-hearted a killer as there has ever been as, unusually among serial killers, he was capable of committing two distinct kinds of murder. On the one hand, he was a career criminal who murdered for purely business reasons. On the other, he was a sex killer, preying on both men and women. Street smart and utterly amoral, Gaskins became a virtual killing machine.

REGULAR BEATINGS

Gaskins was born in South Carolina on 31 March 1933, in the middle of the Depression. His mother's name was Parrott, and Pee Wee was the last in a string of illegitimate children. His early life was characterized by neglect and regular beatings from assorted 'stepfathers'. Small for his age, he was immediately nicknamed Pee Wee; his

◄ *Pee Wee Gaskins on the way to showing the police his crime scenes*

mother took so little interest in him that the first time he ever learned his given name – Donald – was when it was read out on the occasion of his first court appearance, in his mid-teens.

The court appearance followed a brief crime spree indulged in by Pee Wee and a couple of fellow school dropouts. They gang-raped the sister of one of their number and committed a string of robberies. They were arrested after a witness was able to identify them to the police after surviving a savage hatchet assault carried out during a botched burglary. Pee Wee was sent to reform school.

There, the diminutive boy was regularly raped by his fellow inmates. He was released when he was eighteen, in 1951, and briefly worked on a tobacco plantation, but was soon arrested again, this time for arson and assaulting a

woman with a hammer. In prison he was raped again. This time, though, he fought back, cutting his rapist's throat. He received an extra three years in prison for this, but from that time on, Pee Wee Gaskins became the aggressor rather than the victim.

He escaped briefly from prison in 1955 but was recaptured and sentenced once again. Finally released in 1961, he was back in prison a year later for statutory rape. In fact, it was not until his release in 1968 that Gaskins finally spent a significant time outside prison. Unfortunately for the rest of the world, he was by now thirty-five years old and absolutely lethal.

He killed for the first time in September 1969, torturing and murdering a hitchhiker he picked up, before drowning her body in a swamp. 'All I could think about is how I could do anything I wanted to her,' he later wrote in his memoirs. She was to be the first of many hitchhikers he picked up and killed on the back roads between Sumter and Charleston. Unbelievably, he used to drive around in a purple hearse with a plastic skeleton hanging from the rearview mirror. When asked why he chose such a vehicle, he used to reply:

◀ *Not even the threat of the electric chair could deter Gaskins from his crimes. He was executed in 1991*

'Because I kill so many people.' Unfortunately, everyone thought he was joking. Further evidence of his maniacal inclinations was the fact that he stored dynamite in his fridge and vats of sulphuric acid in his backyard.

KILLING CLOSER TO HOME

Gaskins' appetite for murder soon led him to kill closer to home. In November 1970 he raped and murdered his own fifteen-year-old niece Janice Kirby and a friend of hers. The following month he is thought to have tortured and murdered the thirteen-year-old daughter of a local politician; a crime Gaskins later confessed to. In 1973, in the most horrifying of all his murders, he raped and murdered two of his neighbours: Doreen Dempsey, aged twenty-three and eight months pregnant, and her one-year-old daughter.

No one yet suspected that Pee Wee was a serial sex killer, but some of his acquaintances knew that he was prepared to commit murder for a reasonable reward. In February 1975 a woman named Suzanne Kipper Owens hired Gaskins to kill her boyfriend, wealthy farmer Silas Barnwell Yates. The pair briefly considered marriage, but events conspired against them: in order to cover up the murder, Gaskins ended up killing four more times. One of the victims was a woman called Diane Bellamy Neely, who had helped set up Yates for his murder. Her brother Walter Neely, who was involved in Gaskins' main business, a stolen car racket, initially helped Gaskins to cover up the killings.

It was the stolen car business that led to Gaskins' arrest at the end of the year. At this point, Walter Neely lost his nerve and confessed to his involvement in the cover-up murders and testified that Gaskins was responsible for them.

From now on, Gaskins' main priority was to avoid the death penalty. He made endless deals with the police, if they guaranteed that he would not be put to death. In May 1976, he was convicted of one murder, and then received nine more life sentences in 1978. In return for his confession, the sentence was indeed kept down to life imprisonment.

That should have be the end of the Pee Wee Gaskins story. Instead, his lust to kill was such that, while serving his sentence, he accepted a contract to kill Randolph Tyner, a prisoner on death row. Gaskins managed to rig up a bomb in the radio belonging to Tyner, and it did indeed kill him. This time, however, Gaskins had no bargaining power. He was sentenced to death, a punishment that was finally carried out in the electric chair in 1991.

Ed GEIN

Ed Gein is far from the most prolific of serial killers. There are only two murders for which he was undoubtedly responsible, yet he occupies a peculiarly terrifying place in our collective psyche. Not only was he the inspiration for the murderer in Hitchcock's Psycho, but his crimes also inspired the Texas Chainsaw Massacre and the Buffalo Bill character in Thomas Harris' *The Silence of the Lambs*. So why does this inoffensive-seeming little man inspire such horror?

HOUSEHOLD 'DECORATIONS'

The simple answer is this: because of the things he kept in his kitchen and in his wardrobe. Things like bowls made of human skulls; a wastepaper basket made of human skin; a full breastplate made out of a woman's skinned torso; and even, perhaps most disconcertingly of all, a belt constructed entirely from female nipples. Not until the police raided Jeffrey Dahmer's apartment thirty years later would investigators find themselves in quite such a house of horror.

Ed Gein was born in La Crosse, Wisconsin, on 27 August 1906, the second son of Augusta and George Gein. Soon after his birth the family moved to a remote farm outside nearby Plainfield. His father George was a feckless drinker who worked as a tanner and carpenter, while Augusta was an extremely religious woman who dominated the family and ran a grocery in La Crosse.

Augusta drilled into young Ed and his older brother Henry the sinfulness of women and the utter evil of premarital sex (or by implication any kind of sex at all). She disapproved of her children having friends, not that there were any children nearby. Ed Gein grew up, unsurprisingly enough, a sexually confused loner, with a great fondness for escapist books and magazines. Even as an adult, Ed continued to have an isolated existence working on the farm alongside his parents and brothers. As long as that set-up continued, Ed appears to have been harmless enough. Things only really went off the rails when family members started to die off.

In 1940 George died, and his sons started to take on odd jobs in town to help make ends meet. Ed worked as handyman and even as a babysitter, and townspeople found him likeable and trustworthy. Then, in 1944, Henry died under what seem, with the benefit of hindsight, to be suspicious circumstances. Ed and Henry were fighting a fire in the nearby marshes when the two got separated and, when the fire cleared, Henry was found dead. What was odd was that his body was lying in an unburned area and there was bruising to his head. The cause of death, though, was recorded as smoke asphyxiation.

GRAVE ROBBING

That left only Ed and his adored mother Augusta on the farm. Little more than a year later, however, she was dead too. She died of a stroke on 29 December 1945 following an argument with a neighbour. Ed's first response was to nail her bedroom door shut, leaving the room inside just as it was the day she died. His second response was to take up grave robbing. He became fascinated with human anatomy. He was particularly interested in reading about the first sex-change operation, undertaken by Christine Jorgensen, and even considered having a sex-change operation himself. Then, in consort with a disturbed local named Gus, he started visiting graveyards and taking souvenirs; sometimes whole bodies, more often selected body parts. He would scour the obituary column of the local newspaper in order to learn of freshly buried female corpses.

▲ *Ed Gein confessed as soon as he was arrested*

RESEMBLANCES

During these years, Gein started to manufacture his macabre household decorations, and eventually his grave-robbing expeditions failed to satisfy his strange obsession. In December 1954, a fifty-one year old woman called Mary Hogan disappeared from the bar she ran in Pine Grove, Wisconsin. There was blood on the floor and a spent cartridge was found at the scene. Gein was among the potential suspects but there was no hard evidence to connect him, and the police saw no reason to visit his home.

This was the first of only two murders that can certainly be credited to Gein. The next came three years later. Once again the victim was a woman in her fifties, and once again she looked like Ed's mother. Her name was Bernice Worden and on 16 November 1957 she was abducted from her hardware store in Plainfield. Again, there was blood on the floor. This time, however, the police had a pretty good clue as to who was responsible. The victim's son told them that Ed Gein had asked his mother for a date, and another local resident recalled Ed saying he needed to buy some antifreeze from her store on the day she died. A receipt for antifreeze was found lying in the store and the police decided to pay Ed Gein a visit.

Bernice Worden's corpse was hanging from the rafters. Her head was cut off, her genitalia removed and her torso slit open and gutted. On further investigation they found her head turned into a makeshift ornament, and her heart sitting in a

▶ *The contents of Gein's house were a macabre mess, and in sharp contrast to his dead mother's room, which was immaculate*

▲ *The classic film* Psycho *was based on a book inspired by the Ed Gein story*

saucepan on the stove. They also discovered a pistol that matched the cartridge found at the scene of the Mary Hogan murder.

On arrest, Gein immediately confessed to the murders of Worden and Hogan as well as to his grave-robbing activities. A judge found Gein incompetent for trial and he was committed to a secure mental hospital. Meanwhile, his house was razed to the ground to prevent it from becoming the focus of macabre cults.

Soon after, Ed Gein's immortality was ensured when local writer Robert Bloch wrote a book called *Psycho*, inspired by the case, and Alfred Hitchcock picked it up for the movies. In 1968, Gein was once more submitted for trial but was again found insane. He ended his days in the mental hospital, dying of respiratory failure on 26 July 1984.

Erminia GIULIANO

Erminia Giuliano is one of a new breed of women who head the Mafia families of Sicily. She breaks the traditional stereotype of the Italian wife and mother as a docile homemaker who leaves the business side of things to the men. Like other female Mafia bosses, Giuliano came into a position of power because so many of her male relatives had been killed in feuds between the warring Mafia families. And once she was there, she proved as strong a force – if not stronger – than her male counterparts.

Giuliano came to prominence as head of the Comorra, the loosely connected group of Mafia families operating in and around Naples. The Italian police viewed her as one of Italy's most dangerous criminals, and ranked her among the country's top thirty most wanted. Neapolitan police chief Carlo Gualdi regarded her as 'a true leader' and said that she had the ruthless qualities associated with the male Mafia Godfathers of the past.

Giuliano became boss after her brothers were arrested and jailed. One by one, brothers Luigi 'O Re' ('The King'), Carmine, Raffaele, Guglielmo, and Salvatore, had been incarcerated for a variety of crimes, mostly connected to the running of their illegal gambling operations. Also wanted by the police, Erminia went on the run for ten months and was finally discovered hiding in her daughter's home, behind a secret trap door under the kitchen. She made headlines by refusing to be escorted to Pozzuoli jail before taking a shower and changing. A beautician was called to the house to do her make up, and she had her hair done. She then donned a fake leopard-skin outfit and, suitably attired for media attention, then agreed to leave. Erminia was determined, even when arrested, to live up to her nickname, Celeste – 'heavenly'.

Erminia is not the only 'Godmother', or 'Madrina', as these female heads of the family have become known. Others include Maria and Teresa Zappia, who led the Ndrangheta, a Calabrian crime syndicate; Concetta Scalisi, who took power after her well-known father Giuseppe and brother Salvatore were gunned down; and Pupetta ('Little Doll') Maresca. Maresca's husband was murdered while she was still a teenager, and she got her revenge by murdering the killer. So violent was Maresca that, when she was jailed, four prison officers were detailed to guard her at all times.

Fritz HAARMANN

Fritz Haarmann was one of the first serial killers to hit the headlines in modern times. He confessed to the murders of at least twenty-seven young men and boys in the town of Hanover, Germany, between 1918 and 1924. What made Haarmann uniquely terrifying was the mixture of frenzy and orderliness that characterized his crimes. He would kill his victims in a savage onslaught, biting through their windpipes as he raped them. Then, with considerable care, he would remove their clothes and sell them, dismember the bodies, dispose of the bones, and finally cook the flesh and sell it on the black market as pork. If that seems hard to believe, one should remember that Germany in the years after the First World War was on the brink of starvation; food was food, and people at that time did not ask too many questions as to its provenance.

MOTHER'S FAVOURITE

Fritz (Friedrich) Haarmann was born on 25 October 1879 in Hanover, the sixth child of Olle and Johanna Haarmann. Ole was a drunk and a womanizer; Johanna was older than her husband, forty-one at the time Fritz was born, and in poor health. Fritz, the baby of the family, was his mother's favourite and he constantly sided with her against his father. As a child he preferred dolls to boys' toys. More worrying at the time was a fondness for frightening people, particularly his sisters. He liked to play games that involved tying them up or scaring them by tapping on their windows at night.

Fritz's mother died when he was twelve and his feuding with his father intensified. After school, he became apprenticed to a locksmith. When that did not work out he was sent to military school. After six months there, he was sent home because he seemed to be suffering from epileptic fits. Back in Hanover, he took to molesting children. Complaints were made, and Haarmann was examined by a doctor, who sent him to the insane asylum. This was a deeply traumatic experience for Haarmann. He eventually escaped and fled to Switzerland, before returning to Hanover in 1900. By this time, he appeared to be a reformed character. He married a woman named Erna Loewert and seemed ready to settle down. But, when she became pregnant, Fritz left her, joined the army and became involved in petty crime. He was soon arrested for burglary, pick-pocketing and small-scale cons. In 1914

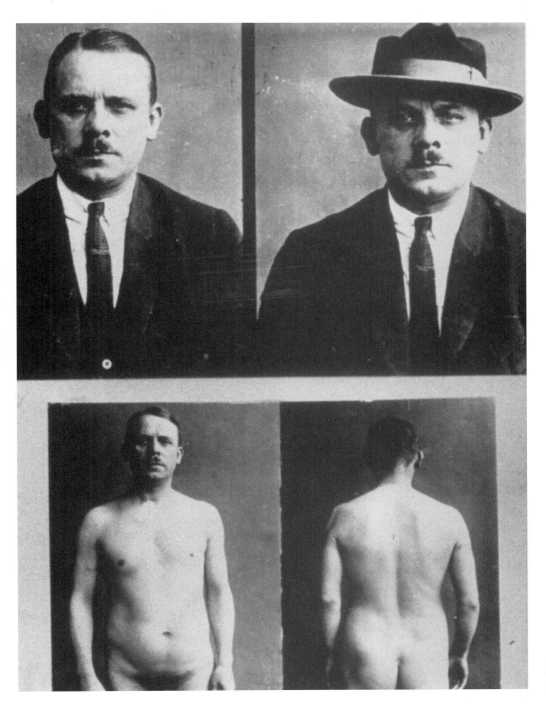

◀ *Photographs of Haarman both dressed and naked were taken by police*

▲ *Haarmann's apartment: there wasn't much to search but police still managed to miss vital evidence that the man was a killer*

Fritz was convicted of a warehouse burglary and sent to prison for his longest stint yet, enabling him to see out the First World War from his prison cell. On release in 1918 he found himself in a poverty-stricken society as Germany struggled to recover from the war.

Crime was flourishing as people desperately sought means of survival. This was the ideal environment for Haarmann. He immediately joined a smuggling ring and simultaneously became a police informer, managing to profit from both sides at once.

POST-WAR CRIMES

A salient feature of the post-war years was the number of homeless and displaced people milling around the city. Many of them resorted to prostitution, so it was easy for Haarmann to pick up boys and youths. In particular he liked to frequent the railway station and find likely prospects there. Often he would introduce himself as 'Detective Haarmann' and use that pretext to get the boys to go with him. At one time, he had been satisfied with sexual abuse, but now his sickness had deepened and he needed to kill his victims to satisfy his lust.

One of his first victims was named Friedel Rothe. Rothe's parents found out that their son had gone with 'Detective Haarmann' and the police went round to Haarmaan's apartment but failed to notice the boy's severed head, hidden behind the stove. Shortly afterwards, Haarmann received a nine-month prison sentence for indecency. On release he met a young homosexual called Hans Grans. They became lovers and moved in together. Next they became business partners, trading on the black market as Fritz continued to act as a police informer. Over the next couple of years their business began to include a gruesome new sideline: selling the clothes and cooked flesh of Haarmann's victims.

For the most part the pair's victims were not missed. Even when they were, the authorities seemed to make elementary blunders in following up clues: the parents of one victim told the police they suspected Grans of having been the murderer, but Grans was in prison at the time; however, Haarmann was never investigated, even though he visited the parents pretending to be a criminologist and laughed hysterically as they told him of their fears. Another time, a suspicious customer took some of Haarmann's meat to the authorities for examination; the police expert duly pronounced it to be pork. It seems that, as long as the murders were confined to a homosexual netherworld, people in general preferred to look the other way.

All that changed in May 1924 when several human skulls were found by the River Leine. At first, the authorities tried to calm the public's fear, suggesting that this was some kind of macabre joke, the skulls having been left there by grave robbers. However, when, on 24 July, children found a sack stuffed full of human bones, there was no stopping the panic. In all the police found 500 bones belonging to at least 27 bodies.

The police investigated all the local sex offenders, among them Fritz Haarmann, but still found no evidence to connect him to the apparent murders. In the end it was Haarmann's own arrogance that led to his downfall. For some reason — conceivably to stop himself from committing another murder — he took a fifteen-year-old boy to the police to report him for insolent behaviour. Once under arrest, the boy accused Haarmann of making sexual advances. Haarmann was

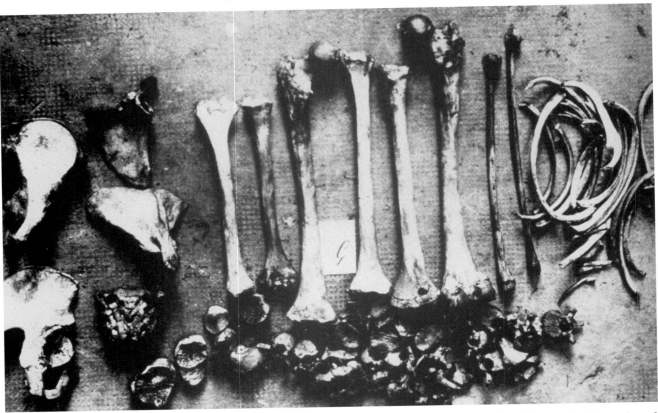

▲ *Some of the bones of Haarmann's victims. Their discovery caused widespread panic*

arrested and his flat searched. The police found garments belonging to missing children, some of them bloodstained. Haarmann at first explained them away by saying that he was a dealer in used clothing and that he had no idea where the blood had come from. However, after a week in custody, under questioning, Haarmann finally confessed to the murders. He took detectives to a number of sites around Hanover where he had buried further bodies, seeming to take pride in his crimes. His testimony only varied when it came to the role of Hans Grans, whom he alternately blamed and exculpated.

When the case came to court, Haarmann was tried and sentenced to death. The jury decided that Grans was no more than an accessory after the fact and sentenced him to twelve years in prison. Haarmann appeared to enjoy his trial, conducting his own defence, smoking cigars and complaining about the presence of women in the courtroom. It was his final act of bravado, however. On 25 April 1925 he – like so many of his victims – was put to death by beheading.

John HAIGH

In 1949, when he came to trial, John Haigh was headlined in the British press as The Vampire Killer. But the only evidence that he ever drank his victims' blood was his own – part of a ploy to have himself declared insane. In fact, he killed for money.

In 1944, as the Second World War was drawing to an end, Haigh, 34, was an independent craftsman, working part-time in a London pin-ball arcade owned by a man called Donald McSwann. It was McSwann who was his first victim. On some pretext, Haigh lured him down to the basement-workshop in the house he rented, and there beat him to death with a hammer. Then he dissolved his body in a vat of sulphuric acid, and poured what remained, grisly bucket by bucket, into the sewage system.

Nobody seemed to pay any attention to McSwann's disappearance. Haigh, who took over the pinball arcade, told his parents that their son had gone to ground in Scotland to avoid the draft; and he himself went to Scotland every week to post a letter to them purporting to be from him. This worked so well that in July 1945 he sent them a further letter,

asking them to visit 'his' dear friend, John Haigh, at his home. They did. They went downstairs to inspect the basement workshop – and followed their son into the sewers.

Haigh, with the help of forged documents, made himself the McSwanns' heir, the master of five houses and a great deal of money. But he was a gambler and a bad investor; and within three years he was once more broke. So he searched out a new inheritance. He invited a young doctor and his wife to look at a new workshop he'd set up in Crawley in Surrey. They agreed. . .

By the time a year had passed, though, the pattern had repeated itself. Once

◀ *John Haigh is led to court*

John HAIGH

135

▲ *Haigh was dubbed the Vampire Killer by the British press*

again unable to pay his bills at the London residential hotel he by now lived in, he badly needed a fresh victim — and this was when he made his first mistake. For he chose someone much too close to him: a fellow-resident of the hotel, a rich elderly widow called Olive Durand-Deacon. Mrs. Durand-Deacon, who ate her meals at the table next to him, was thought that Haigh was an expert in patenting inventions; and she had an idea, she said, for false plastic fingernails. He charmingly invited her to his Crawley 'factory' to go over the details.

It took several days for the acid-bath to do its work on Mrs. Durand-Deacon; and in the meantime Haigh had to go to the police, with another resident, to declare her missing. The police, from the beginning, were suspicious of him and, looking into his record, they found that he'd been imprisoned three times for fraud.

So they searched the Crawley 'factory;' and though they didn't find Mrs. Durand-Deacon, by now reduced to a pile of sludge outside in the yard, they did find a revolver and a receipt for her coat from a cleaner's in a nearby town. They later discovered her jewellery, which Haigh had sold to a shop a few miles away.

When arrested and charged, Haigh blithely confessed, believing that, in the absence of his victim's body, he could never be found guilty. But when a police search team painstakingly went through the sludge, they found part of a foot, what was left of a handbag and a well-preserved set of false teeth, which Mrs. Durand-Deacon's dentist soon identified as hers.

In the end, Haigh pleaded insanity, inventing gruesome stories to back up the plea. But after a trial that lasted only two days, the jury took fifteen minutes to decide that he was both sane and guilty. The judge sentenced him to death. Asked if he had anything to say, Haigh said: 'Nothing at all.' He was hanged at Wandsworth prison on August 6th 1949.

Gary HEIDNICK

Transplanted Clevelander Gary Heidnik was the 'bishop' of a one-man, tax-registered Philadephia church, the United Church of the Ministries of God – and a shrewd investor. But he had a fixation for women he thought beneath him. His congregation – and his lovers – were mostly down-and-outs and women from a nearby home for the retarded.

In December 1978, when he was tried for the kidnapping and rape of a severely brain-damaged woman he had abducted from a home in Harrisburg, the judge said of him:

> 'He appears to be easily threatened by women whom he would consider to be equal to him either intellectually or emotionally.'

Heidnik, who'd served as a medical corpsman in the Army and had trained as a practical nurse outside, spent almost four-and-a-half years in prison on the kidnapping and rape charge. He was released, aged 39, to go back to his 'ministry,' his investments, and what turned out to be his murderous career.

First, he moved house, to a stand-alone building on a street of row houses in north Philadelphia; and then, a year later, he married a twenty-two-year-old mail-order bride from the Philippines the day after she got off the plane from Manila. He used her as his slave; he raped and assaulted her. She escaped – but failed to press charges. So he was free to move on to his next dark fantasy: the acquisition of a harem.

He dug a pit in his basement floor; and when he was ready, on Thanksgiving Day 1986, he picked up and took home his first victim, a part-time prostitute – half Afro-American, half Puerto Rican – called Josephina Rivera. He choked her unconscious and then imprisoned her, naked and chained, in the basement – where he raped and sodomised and beat her daily.

By New Year's Day 1987, Heidnik had abducted three other black women, all of whom were subjected to exactly the same fate. The latest addition to Heidnik's harem, twenty-three-year-old Deborah Dudley, was feisty, though, and fought back. So she was given special treatment: beaten up and either confined to the pit with a heavy weight on top of her or else suspended by a handcuffed wrist from the ceiling. The others were threatened with, and sometimes given, the same punishment if they stepped out of line: if

▲ *Gary Heidnick acquired a 'harem'*

body with a power saw, fed what he could to his dogs and to the women in the basement, and kept the rest in the freezer. Josephina Rivera was beginning to be seen as an ally, but Deborah Dudley he electrocuted to death.

At this point, he forced Josephina Rivera to sign with him a joint confession to Lindsay's murder and, with the confession in hand as an insurance policy, gave her more freedom. He took her with him when he got rid of the body; and then out to meals in fast-food restaurants. During one of these expeditions, he even picked up another prostitute she knew and added her to the harem.

The next day, though, saying that she needed to see her family, Rivera escaped. She went to see a former boyfriend, and together they went to the police. Within minutes the police had all the evidence they ever needed against Heidnik. He was picked up a few blocks away.

Was Heidnik sane? At his trial, a broker gave evidence of his shrewdness: at the time of his arrest, as well as owning several showy Cadillacs and a Rolls-Royce, his 'church' had over half a million dollars. The jury decided that his defence's plea of legal insanity wouldn't wash, and convicted him of murder in the first degree. He was sentenced to the electric chair.

they resisted the continuing rapes, for example, or complained about the dog food they were increasingly fed on.

He picked up a fifth victim, an eighteen-year-old prostitute, on January 18th. The retarded twenty-five-year-old Sandra Lindsay died after being kicked into the pit. Heidnik dismembered her

David HENDRICKS

When police entered the home of Illinois businessman David Hendricks on 8 November 1983 they found a scene of sickening slaughter. Hendricks' wife Susan and their three children had been brutally slain with blows from a butcher's knife and an axe which the killer had had the presence of mind to clean before he left. The walls and ceiling were running with blood and the mattresses were caked in splatter and brain tissue.

So when the distraught father pulled into his driveway later that night having returned from a business trip, police prevented him from entering the house to spare him the grisly sight. They also told him as little as possible about the horrific injuries his loved ones had suffered at the hands of their deranged attacker. It was therefore highly suspicious when very shortly afterwards Hendricks recovered sufficiently to talk to reporters and describe the scene in detail as if he had been there when the murders were committed.

Questioned again at length, Hendricks appeared to have an airtight

▲ *David Hendricks outside prison in 1990*

alibi. He had left home at midnight on Friday 4 November and driven through the night to Wisconsin to have meetings with potential customers first thing the next morning. Over the weekend he made repeated calls to his family and neighbours after failing to get through to his wife on the phone. None of them had seen Susan or the

▶ *Hendricks gets a kiss from his second wife Pat*

children since the night he had left home, but they were all confident that his fears were unfounded. Apparently not satisfied with their reassurances, he called the police and asked them to check on his family to put his mind at rest.

The phone company's record of the calls placed him across the state line, confirming his story. In addition, microscopic analysis of his clothes and his car failed to find any incriminating traces of blood. Of course he would have had time to clean himself up and discard any bloodstained clothing, but even to cynical homicide officers such a scenario seemed too unlikely to be worth considering seriously.

SUSPICIONS AROUSED

However, Hendricks' willingness to speculate with reporters on who might have been responsible for butchering his family aroused the interest of detectives whose first impressions had been that the scene had been staged. A deranged maniac would have ransacked the house in his rage, but the Hendricks' home did not betray signs of wanton destruction, nor even of a burglary that had gone tragically wrong.

But what reason would an apparently devoutly religious and successful businessman have for murdering his own family? Hendricks appeared to have neither the motive nor the temperament for committing such a horrific act.

But, as investigators discovered, it was his new-found success that had created the urge to kill. As the profits from Hendricks' orthopaedic equipment company grew he began to acquire a taste for good living, sharp clothes and the company of beautiful women. He became estranged from his wife whom he was forbidden from divorcing by his Christian fundamentalist faith and this conflict precipitated a breakdown which led him to butcher his family and then calmly walk away as if someone else had done it. However, suspecting that he had done it and proving it in a court of law were two different things.

The case hinged on the victims' time of death, because if it could be proven that they were killed before midnight then detectives could discard the deranged intruder theory and place David Hendricks at the scene of the crime. At the autopsy the pathologist examined the stomach contents of the three children which contained half-digested pizza which they had eaten between 6.30 and 7.30pm.

One would expect that the meal would have passed into the lower intestine after two hours but the fact that it hadn't travelled that far meant that they had been killed before 9.30, when their father was still at home. The best the defence could do at the trial was to argue that the children had been playing energetically after their meal and that exercise is known for slowing the digestive process, but the experts concurred that this would delay digestion by only an hour.

Whatever sympathy the jury might have had for David Hendricks evaporated when they were presented with the image of a callous father who calmly fed his children then slaughtered them so that he could be free to pursue other women. It is an image Hendricks will have to live with every day for the full term of his life sentences, all four of them.

JACK the RIPPER

Now that London's famous fogs have disappeared – and with them the gas-lamps, the brick shacks, the crammed slums, the narrow streets and blind alleyways of the city's East End – it's hard to imagine the hysteria and terror that swept through the area when The Whitechapel Murderer – later known as Jack the Ripper – went to work. Already in 1888 two prostitutes had been murdered. So when the body of another was found, her throat cut and her stomach horribly mutilated, on August 31st, she was immediately assumed to be the brutal killer's third victim. And brutal he was:

'Only a madman could have done this,'

– said a detective; and the police surgeon agreed.

'I have never seen so horrible a case,'

– he announced.

'She was ripped about in a manner that only a person skilled in the use of a knife could have achieved.'

A week later, the body of 'Dark Annie' Chapman was found not far away, this time disembowelled; and a fortnight after that, a letter was received by the Central News Agency in London which finally gave the killer a name. It read (in part):

'Grand job, that last job was. I gave the lady no time to squeal. I love my work and want to start again. You will soon hear from me, with my funny little game. . . Next time I shall clip the ears off and send them to the police just for jolly.'

It was signed —

'Jack the Ripper.'

Five days later, he struck again – twice. The first victim was 'Long Liz' Stride, whose body, its throat cut, was discovered on the night of September 30th by the secretary of a Jewish Working Men's Club whose arrival in a pony trap seems to have disturbed the Ripper. For apart from a nick on one ear, the still-warm corpse was unmutilated. Unsatisfied, the Ripper went on to find another to kill. Just forty-five minutes later – and fifteen minutes' walk away – the body of Catherine Eddowes, a prostitute in her 40s, was found. Hers was the most mutilated so far. For her entrails had been pulled out through a large gash

◄ The crimes of the Ripper were luridly reported in the national press

running from her breastbone to her abdomen; part of one of her kidneys had been removed; and her ears had been cut off. A trail of blood led to a message written in chalk —

'The Juwes are The men That Will not be Blamed for nothing.'

By this time 600 police and plain-clothes detectives had been deployed in the area, alongside amateur vigilantes; and rumours were rife. The Ripper was a foreign seaman, a Jewish butcher, someone who habitually carried a black bag; and there were attacks on anyone who fitted this description. He could even be — for how else could he so successfully avoid apprehension? — a policeman run mad. There was plenty of time now for speculation. For the Ripper didn't move again for more than a month — and when he did, it was the worst murder of all. His victim was twenty-five-year-old Mary Jane Kelly; and her body, when it was found in the wretched hovel she rented, was unrecognisable: there was blood and pieces of flesh all over the floor. The man who found her later said:

'I shall be haunted by [the sight of it] for the rest of my life.'

This time, though, there was a clue. For Mary Jane had last been seen in the company of a well-dressed man, slim and wearing a moustache. This fitted in with other possible sightings and could be added to the only other evidence the police now had: that the killer was left-handed, probably young — and he might be a doctor for he showed knowledge of human dissection.

After this last murder, though, the trail went completely cold. For the

▼ *The Whitechapel Murders appalled the public*

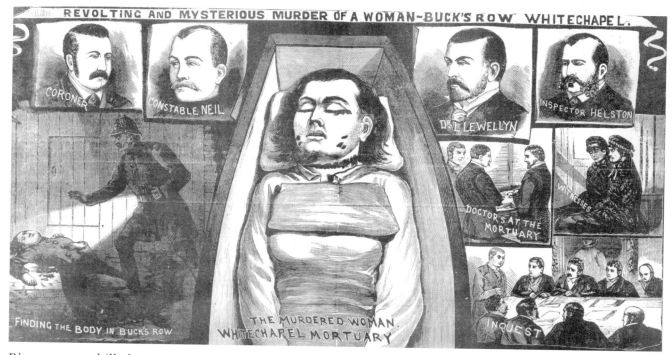

REVOLTING AND MYSTERIOUS MURDER OF A WOMAN-BUCK'S ROW WHITECHAPEL.

CORONER

CONSTABLE NEIL

D^R L LEWELLYN

INSPECTOR HELSTON

DOCTORS AT THE MORTUARY

WITNESSES

FINDING THE BODY IN BUCK'S ROW

THE MURDERED WOMAN. WHITECHAPEL MORTUARY

INQUEST

Ripper never killed again. The inquest on Mary Jane Kelly was summarily closed and investigations were called off, suggesting to some that Scotland Yard had come into possession of some very special information, never disclosed. This has left the problem of the Ripper's identity wide open to every sort of speculation.

The finger has been variously pointed – among many others – at a homicidal Russian doctor, a woman-hating Polish tradesman, the painter Walter Sickert, the Queen's surgeon and even her grandson, Prince Albert, the Duke of Clarence. The theory in this last case is that Albert had an illegitimate child by a Roman Catholic shopgirl who was also an artist's model. Mary Jane Kelly had acted as midwife at the birth, and she and all the friends she'd gossiped to were forcibly silenced, on the direct orders of the Prime Minister of the day, Lord Salisbury.

The probable truth is that the Ripper was a man called Montagu John Druitt, a failed barrister who had both medical connections and a history of insanity in his family. He'd become a teacher, and had subsequently disappeared from his school in Blackheath. A few weeks after the death of Mary Jane Kelly — when the killings stopped — his body was found floating in the river.

▲ *An artist charts the people and events of the Ripper's crimes*

Jesse JAMES

In the Civil War, Jesse James, his brother Frank and his cousin Cole Younger fought – nominally, at least – for the South. They joined Quantrill's Raiders, led by William Clarke Quantrill, riding with him on raids into Kansas and attacks on wagon trains further south. After Quantrill was killed in Kentucky and the war ended, they simply continued his work. Still wrapped in the Confederate flag – and joined by other ex-members of the Raiders – they robbed banks by day, held up trains at night – and killed anyone who stood in their way. For sixteen years, protected by ordinary Missourians, they terrorised a vast area in and around their home state – until Jesse was shot in the back of his head while hanging a picture in his front room.

Jesse Woodson James was born in Clay County, Missouri on September 5th 1847, and walked into legend twenty-two years later, when his horse was taken and recognised in the aftermath of a bank raid in Galatin, Missouri. From that point on, newspapers and word of mouth turned him into the baddest of all bad men, not only the leader of the famous James Gang – which was probably led in fact by his elder brother Frank – but responsible for every major robbery that took place in Missouri, Kansas, Iowa and beyond.

He also acquired a reputation – probably just – for devil-may-care boldness. When in 1871 a robbery of the county office in Corydon, Iowa failed – the treasurer, who had the combination of the safe, was out at a meeting – Jesse simply walked across the street to rob the bank opposite, holding out a $100 bill and asking for change. He and the gang got away on this occasion with $15,000.

With money like this, the James Gang could afford to be choosy about the jobs they took on – probably no more than about twenty-six over sixteen years. They committed their first train robbery in 1873, on the Chicago, Rock Island and Pacific Railroad near Council Bluffs, Iowa, killing the engineer, looting from the passengers and escaping with a large pile of cash from the express car. The following year, this time on the Mountain Railroad, they flagged down another train and took off with $10,000. In the aftermath of this robbery, Jesse and another Gang member kidnapped and killed a Pinkerton detective sent after them. They left his body, as a

◀ *Jesse James was a member of Quantrill's Raiders in the Civil War*

warning, at a crossing of yet another railroad company.

In 1875 and 1876, the Gang mounted two more major train robberies, netting $55,000 and $17,000 respectively. But then they went back to robbing banks — with disastrous consequences. In July 1876, in Northfield, Minnesota, after they'd killed a cashier, the townspeople opened fire on them as they were escaping. Three of the Gang members were killed; Cole Younger and two of his brothers were surrounded and captured a few days later; and Jesse James, who'd

▲ *Rumours persist that James wasn't shot and actually lived to a ripe old age*

On April 1, 1882, two men, Charles and Bob Ford, friends of the Jameses, shot Jesse from behind for the money; and six months later Frank gave himself up to the Missouri authorities.

There are two extra wrinkles to the Jameses' story, though. For Frank James was actually acquitted; and the Missouri governor who'd put a reward on his head refused to extradite him to Minnesota, where he faced more charges. From then on, he lived a peaceful life as a rancher; and almost 20 years later joined a tent show with Cole Younger – after Younger's release from a Minnesota prison – to reminisce in public about the bad old days. He died in 1915.

And the second wrinkle? In November 1889, Martha Jane Canary – Calamity Jane, no less – wrote in her diary:

'I met up with Jesse James not long ago. He is quite a character – you know he was killed in '82. His mother swore that the body that was in the coffin was his but (I know) it was another man they called either Tracy or Lynch. He was a cousin of Wild Bill [Hickok].'

been wounded, only escaped back to Missouri through the resourcefulness of brother Frank.

The Gang's glory days were finally over. But there was still a reward out for the James brothers, either dead or alive.

Jesse James, she wrote, was 'passing under the name of Dalton' and said that if he turned 100, he would give himself in. In the mid-1940s, a very old man called J. Frank Dalton claimed to be Jesse James.

George JUNG

The story of George Jung is a fascinating one. It is the story of how the hippy idealism of the 1960s, based on love, peace and cannabis, slowly developed into a violent culture based on greed, guns and cocaine. The man in the middle of it all was George Jung, who became almost single-handedly responsible for flooding the United States with cocaine in the 1970s. Along the way, Jung lost his ideals, his family and his freedom, and today serves out his sentence in a prison cell.

George Jung grew up in the 1960s in Massachusetts. His father was an honest, hard-working man; his mother a dissatisfied woman, who constantly berated her husband for not earning enough money. The young George left home with a burning desire, above all else, to be rich – an aim he soon achieved. He began by selling marijuana to students in the northeast, before realizing the financial potential of buying it cheap in southern California and Mexico and then transporting it to the east coast of the US, where the street price was much higher. His operation expanded rapidly, until finally one day he was caught. He was tried and sentenced to prison.

'WHITE-COLLAR CRIMINALS'

It was in prison that Jung met the men who were later to become his partners in the cocaine trade. At the time, cocaine was a little-known drug in the US, and was hardly used at all. However, from his cell mate, an English-speaking Colombian named Carlos Lehder, Jung learned that cocaine was available cheaply in Colombia and could fetch a very high price in the US. Together, the pair devised a plan for smuggling cocaine from South America into the US. In pursuit of this aim, they met with a number of other prisoners – 'white-collar criminals' as Jung called them – ranging from lawyers and bankers to Indian tribesmen. From a drug smuggler, they learned all they could about navigation, and from a banker, they found out about money laundering.

Once they were released from prison, Lehder and Jung used their new contacts to build up a massive cocaine-trafficking operation. They and the members of their cartel, the Medellin cartel, became responsible for introducing an astonishing eighty-five per cent of the entire amount of cocaine smuggled into the US from the late 1970s to the early 1980s.

▲ *George Jung went from being a small-time pot dealer in California to amassing a million dollar fortune from the cocaine industry. His story was made into the film* Blow, *starring Johnny Depp (left)*

Pablo Escobar, who supplied the cocaine from Colombia. Escobar not only carried guns but thought nothing of using them; in fact, he once went outside to execute a man during dinner, mentioning to Jung that the man had 'betrayed' him. He then continued his dinner. It was incidents like these that made Jung realize that the hippy ideals of love and peace he had started out with had long since vanished, and in their place was a terrifying, evil world of greed, paranoia and violence.

ADDICTED TO FEAR

By this point, Jung was living a life of luxury, having amassed over a hundred million dollars. His money, and his glamorous lifestyle, attracted many female admirers. He met and married a beautiful woman named Mirtha, and the couple had a baby daughter. On a financial and social level, Jung had achieved more than he could ever have hoped for. However, in the process, he had completely lost control of his life. He was addicted to cocaine. He was also addicted, as he later put it, to 'fear': the constant fear of getting caught provided an adrenaline rush that he could not do without, even though he knew that his activities were a threat to his family.

Jung was also fearful about the company he was keeping: by now, he was surrounded by violent criminals such as

THE FINAL COLLAPSE

As the cocaine operation became bigger, the risks also grew. Eventually, Jung was arrested. His wife left him, taking their baby daughter with her, and he ended up serving a long prison sentence. Everything that he had built up collapsed. Jung had never been a violent man, and was known for his kindness and straight dealing, yet he had allowed himself to become part of a world that had absolutely no moral scruples whatsoever.

Jung's story was later told in a movie, *Blow*. Unusually, the film tried to avoid the stereotype of drug dealers as sleazy lowlifes, and instead portrayed the main characters as dynamic, intelligent men trying to make a success of their lives but eventually succumbing, through greed, to violence and corruption.

George KELLY

George 'Machine Gun' Kelly was one of the celebrity gangsters during Prohibition. An undistinguished man in early life, when he turned to crime he became famous, largely as a result of his wife Kathryn's relentless publicity campaign on his behalf.

Kelly committed a series of flamboyant bank robberies before kidnapping a millionaire, which led to a national manhunt and his eventual capture. He died in 1954, while serving out a sentence of life imprisonment.

Kelly was born George Kelly Barnes on 18 July 1895 in Memphis, Tennessee. Unlike most gangsters of the period, he was not tempted into a life of crime through growing up in

◀ *Behind every great man... Kathryn Thorne was Kelly's unofficial public relations manager, building him a fearsome reputation as a highly skilled machine gunner*

▲ *At the other end of a machine gun, for once, George Kelly (handcuffed, centre) leaves the courthouse accompanied by a bevy of heavily armed guards*

poverty; on the contrary, his father was an insurance company executive and he came from a wealthy, middle-class family. As a child, Kelly was very fond of his mother, but did not get on with his father. During his teenage years, he found out that his father was having an affair and, when his mother died while he was in high school, he blamed his father for her death.

THE BOOTLEGGING TRADE

After leaving high school, Kelly enrolled at Mississippi State University to study agriculture. He was not a good student, and showed no interest in his work. When he met a girl called Geneva Ramsey and fell in love, he decided to quit university and marry her. The couple went on to have two children, and Kelly had to support his new family. He worked as a cab driver in Memphis for a while, but his earnings were not enough, and he soon began to look around for other opportunities. Before long, he met a local gangster and turned to crime, working in the bootlegging trade and changing his name so as not to bring shame on his respectable family.

Kelly was arrested several times as a result of his illegal activities, and each time his wife and other relatives had to bail him out. He began drinking heavily. To get him away from his underground cronies, the family moved to Kansas City, where for a short time Kelly went straight and worked in a grocery store, before his wife found out that he was stealing from the till. Realizing that he was incapable of staying in a straight job, his wife left him, and the couple later divorced.

Now on his own, Kelly stayed in Kansas City and began to build up a bootlegging business there. He gained a reputation in the trade, expanding his operations across several states, but in 1927 he was caught and arrested. The following year, he was sentenced to three years imprisonment for smuggling liquor into an Indian reservation. He then served out another sentence for bootlegging before moving to Oklahoma City, where he met his future partner in crime.

THE OUTLAW BRIDE – AND PR GIRL

Kathryn Thorne was the mistress of a bootlegger named Steve Anderson, but she was also a hardened criminal in her own right. She came from a family of outlaws: her mother was a bootlegger, her aunt a prostitute and several other members were known to police for robbery offences. Thorne was a divorcee who had been married twice, and it was rumoured that she had shot her second husband dead for infidelity. Kelly immediately became enamoured of the worldly wise Thorne, and the pair were married in 1930. From that time on, Kelly rose from being a small-time criminal to a well-known gangster, reaching a pinnacle of infamy when he became 'Public Enemy Number One'.

Thorne bought her husband his first machine gun and encouraged him to practise shooting it, distributing the used cartridges to the denizens of underground drinking clubs as souvenirs from 'Machine Gun' Kelly. In this way, she built up a reputation for her husband as a cold-blooded killer and an expert gunman.

Kelly went on to perform a series of bank robberies, resulting in a series of 'Wanted' posters that emphasized his prowess as an 'expert machine gunner'. The public was terrified, and Kelly hit the headlines as America's most wanted gangster.

In July 1933, Kelly kidnapped a wealthy oil man, Charles Urschel. He demanded a ransom of two hundred thousand dollars. Once the money was delivered, Urschel was freed. A huge investigation was launched, aided by Urschel, who had carefully laid as many clues as he could during his ordeal. Kelly and his cronies were now on the run.

THE LAW CLOSES IN

The other members of the Kelly gang were soon arrested and charged as accomplices in the kidnap. Meanwhile, Kelly and his wife moved around from state to state, living a life of luxury on the ransom money. However, the police were steadily closing in.

When the couple paid a visit to an old friend in Memphis, the FBI managed to catch up with them, surrounding the house and forcing their way in. Kelly, terrified of being killed, was reported to have pleaded for mercy. The couple was arrested, tried and convicted. They both received life sentences.

Initially, Kelly was jailed at Leavenworth in Kansas, but while he was there he continually boasted about how he would escape from the prison. His threats were taken seriously, and in 1934 he was transferred to Alcatraz. There, he continued to boast, this time about crimes he had never committed, which irritated his fellow prisoners immensely but in most ways he served out his sentence as a model prisoner.

In 1951, he was sent back to Leavenworth for the rest of his term. Three years later, on 18 July – which happened to be his birthday – he died of a heart attack.

Ned KELLY

Ned Kelly is perhaps the most famous folk hero of Australia. He was a bushranger who rose from poverty during the late nineteenth century to become a thorn in the side of the police. His career of crime, and his letters to the press explaining his actions, drew attention to the authorities' persecution of the country's poorest farming families, who were trying to scratch a living in the harsh conditions of the Australian outback at the time.

Kelly was born near Melbourne in Beveridge, Victoria, in 1854. His parents, John and Ellen, were Irish immigrants; his father was an ex-convict, now doing his best to go straight. Ned was the eldest boy, and the third of eight children. As a child, he saved a schoolmate from drowning, and for his bravery was awarded a green sash, which he later wore under his armour when he clashed with police.

THE OUTLAW CLAN

When Ned was twelve years old, his father died, and the family moved to Glenrowan in Victoria, which today is known as 'Kelly Country'. Ned was forced to leave school to provide for his large family. The family became 'selectors', landless farmers who were allowed to live on small, often barren areas of land set aside by the government. The idea was that the selectors could improve the property and buy the land bit by bit, but

▲ Ned Kelly was Australia's best-known outlaw. This picture was taken the day before he was hanged at the Old Melbourne jail, in November 1880, aged just twenty-five years

◄ *Ned Kelly's infamous armour was made from beaten-out farm implements*

inevitably, they were too poor to make the necessary improvements, and often the land was taken back from them. Faced with ruin, the selectors sometimes took to stealing livestock from richer farmers, and then escaping into the bush and living as 'bushrangers' – bandits and cattle rustlers.

As the twelve-year-old head of the family, Ned was faced with an impossible task. He did his best, struggling to earn a living in the harsh weather conditions of the country. As well as the poverty, the Kelly family had to endure persecution by the police, because their mother, Ellen Quinn, came from an extended family of outlaws that had a reputation in the area. The Kellys were constantly being charged with one offence or another, although often when the cases came to court the charges did not stick.

THE BATTLE OF STRINGY BARK CREEK

At the age of fourteen, Ned was arrested for assaulting a pig farmer, but found not guilty. The following year, he was again arrested for assault, and this time he was sentenced to six months' hard labour. After he was released, he was arrested again for being in possession of a stolen horse, although it seems that he did not know

▲ *A mock-up of the Kelly Gang's last stand still draws crowds of tourists each year, proving the enduring appeal of this gang of desperadoes*

the horse was stolen. This time, he was sentenced to three years in prison.

In 1878, a policeman, Constable Alexander Fitzpatrick, assaulted Kelly's sister, Ellen, at the family's home. Fitzpatrick then accused Kelly of trying to murder him. Kelly fled with his brother Dan into the bush. Some months later, they and their friends Joe Byrne and Steve Hart, came across police camped at a place called Stringy Bark Creek. A fight ensued and, in the process of it, Kelly shot dead three policemen. From that time on, Kelly was a fully fledged outlaw, constantly on the run. Police put up a huge reward for his capture, but the Kelly Gang, as they became known, had many friends in the area, and nobody turned them in.

HOME-MADE ARMOUR

In 1879, having run short of funds, Kelly robbed a bank at Euroa. The same year, he also committed a bank robbery at Jerilderie. He then composed a long letter to the press, which became known as the 'Jerilderie Letter'. It set out his views on the police and the way they had treated his family, and listing the way in which Protestant police ill-treated Catholic families in Australia. It also predicted uprisings in Australia, Ireland and the US against the persecution that he felt the Catholics had suffered.

In 1880, Kelly and his men came back to Glenrowan, bringing armour that they had fashioned themselves. The armour had been made out of agricultural machinery parts, and weighed about eighty pounds per suit. The gang held about sixty hostages prisoner in a local inn, and then attempted to derail a police train. The plan was foiled by a hostage, schoolmaster Thomas Curnow, who stood on the rails waving a red scarf and holding a lighted candle to warn away the train.

AN ALMIGHTY SHOOT-OUT

When police caught up with the Kelly Gang at Glenrowan, there was an almighty shoot-out, in which Kelly himself was shot many times in the legs, the only part of him not protected by his armour. Other gang members, namely Dan Kelly, Joe Byrne and Steve Hart, died in the inn. Ned managed to survive his injuries long enough to stand trial, and was later sentenced to death. A petition was signed by over thirty thousand people, asking for his sentence to be repealed, but it was to no avail. The flamboyant Ned Kelly was hanged on 11 November 1880, at the age of twenty-five.

After his death, Kelly became a folk hero in his native land. During his life, Kelly had developed a reputation as a polite man who treated his neighbours well. The hounding of his family by the police had also attracted a great deal of sympathy from the public. The outcry that accompanied his hanging eventually caused the authorities to launch an enquiry, and as a result all the police officers connected with the case were either dismissed or brought down in rank.

FREEDOM FIGHTER...
OR COMMON CRIMINAL?

Today, Kelly is a controversial figure. Some see him as a common criminal who robbed and murdered for his own gain; but to others, he is a romantic figure who continues to embody the Australian settlers' values of self-reliance, independence and freedom from persecution in a land of opportunity.

Edmund KEMPER

Edmund Kemper, 'the co-ed killer', was a disturbed child who grew up very tall, very bright and very dangerous. He earned his nickname by killing six young women whom he picked up hitchhiking. There may well have been more victims, but Kemper very carefully avoided leaving any clues. However, he eventually lost all sense of caution when his killing rage turned on his own mother. This time, there was only one obvious suspect.

TROUBLED CHILDHOOD

Edmund Kemper was born in Burbank, California, on 18 December 1948, one of a cluster of serial killer baby boomers. Something else he had in common with other serial killers was a troubled childhood. His father, known as E.E., was a Second World War hero and gun collector; his mother was named Clarnell. The couple split up when Ed was nine and his mother took him, along with his sister, to live in Helena, Montana. Ed reacted badly to the break-up and began to manifest some of the warning signs of serious disturbance. He killed the family cat by burying it alive in the back garden,

then he dug it up, cut off its head and mounted it on a stick, keeping it in his bedroom as a trophy. He also took to mutilating his sister's dolls. Once he confided in his sister that he had a crush on a female teacher. Joking, his sister asked him why he did not kiss her. Edmund answered, in all seriousness, that if he did that 'I would have to kill her first'.

It was not just Edmund's behaviour that was disturbing: his size was also a problem. Both his parents were very tall and, as he reached his teens, Edmund became far taller than his peers, although despite his size, he was also unusually afraid of being bullied. His relationship with his mother deteriorated until she could take no more. Branding him a 'real weirdo' she sent him to live with his father. His father could not handle him either and in turn sent him, aged fifteen, to live with his paternal grandparents on their California farm. This arrangement worked tolerably well for a while, country living at least providing Edmund with plenty of opportunity to shoot animals and birds; but on 27 August 1964 Kemper moved from animals to humans. He shot dead first his grandmother and then his grandfather.

Kemper was promptly arrested and, when he explained his actions by saying 'I just wondered how it would feel to shoot Grandma', he was judged to be mentally ill and placed in a secure hospital at Atascadero. Five years later, in 1969, Kemper, who was by now 6 feet 9 inches tall and 300 pounds in weight, managed to persuade doctors that he was a reformed character, and he was paroled to his mother's care.

CUSTOMIZED CAR

This was, to put it mildly, a mistake. His mother, Clarnell, had now relocated to Santa Cruz, a college town in the San Francisco Bay area. For the next two years Kemper bided his time. He applied to join the police, but was turned down on the grounds that he was too tall. Undeterred, he became a regular drinker at a police bar called the Jury Room, where he befriended numerous detectives. He also worked odd jobs and bought himself a car, similar to those used by the police as undercover vehicles. He started using the car to pick up young female hitchhikers, gradually getting the hang of learning to put them at ease. Next he customized the car, making it impossible to open the passenger side door from the inside. In retrospect it is obvious that he was just waiting for his moment.

The moment finally arrived on 7 May 1972, when he picked up two eighteen-year-old students, Mary Ann Pesce and Anita Luchessa, who were hitching to Stanford University. He drove them down a dirt road, stabbed them both to death, and then took them back to his apartment. There he sexually assaulted the bodies and took photographs of them, before cutting off their heads, putting the bodies in plastic bags, burying them on a nearby mountainside and throwing the heads into a ravine.

It was four months before he killed again. This time the victim was fifteen-year-old Aiko Koo. He strangled her, raped her corpse, and then took her body home to dissect. He had her head in the trunk of his car the next day when he went for a meeting with court psychiatrists – who were pleased with his progress and declared him officially 'safe'.

They could, of course, hardly have been more wrong. Another four months went by and Kemper murdered another student, Cindy Schell. By this time he had acquired a gun that he used to shoot Schell dead after forcing her into the trunk of his car. Now following a pattern, he raped, beheaded and dissected her before disposing of the corpse. He buried her head in his mother's garden.

Less then a month passed before Kemper struck again. This time, it was two more hitchhikers, Rosalind Thorpe and Alice Lin. They hardly had time to get into the car before he shot them both dead. He put both bodies in the trunk and left them there while he went to have dinner with his mother, returning to the car afterwards to decapitate them, then taking Lin's headless corpse inside to rape.

Kemper's madness was now a long way out of control. At this point he apparently contemplated trying to murder everyone on his block. Instead, though, he decided to stay closer to home. Over the Easter weekend, 1973, he murdered his mother with a hammer, decapitated and raped her, and tried to force her larynx down the waste disposal unit. In a muddled attempt to cover up his crime, he then invited one of his mother's friends over, Sally Hallett. He murdered Hallett, and then, on Easter Sunday, he got in his car and started driving west.

By the time he reached Colorado he realized the game was up. At this stage, he telephoned his friends on the Santa Cruz police force and told them what he had done, where and when.

Kemper's confession left no room for legal manoeuvring, except on grounds of insanity. The jury eventually decided that he was sane and found him guilty on eight counts of murder. Asked what the appropriate punishment would be, Kemper reportedly said 'death by torture'. In fact the judge sentenced Kemper to life in prison, a sentence he is still serving.

▲ *Kemper is led to the courtroom during his trial*

Fuelling the court's belief that here was a sociopath not a psychopath, Kemper enjoys his notoriety. He has given regular interviews (including one shared with John Wayne Gacy that was broadcast live). Asking himself the rhetorical question, 'What do you think when you see a pretty girl walking down the street?' Kemper provided this for an answer: 'One side of me says I'd like to talk to her, date her. The other half of me says "I wonder how her head would look on a stick." '

In the light of such remarks, it is unsurprising that Kemper's parole requests have been turned down.

Paul KNOWLES

Journalists usually only meet serial killers once they are safely locked behind bars. British journalist Sandy Fawkes had a rather different experience when she met a good-looking young man named Paul Knowles in an Atlanta bar, and ended up spending several days with him. Ten days later, she was to see her lover's mugshot on the cover of the newspaper – arrested for the latest in a string of at least eighteen murders.

A native of Florida, Paul Knowles was a serial killer who lacked the usual patterns of behaviour common to murderers of this type. He roamed from place to place, killing young and old, men and women. Sometimes he raped his victims, both men and women; sometimes he did not. Sometimes his crimes were financially motivated, sometimes sexually. The only common thread in his actions was an utter lack of moral scruple.

Born in 1946, from his teenage years Knowles was consistently in trouble with the law. He served his first prison sentence when he was nineteen and from then on was constantly in and out of jail, mostly for burglary or car theft.

His first verified murder came shortly after being arrested following a bar fight in Jacksonville, Florida, on 26 July 1974. He escaped from prison using his lock-picking expertise and broke into the house of sixty-five-year-old Alice Curtis. He stole her money and possessions, including her car, and left her bound and gagged. Later, she choked to death on the gag and, when news of her death hit the local media, Knowles decided to dump the car. As he did so, he saw two young girls, aged seven and eleven, whom he thought had recognized him. He abducted them both, strangled them and dumped their bodies in a swamp.

ON THE ROAD

Next, he headed south to Atlantic Beach, Florida, where he broke into another house and strangled the occupant. From there he went north, picking up a hitchhiker and raping and strangling her along the way, before stopping off in Musell, Georgia, to break into yet another house where he strangled Kathie Pierce as her three-year-old son watched. He did, however, leave the boy unharmed.

Knowles spent the next two months driving aimlessly around the country, killing, raping and stealing as he went. On 3 September 1974, he robbed and killed a businessman named William Bates in Lima, Ohio. On 18 September, he

◄ *Paul Knowles was charged with six slayings in November, 1974*

murdered two campers in Ely, Nevada. On 21 September, in Texas, he saw a stranded motorist looking for help. He stopped to rape and kill her. Two days after that, heading back towards his home, he met a beautician named Ann Dawson in Alabama. They spent six days together as lovers, Dawson paying the bills, until he killed her.

Three more weeks of drifting elapsed before Knowles found his next victim, Doris Hovey, whom he shot dead a little way north of Woodford, Virginia. Back south in Macon, Georgia, on 6 November, a man named Carswell Carr made the mistake of inviting Knowles back to his house for drinks. Knowles stabbed Carr to death and then strangled his fifteen-year-old daughter Mandy, attempting to have sex with her corpse.

ROAD BLOCK

Two days later, Knowles was in Atlanta, where he met Sandy Fawkes. She was

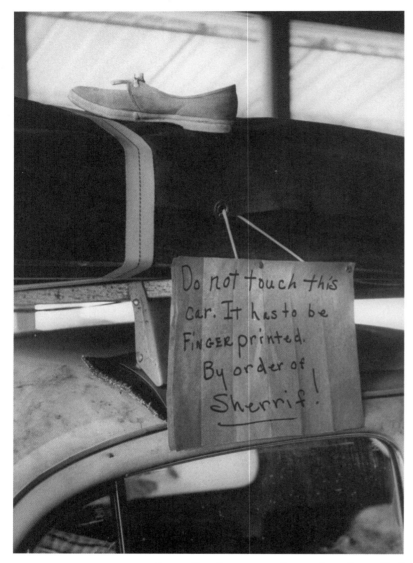

▲ *A police chase was a fitting end to the career of the killer who had spent so much of his time on the move*

picked up one of her friends, Susan Mackenzie, and pulled a gun on her before demanding sex. Mackenzie managed to escape and alert the police, who were soon on Knowles' trail.

The chase lasted several days. Finally apprehended by a police officer, Knowles managed to draw his gun first and kidnap the officer, stealing his car. He then used the police car to stop another motorist, whose car he stole in turn.

Now he had two hostages, the policeman and the hapless motorist, James Meyer. He soon tired of them, and tied the two men to a tree in Pulaski County, Georgia, before shooting them both in the head.

Time was running out for Knowles, however. He ran into a police roadblock, and tried to escape on foot before finally running into an armed civilian who took him prisoner.

Knowles did not live long enough to provide the police with a very detailed confession. The day after his arrest, he was taken by police officers to the site of one of his murders. As they drove along Knowles managed to unlock his handcuffs using a paperclip. He then made a grab for the gun in the holster of the driver, Sheriff Earl Lee. As they struggled, the FBI agent who was also in the car, Ron Angel, drew his own gun and shot Knowles dead.

immediately attracted to what she called his 'gaunt good looks'. Knowles was unable to perform sexually, however, and failed repeatedly over the next few days. When they parted, Fawkes had no idea how lucky she was to be alive; she found out when, on the following day, Knowles

Ronnie and Reggie KRAY

The Kray Twins masterminded the world of organized crime in London's East End during the 1960s. Their fearsome reputation for ruthless violence protected them from the law for many years, but in the end they were arrested, convicted of murder and sentenced to life imprisonment.

Both of the Kray twins later died while serving their sentences. Although they were both vicious criminals, they have often been depicted as 'rough diamonds', essentially good-hearted cockney characters who kept a certain amount of law and order in the East End underworld – but their law and their order. The demise of their reign of terror coincided with the fragmenting of the close-knit, colourful East End community at the end of the 1960s, which perhaps explains why these legendary villains have been sentimentalized to such a degree by the popular media, both in Britain and internationally.

DODGING THE DRAFT
Ronald and Reginald, or Ronnie and Reggie as they were known, were born in

◀ *Ronnie and Reggie, with their beloved mum, Violet*

1933. Their father, Charlie, was seldom at home, but travelled the country as a trader, knocking at people's doors to buy and sell goods. Although he was a hard drinker and gambler, he earned a good living, and made sure that his family lived well. His wife, Violet, and his children were always comfortably housed, clothed and fed, and the children were surrounded by a close network of relatives and neighbours. As well as the twin boys Ronnie and Reggie, there was an older brother, Charlie, who often took responsibility for his younger brothers in the absence of their father.

When Charlie Snr was called up to fight in the Second World War, he repeatedly dodged the draft, which meant that military police often called at his home to find him. This situation gave the brothers a lifelong hatred of authority that was later to become a hallmark of their criminal behaviour.

ARMED ROBBERIES AND ARSON ATTACKS

In their early days at school, both twins were co-operative pupils. Encouraged by their grandfather, Jimmy 'Cannonball' Lee, they took up amateur boxing and did well at it. However, the pastime spurred

◀ *A close-knit family – Reggie, Charles Jr and Ronnie Kray*

them to fight constantly on the streets, and they became known as notorious bullies among the youth of the East End. In 1951, the pair was called up for state military training, or National Service as it was called, but like their father, they were unwilling to become soldiers. They both escaped from army camp several times, and eventually ended up in military prison for assaulting a police officer who noticed that they were on the run and tried to arrest them. They were imprisoned for the assault, but behaved so badly that eventually they were given a dishonourable discharge from the army.

As a result of their anti-social behaviour, the twins now had few career options. They bought a nightclub in Bethnal Green, in the East End, and from there ran a variety of criminal enterprises, including protection rackets, armed robberies and arson attacks for insurance claims. The operation expanded quickly, and more gang members were brought in. However, as it transpired later during their trial, their empire could have been much bigger and more efficient had they not argued with each other constantly.

A REIGN OF TERROR

Even so, through their many nefarious activities the Krays became rich, and went on to acquire several more nightclubs. The clubs became part of the newly emerging 'swinging London' scene of the 1960s. Ronnie in particular enjoyed having his photo taken with celebrities of the day, and in this way the twins started to become famous, not only within the East End, but nationally. As a homosexual, Ronnie made friends with several high-profile figures of the day, including Lord Boothby, a high-ranking Conservative, who was the centre of a tabloid scandal at that time.

As the Krays' fame and fortune increased, so did their criminal activities. However, it was difficult for the police to get witnesses to testify against the brothers, because of their increasing reputation for violence. Ronnie in particular was feared by everyone in the East End. He was by this time suffering from mental illness, and was brutally savage in his attacks on rival gangsters, informers and others. It was only when the pair started to turn on their own followers that the law was able to catch up with them.

STABBED TO DEATH

In 1967, Reggie killed a member of the Kray gang, Jack 'The Hat' McVitie, so called because he always wore a hat to cover a bald patch in the middle of his head. A minor player in the Krays' gang, McVitie was a seedy drunkard who often criticized the twins, disobeyed orders and

generally refused to be intimidated by his bosses. To punish him, members of the gang lured him to a house in the East End, where they stabbed him to death.

Inspector Leonard 'Nipper' Read of Scotland Yard had been trying to bring down the Krays for several years, but only now did he begin to get incriminating statements from witnesses about the brothers' activities. In 1968, Scotland Yard managed to build up enough evidence to arrest the twins and several important members of 'The Firm', as their gang was known. As the police had hoped, once the Krays and their henchmen were in custody, many more witnesses came forward to testify against them.

PSYCHOTIC CRUELTY

After a long trial at the Old Bailey in London, the twins were both convicted of murder and given life sentences. Several other men from 'The Firm' were also found guilty of murder: John 'Ian' Barrie, Tony Lambrianou, Christopher Lambrianou, and Ronnie Bender. The Krays' elder brother Charlie and two other men were found guilty of being accessories to the murder of Jack McVitie.

During the trial, the psychotic cruelty of the twins came to light. As well as the murder of McVitie, Ronnie had shot dead a man named George Cornell at the Blind Beggar public

◄ Savile Row-suited London gangsters Ronnie and Reggie Kray walking along an East End street, London, 1965

house in the East End, in full view of all the customers, for calling him 'a fat poof'. (No witnesses to this murder ever came forward until the twins were in custody, so terrified were they of the consequences.) Reggie was also shown to be an extremely violent man, though most often committing his crimes as a result of Ronnie's influence. In the McVitie murder, Reggie had repeatedly stabbed the victim in the face, neck and stomach, while being urged on by Ronnie, who was holding the victim down.

THE DEATH OF THE KRAYS

Ronald Kray died in 1995 in a mental institution, having been certified insane. Reginald was let out of prison in 2002 on compassionate grounds because he had terminal cancer, but he died the same year. Thus the career of the Kray twins, once feared throughout the London underworld, came to an ignominious end.

Joachim KROLL

Joachim Kroll, the 'Ruhr Hunter', was in some ways the archetypal serial killer. He was a nervous, sexually inadequate loner who preyed mostly on young girls and teenagers. What made him unusual was that his killing spree did not burn itself out in a frenzy, but went on at a steady pace for over twenty years before he was finally caught.

Joachim Georg Kroll was born on 17 April 1933 in Hindenburg, towards the east of Germany near the Polish border. Much of his childhood spent during the terrible years of the Second World War and its aftermath was a time of great poverty and widespread starvation in Germany. Kroll's father was taken prisoner by the Russian Army during the war and never returned. In 1947, Kroll and his mother fled Russian-occupied East Germany to live in the heavily industrialized Ruhr area of West Germany.

MOTHER'S DEATH

The event that seems to have tipped the shy, withdrawn Joachim Kroll into madness was the death of his mother in January 1955. Just three weeks later, on 8 February, Kroll killed for the first time, raping and stabbing to death nineteen-year-old Irmgard Srehl in a barn near the town of Lüdinghausen.

Just how many people he went on to kill over the next two decades will never be known. The only murders that can be traced to him are those he confessed to after his eventual arrest, and he was not sure that he remembered all of them. However, we do know that his next victim was twelve-year-old Erika Schuleter, whom he raped and strangled in Kirchellen.

In 1957, Kroll moved to Duisburg, an industrial city in the Ruhr, where he lived until his eventual arrest. On 16 June 1959 he marked his new territory with the rape and murder of Klara Frieda Tesmer in the Rheinwiesen district of the city. Little more than a month later, on 26 July, he raped and strangled sixteen-year-old Manuela Knodt in Essen, another major Ruhr town. This time, however, Kroll took his perversion one step further. He cut slices from her buttocks and her thighs, took them away and ate them. The police later arrested a compulsive confessor named Horst Otto for this murder.

TASTE FOR HUMAN FLESH

Then came a three-year gap before, sometime in 1962, Kroll raped and

strangled Barbara Bruder in the town of Burscheid. That same year, on 23 April, Petra Giese was abducted from a fair in Dinslaken-Brückhausen, raped and strangled. Once again, he cut off the girl's buttocks to eat. From now on this was a regular trademark. Kroll had clearly acquired the taste for human flesh. Little more than a month later, on 4 June 1962, he indulged himself once again. This time the victim was thirteen-year-old Monika Tafel, who was found dead in a cornfield in Walsum with portions of flesh once again removed from her buttocks. This

rash of murders provoked an uproar, and the people of the town of Walsum soon identified Walter Quicker, a 34-year-old paedophile, as a suspect. He hanged himself soon afterwards.

LOVERS LANE

Kroll appears to have lain low for the next three years, perhaps scared by the investigation. Then, on 22 August 1965, he crept up on a couple parked in a lovers lane in Grossenbaum-Duisburg. He stabbed the man to death, but before he could attack the woman she escaped.

▲ *Sentenced to nine life terms, Kroll died of a heart attack in prison in July 1991, having served only fourteen years of his sentence*

Another year passed and then, on 13 September 1966, Kroll strangled Ursula Rohling in a park in Marl, north of Duisburg. Ursula's boyfriend Adolf Schickel was the suspect this time, and he too soon killed himself. Three months later, Kroll returned to Essen and abducted his youngest victim yet, five-year-old Ilona Harke. He took her by train and bus to a woodland area called the Feldbachtal. There Kroll raped her then, in a variation that he later put down to simple curiosity, he drowned her.

The following year, on 22 June, Kroll lured ten-year-old Gabrielle Puetman into a cornfield and showed her pornographic pictures. She fainted but was saved by the arrival of passers-by. Kroll managed to escape from the scene.

INNOCENT VICTIMS

Once again, he waited before raping and murdering his next victim. This time it was an older woman, 61-year-old Maria Hettgen, whom he raped and strangled in her home on 12 July 1969. Two years later, on 21 May 1970, he raped and strangled thirteen-year-old Jutta Rahn as she walked home from school. Her neighbour, Peter Schay, was suspected and spent fifteen months in prison for the crime.

This time, six more years went by before Kroll raped and strangled another schoolgirl, Karin Toepfer, in Dinslaken-Voerde. Then, on 3 July 1976, he took his final and youngest victim, four-year-old Marion Ketter, whose disappearance provoked a large investigation by neighbours and police.

At this point, it seems that Kroll was crying out to be caught. A local resident in the block of flats where he lived complained to him that his toilet was blocked; Kroll apparently replied that the reason for this was that it was 'full of guts'.

The neighbour did not know what to make of this, but a call to a plumber soon showed that Kroll was not joking. The child's lungs and other organs were blocking the pipe. The police were immediately called to Kroll's apartment, where they found bags of human flesh in the refrigerator, and a child's hand boiling on the stove, along with some carrots and potatoes.

Kroll was arrested and promptly confessed to his whole twenty-year history of murder. Three years later, the case finally came to court and, after three more years of drawn-out proceedings, he was finally found guilty on eight counts of murder and one of attempted murder. He was duly sentenced to nine terms of life imprisonment. On 1 July 1991, he died of a heart attack in prison.

Peter KÜRTEN

Peter Kürten, the so-called Vampire of Düsseldorf, was an indiscriminate murderer: he attacked and killed everything – men, women, children, animals – that came his way. Yet he was described by a psychiatrist at his trial in 1930 – where, from behind the bars of a specially-built cage, he spelled out the details of his crimes in meticulous detail – as a clever, even rather a nice man.

That he should have been so is astonishing. For Kürten's father had been a drunken, pathological sadist, who was sent to prison for repeatedly raping his wife and thirteen-year-old daughter; and he himself had committed his first murders – the drowning of two playmates – at the age of nine. At about the same time, he later said, he was inducted by the local dog-catcher into the delights of torturing animals – he sometimes decapitated swans to drink their blood.

By the age of 16, he was a petty young hoodlum and occasional arsonist living in a ménage-à-trois with a masochistic older woman and her teenage daughter. He was arrested and sent to prison twice – first for theft and fraud, and then for deserting

◀ *Peter Kürten was named the Vampire of Düsseldorf*

from the army the day after he'd been called up. In between these two sentences, though, while making his living as a burglar in Cologne-Mullheim, he committed his first murder, when he came across an eight-year old girl in a room over an inn, raped her and cut her throat with a pocket-knife.

'I heard the blood spurt and drip beside the bed,'

— he said calmly at his trial seventeen years later.

His second sentence, for desertion, kept Kürten out of circulation, perhaps luckily, for eight years; and in 1921, when he came out, he seemed on the face of it a changed man. He got married in Altenburg, took a job in a factory and became known in the community as a quiet, well-dressed and charming man, active in trade union politics. Then, though, in 1925, Kürten and his wife moved to Düsseldorf – and the opportunistic attacks on complete strangers began.

'The Vampire,' as he soon became known, attacked people with either scissors or knives, in broad daylight, any time – as if inflamed by the idea and sight of blood. By 1929, he had struck forty-six times and four of his victims had died; and now, far from stopping, he was beginning to step up the rate and violence of his attacks. On the evening of 23 August of that year, he strangled and cut the throats of two young sisters on their way back from a fair; and twelve hours later, after offering to take a servant-girl to another fair, he attacked and stabbed her as they walked through woods nearby. For a while there was a lull, but then he attacked three people, a man and two women, within a single half-hour; and later he bludgeoned a pair of serving women to death. Finally, on 27 November, he killed a five-year-old girl, slashing her body no fewer than thirty-six times.

The city of Düsseldorf was by now in a state of panic. But again, for a while, nothing more was heard from 'The Vampire.' Then, on May 14th 1930, Maria Budlick, a young girl looking for work in the city, arrived from Cologne and was picked up at the station by a man who offered to show her the way to a women's hostel. When he tried to take her into a nearby park, though, she refused on the grounds that she didn't know who he was – he might even be 'The Vampire.' While they were arguing, a second man stepped up and asked her if she was all right. This second man was charm itself, Maria later said, and, when the first man left, he offered her something to eat before taking her to the hostel.

She agreed; and after a glass of milk and a sandwich at his house, they duly took a tram to the edge of the city. Still believing she was on the way to the hostel, Maria began walking with him through the Grafenberg Woods. Then, suddenly, he said,

'Do you know where you are? You are alone with me in the middle of the woods. You can scream as much as you like and no one will hear you!'

He seized her by the throat and threw himself on her. She fought back; and then, quite unexpectedly, he let go of her, and asked her if she could remember where he lived. Maria, in fact, could remember, but she said no, she couldn't. Satisfied, the man then stood

up and calmly showed her towards the woods' exit.

When the police found out about this incident – through a mis-addressed letter in which Maria had confided to a friend – they located her and asked her to take them to the house she'd visited. She did, and saw the man she'd met – Peter Kürten – going in.

Kürten, having recognized her too, must have known immediately that his days of freedom were numbered. For he soon left, went to the restaurant where his wife worked and coolly confessed to her that he was 'The Vampire' – she could now claim the reward. A few days later,

she went to the police and told them where he was.

The trial was a formality, consisting almost entirely of Kürten's detailed confessions to the nine murders and seven attempted murders he'd been charged with. Yes, he'd drunk blood. Yes, he was a sadist, an arsonist, a rapist, a vampire. He was sentenced to death nine times. On July 1st 1931, before his walk to the guillotine, he asked the prison psychiatrist whether he'd be able to hear, if only for a second, the gouting of his own blood as the blade cut through his neck. 'That,' he said, 'would be the greatest of all pleasures.'

▲ *Kürten's crimes threw Düsseldorf into a state of panic*

Henri LANDRU

Henri Landru, the French 'Bluebeard,' was a conman, a fraudster, specializing in lonely widows and spinsters; and by 1914, when he was 45 he'd already been in prison four times for swindling and abuse of confidence.

In 1914, he seems to have made one more important decision: from now on, he'd kill his victims, rather than leave them

▶ Henri Landru – aka Bluebeard

alive to give evidence against him. His first victim of this new resolution was a 39-year-old widow and her 18-year-old son. Calling himself Monsieur Diard, he moved them into a villa on the outskirts of Paris, where they both disappeared.

By this time Landru was placing ads in newspapers, claiming to be a widower of 43, with 'a comfortable income,' 'moving in good society' and desirous 'to meet widow with a view to matrimony.' He recorded replies in a black notebook. One of them was his next prey: a 51-year-old ex-governess with a considerable legacy. When she disappeared, Landru, together with her legacy, moved to the Villa Ermitage in the village of Gambais.

The widows came – and went – over a period of over three years. But then the sister of one of Landru's victims recognized the man she knew as 'Monsieur Fremyet' walking, with a young girl on his arm, in Paris. 'Monsieur Fremyet' was arrested. In a stove at the Villa Ermitage, police discovered fragments of human bone.

Landru, was tried for ten of a suspected 300 murders and was found guilty. On 30 November 1921, still maintaining his innocence, he walked to the guillotine with some hauteur. But more than 40 years later, a confession he'd written on the back of a drawing he'd given to his lawyers was found.

Meyer LANSKY

Meyer Lansky, born Maier Suchowjansky in Grodno, Poland, is the most shadowy and indistinct of all the great American Mafia bosses of the twentieth century. But it was he more than anyone else who was responsible for creating the structure and outreach of the modern Mafia – first by masterminding the alliance between New York's Italian and Jewish mobs that created the central commission, the Syndicate, and then by expanding the Syndicate's reach and influence across the United States and beyond. It was he, the grand strategist, who moved the Mafia's money and power into Las Vegas, movies and legitimate businesses all across the country. He said in the 1970s – and only he perhaps knew:

'We're bigger than US Steel.'

In about 1918, sixteen-year-old Lansky arrived in New York and seems to have taken a job as an engineering apprentice. But he was soon part of the rough-and-tumble of the Lower East Side's streets, running with the Jewish gangs and fighting for both territory and survival.

The turning point came when he met and outfaced another tough street kid called Charlie Luciano, who took him under his wing. Many of the underground rackets in the city were then run by Jewish gangsters, and Lansky became in time Luciano's bridge to their operations and muscle. 'We had a kind of instant understanding,' Luciano later said.

'It may sound crazy, but if anyone wants to use the expression "blood brothers," then surely Meyer and I were like that.'

Both Luciano and Lansky in due course made it to the big time: they went to work for the visionary Arnold Rothstein, the first great bootlegger of the Prohibition era – and the first man, it's said, to recognise the potential of dope. Rothstein – Lansky's said to have met him at a bar mitzvah – taught both men a good deal about style, and gave Lansky his first taste of what was later to become his main operation: casino gambling.

Rothstein was assassinated in 1928; and left the field open to the fastest learners among his apprentices, Luciano and Lansky. They largely sat out the score-settling wars that followed. But then, in 1931, Lansky organised the Jewish hit-men who disposed of the first self-styled *capo di tutti capi*, Salvatore Maranzano, who'd set himself up as the

▶ *Meyer Lansky masterminded the alliance of the Jewish and Italian gangs in New York*

ultimate authority over what came to be known as 'the five families.' He and Luciano took over Maranzano's five-family structure, but instead of appointing a boss of all bosses, they created a board of directors, the Syndicate, backed by the enforcement arm of Murder Incorporated. Both sat on the Syndicate board, and met every day they could, it's said, for breakfast at a

delicatessen on Delancy Street. Luciano and Lansky: they were the real power.

They moved the Mafia into dope – it's said that Lansky himself got hooked on heroin after his son was born crippled, and then did cold turkey in a hide-out in Massachusetts, watched over by a hood called Vincent 'Jimmy Blue Eyes' Alo, ever after a close friend. They became the ultimate authority in policy and peace, ruling Mafia activity nationwide. But then in 1936, Lucky Luciano was tried on a trumped-up charge of prostitution and sentenced to thirty to fifty years in jail.

After Luciano's fall, Lansky more and more took to the shadows, living apparently quietly in a tract house in Miami, as he moved the Mafia into gambling operations in Las Vegas, the Bahamas and Cuba.

In 1970, after hearing that he faced tax-evasion charges, Lansky, by now 68, fled to a hotel in Tel Aviv, before being extradited, by order of the Israeli Supreme Court, back to the US. In the end, he was acquitted; and in the late-70s and early-80s, he could be seen walking his dog along Miami's Collins Avenue or having a meal in a diner with his old friend 'Jimmy Blue Eyes.' He died from a heart attack in 1983, at the age of 81.

◄ *Lansky was one of the first bosses to move the Mafia into dope smuggling*

Louis LEPKE

Louis Lepke, the boss of the Jewish arm of Murder Incorporated, is the only American Mafia chieftain to have been executed. After two years hiding out in Brooklyn, he gave himself up to the FBI, persuaded into doing so, it's said, by Albert Anastasia. He, Lucky Luciano and the other members of the Syndicate wanted him dead.

Lepke, short for 'Lepkele' or 'Little Louis,' was born Louis Buchalter in Williamsburg, Brooklyn in 1897. His father, the owner of a hardware store on the Lower East Side, died of a heart attack when he was 13, and his mother moved soon afterwards to Colorado. Little Louis, then, came of age in the streets. He hung out with hoodlums, and was soon in trouble with the law. He was sent out of town to live with his uncle in Connecticut, and then to a reformatory, from where he soon graduated, around the time of his 21st birthday, first to New York's Tombs prison, and then to Sing Sing, where he acquired the nickname 'Judge Louis.'

Back on the streets again in 1923, he went into the protection business with an old pal, Joseph 'Gurrah' Shapiro – they were known as 'the Gorilla Boys' and specialised in bakeries. But they didn't hit the big time until they went to work for Arnold Rothstein, who dealt large in liquor and drugs. Soon they were moving into the union rackets, backing the workers against the bosses with goon squads, and then taking over from both. They started out in this with a real expert, 'Little Augie' Orgen, as their principal mentor. But by 1927, Orgen simply stood in their way. So on 15 October they gunned him down in front of his clubhouse; and by the beginning of the 30s they ruled the labour roost: they controlled painters, truckers and motion-picture operators; they were expanding their drugs business; and they still took in $1.5 million a year from bakeries. They were now known, not as 'the Gorilla Boys,' but 'the Gold Dust Twins.'

In 1933, with the setting up of the Syndicate, Lepke became a board-director and one of the founding members of Murder Incorporated, its enforcement arm of contract-killers, among whom was a Brooklyn thug called Abraham 'Kid Twist' Reles. That same year, though, Lepke was indicted by a federal grand jury for violation of anti-trust laws. And though he ultimately beat the rap on this one, the Feds began closing in with narcotics charges, and the

Brooklyn DA's office with an investigation into racketeering. In the summer of 1937, he – along with 'Gurrah' Shapiro – went on the lam; and he soon became the most wanted man in US history.

He did his best from hiding to silence the potential witnesses against him, but the heat on the streets became too great; and in August 1940, he gave himself up, with the understanding that he'd face federal narcotics charges rather than a state indictment for murder. He was sentenced to fourteen years and shipped to the penitentiary at Leavenworth, Kansas.

Then, though, Abe Reles, 'Kid Twist,' one of the executioners he'd hired in the old days, began to sing. For six months Reles was held at a hotel in Coney Island as he gave evidence at trial after trial. On 12 November 1941, his body was found – apparently he'd jumped from a sixth floor window – but it was too late for Louis Lepke. For Reles had already appeared before a grand-jury hearing to give evidence against him, evidence that could be – and was – used in court.

Louis Lepke and two of his lieutenants, Mendy Weiss and Louis Capone, were tried for murder and condemned to death. They went to the electric chair in Sing Sing prison on 4 March 1944. The murder of Reles – which got Albert Anastasia and Bugsy Siegel off the hook – was probably arranged by Frank Costello.

▲ *Louis Lepke, one-time boss of the Jewish arm of Murder Incorporated*

John LIST

The case of John List has become famous as an example of a crime solved by a particular type of forensic investigation – sculpture. The pioneer of this method of detection is Frank Bender, an artist with an uncanny ability to visualize what a criminal – or victim – might look like.

Working with any clue he can find, from the remains of a mangled, decomposed body to an out-of-date photograph, Bender is able to build up a visual profile of his subject with amazing accuracy. Using a mixture of technical information and artistic instinct, he builds a sculpture of the subject, colours it with naturalistic shades based on information about the individual and photographs it.

The image of the head is then broadcast on television and pictured in the press so that members of the public may come forward with information. In this way, several dangerous criminals have been brought to justice, sometimes after many years of being on the run, and the files on many other wanted criminals constantly updated and revised.

MURDERED ONE BY ONE

One of the most successful of Bender's assignments was the case of John List. List was born in Bay City, Michigan on 17 September 1925. The only child of Lutheran parents, List grew up under the watchful eye of a controlling mother, attending church regularly and leading Sunday school sessions. During the Second World War, he joined the army, and later qualified as an accountant. However, he did not get on well with his colleagues, earning a reputation as a loner, and his lack of empathy caused constant problems in his career. Nevertheless, he married, raised a family, and lived in an expensive home. To the casual observer, he looked like a successful man.

In reality, however, his life was a mess. His wife was suffering from mental illness, and he was having difficulty paying the bills for extravagant items he had bought for the house, such as a Tiffany glass ceiling. He was plagued by guilt, feeling that his career failures had let his family down. He was also anxious about his daughter, who was interested in pursuing a career as an actress, an activity he considered deeply evil. As he explained later to his pastor in a letter, he was overcome by the need to save his family's souls, so that they would not be corrupted by the sinful modern world.

List eventually decided to murder each of them, one by one, laying them out on sleeping bags and praying over them before he left the house. The bodies were not discovered for a month, by which time List had disappeared.

AMERICA'S MOST WANTED

Police investigating the murder followed up hundreds of leads at the time, but to no avail. However, eighteen years later the List case was unearthed and became the subject of the television show *America's Most Wanted*.

It was the oldest, coldest case ever to be featured on the television show, and the producers were aware that the murderer, wherever he was, would by now look very different. The producers asked Frank Bender to help.

By looking at photographs of List's parents taken when they were age that List would be now, as well as List himself, Bender was able to predict how the murderer would have aged. He also analysed the case with criminal psychologist John Walter, building up a picture of List's personality.

▲ *John List with his family, all of whom he murdered in cold blood*

RIGID HABITS

Together, Bender and Walter came up with a picture of List's way of life after the murders. Because List was a man with rigid habits, they predicted that he would move, but not too far away, and that he would marry an easily dominated woman. They thought he would become a member of a Lutheran church, continue to work as an accountant, and still be in debt.

They imagined that he would dress conventionally and still wear glasses, as he had done at the time of the murders, rather than changing to contact lenses, which were now available. Bender intuited, however, that List would by now have changed the style of the glasses. Bender thought that List would now be wearing ones with thick, heavy rims designed to make the wearer look serious and intelligent.

It also seemed likely, from the research they conducted, that List would have done very little, other than change his name, to disguise his identity. List had a scar behind his right ear but probably would not have had cosmetic surgery to cover this up. John List was at heart an unimaginative man who would simply try to forget the past and resume his routine as quickly as possible somewhere else, without taking too much trouble to cover his tracks.

▶ *John List at his trial, by which time he was using the name of Bob Clark*

THE NEED TO DO GOOD

Using this information, Bender built a clay bust of List, adding each detail, such as his hair and glasses, with infinite care. When the clay bust was shown on television, a man recognized and identified him. The FBI followed up the lead, and on 1 June 1989, ten days after the call, List was arrested. He was now living under the name Bob Clark, but – as Bender had predicted – other than that, had done little to disguise his identity. Amazingly enough, all Bender's other predictions were proved right too. List was living less than three hundred miles from his former home, had remarried, was working as an accountant, and still had financial difficulties. He dressed conservatively and had changed to the exact same style of heavy-framed glasses that Bender had added to the clay bust.

John List was taken into police custody and the following year was convicted of all the murders, and sentenced to life imprisonment.

Today, Frank Bender continues to work as a forensic sculptor. Often working using body parts and other clues to build up a visual profile of his subjects, he is committed to his work, saying, 'It's the need to do good and help cut the cancer out of society, and to find truth. I felt that from the very first case.'

Pedro LOPEZ

Pedro Lopez, the 'Monster of the Andes', has a claim to being the most prolific serial killer of modern times. If his own unverified estimate of three hundred victims is to be taken seriously, then only Harold Shipman can rival him for the sheer number of lives brought to an untimely end.

STREET LIFE

Pedro Lopez was born in Tolina, Colombia, in 1949, the seventh of thirteen children born to a prostitute mother. At any time this would have been a hard start in life, but in 1949 Colombia was going through what became known as 'La Violencia', a time of brutal lawlessness and civil war. When Pedro was eight years old, his mother found him making sexual advances to a younger sister and threw him out.

The first person to take him in posed as a Good Samaritan, but turned out to be a paedophile who raped Pedro repeatedly, before casting him back out on to the streets. Utterly traumatized, the boy became a feral, nocturnal being.

He endured this existence for a year, finally ending up in the town of Bogota, where an American couple saw him begging on the streets, took pity on him and took him in. They gave him room and board and sent him to a local school for orphans. This good fortune did not last, however. Aged twelve, Pedro ran away from school after stealing money.

PRISON RAPE

Pedro Lopez was able to survive by a mixture of begging and petty theft, building up, in his mid-teens, to a specialization in car theft. Aged eighteen, he was arrested and sentenced to seven years in prison. After only two days there he was gang-raped by four of his fellow inmates. Lopez, however, was tired of being a victim; he constructed a homemade knife and succeeded in killing three of his attackers. The prison authorities, little interested in the well-being of the inmates, added two years to his sentence.

By the time of his release in 1978, Lopez was a very angry and dangerous individual, with a major grudge against society in general and women in particular – he blamed his mother for everything that had gone wrong in his life. On release, he started to take a perverse form of revenge and embarked on a two-year killing rampage. His targets were invariably young girls, mostly from Indian tribes, as he knew the authorities would be uninterested in their fate. Nor did he confine himself to Colombia; his murderous spree saw him following the Andes south to Peru and Ecuador. In Peru alone he reckoned to have killed as many as a hundred girls before he was captured by Ayachuco Indians while attempting to abduct a nine-year-old girl. They were about to bury him alive when an American missionary intervened and persuaded them to hand Lopez over to the authorities. The authorities simply deported him over the border to Ecuador and let him go.

CAUGHT

For the next year or so, Pedro Lopez moved back and forth between Ecuador and Colombia, killing with apparent impunity. Then, in April 1980, there was a flash flood in the Ecuadorian town of Ambato and the bodies of four missing children were washed up. A few days later, still in Ambato, a woman named Carvina Poveda spotted Lopez in the act of trying to abduct her twelve-year-old daughter. She called for help. Lopez was overpowered and handed in to the police.

Lopez started to confide in the prison priest. After a day of grisly confession, the priest had to ask to be released, as he could not stand to listen any more. The priest told the interrogators what he had learned; they put the new evidence to Lopez and he began to confess.

◀ Tired of being a victim, Lopez turned into a monster – one of the most prolific serial killers of all time

DAYLIGHT MURDER

Lopez told them that he had murdered a hundred girls in Colombia, at least a hundred and ten in Ecuador, and many more than that in Peru. He expressed a particular enthusiasm for Ecuadorian girls, who he said were much more innocent and trusting than Colombians and stated a preference for murdering by daylight so he could see the life leave his victims' eyes as he strangled them.

Further confessions allowed prosecutors to convict Lopez of a hundred and ten murders in Ecuador. He was sentenced to life imprisonment. In the unlikely event that he is ever released, he would be required to stand trial in Colombia, where he would face the death penalty. Today, Lopez does not appear remorseful; rather, he seems proud of his crimes: 'I am the man of the century,' he said in a recent interview.

Henry Lee LUCAS

The case of Henry Lee Lucas is one of the oddest in the annals of serial killers. He was either one of the most prolific killers ever to walk the face of the earth, or was responsible for just three murders. According to the stories he told the police during the mid-1980s, he committed between seventy and six hundred murders, all over the United States. However, the only murders he can conclusively be linked to are the killing of his mother, for which he served time in the 1960s, and the murders of his 15-year-old girlfriend and an 82-year-old woman who had helped the pair. These were the crimes that led to his final arrest.

DESPERATELY POOR

Henry Lee Lucas' background was tailor-made to produce a serial killer. He was born in 1936 in the town of Blacksburg, Virginia, in the desperately poor Appalachian Mountains. He was the youngest of Viola and Anderson Lucas' nine children. Both parents were alcoholics. Viola dominated the home and provided most of the family's income by prostitution; Anderson was known as 'No Legs', having lost his lower limbs in a drunken accident.

Viola Lucas seems to have loathed her youngest child from birth. She sent him to school shoeless and, initially, wearing a dress. When the school gave him some shoes she beat him for accepting them. Later in his childhood he cut his eye with a knife while playing around; Viola let the wound fester until he had to have the eye removed and replaced by a glass one. She would also force her children to watch her having sex with her clients and her lover 'Uncle Bernie'. Lucas' father finally died of pneumonia after spending a night outside the house lying in the snow. His main contribution to his son's upbringing was to introduce him to moonshine whiskey. By the time he was ten, Henry was virtually an alcoholic.

Not long after that, Uncle Bernie and Henry's older half-brother introduced him to bestiality, which involved sexually assaulting animals and then killing them. This was an activity Henry later claimed to have taken to with relish. By his own unreliable account, his first sexual experience with a woman resulted in his first murder; aged fourteen, he raped and strangled an unknown girl.

Almost inevitably, Lucas drifted into crime and in June 1954 he was sentenced to six years for burglary. He twice managed to escape custody but was recaptured both times, and finally released on 2 September 1959. On release, he went to live with his sister in Tecumseh, Michigan. Soon afterwards his mother arrived and tried to persuade Henry to return with her to Blacksburg. This led to a drunken argument that culminated in Henry stabbing Viola Lucas, resulting in her death two days later. Henry was convicted of second-degree murder and served ten years in prison.

ATTEMPTED KIDNAP

He was released in June 1970 but was soon rearrested for attempting to kidnap two teenage girls. Released again in 1975, he was briefly married to Betty Crawford, who divorced him, claiming he had molested her daughters. At around this time, according to his later confessions, he began his epic orgy of killing, travelling the highways of the United States in search of women to rape and murder.

In late 1976, he met Ottis Toole in a soup kitchen in Jacksonville, Florida. Toole, like Lucas, was a sexual deviant and murderer, and also prone to exaggeration. The pair became friends and, by 1978, Lucas was living in Toole's house in Jacksonville, along with Toole's young niece and nephew. Lucas fell in love with the niece, a slightly retarded girl called Becky Powell, despite the fact she was just ten years old when they met.

From 1979 to 1981 Lucas and Toole worked together for a roofing company. If their stories are to be believed, they frequently took time off to rape and slaughter. In 1981, Becky and her brother were taken into care. Lucas and Toole snatched them back and headed out on the road. In May 1982 Lucas and Becky, now fifteen and claiming to be married to Lucas, went to Texas to work for an old lady named Kate Rich. Rich's neighbours kicked the couple out of the house when they discovered that they were cashing cheques in the old lady's name.

Lucas and Powell spent some time in a religious commune nearby, before Becky

▲ *Once in prison Lucas poured out a tale of mass murder that not everybody believed*

decided that she wanted to go home. Lucas appeared to agree and the two left the commune. The next day, he returned alone. Three weeks later the old lady, Kate Rich, disappeared. Lucas left town the following day. He was eventually arrested on 11 June, when he returned to the commune and was found in possession of an illegal handgun.

CONFESSION

After four days in jail Lucas began to confess, first to the murders of Becky Powell and Kate Rich, and then to a string of other crimes. He was convicted of the murders of Powell and Rich and sentenced to seventy-five years in prison. However, this did not halt his stream of confessions. For eighteen months he kept on confessing, his body count spiralling into the hundreds. He implicated Toole in many of these murders.

By this time, detectives from all over the country were queuing up to see if Lucas would help solve any of their murder cases. More often than not Lucas was happy to oblige, particularly if they took him out of prison to tour the murder sites, put him up in hotels and bought him steaks and milk shakes. By March 1985, police across the States had cleared 198 murders as having been committed by Lucas either alone or in tandem with Toole. Alarm bells started to go off in the minds of some prosecutors when Lucas, who had never left the country, started to claim that he had committed murders in Spain and Japan, not to mention having supplied the poison used in the Jonestown Massacre.

A FRAUD?

A series of newspaper articles appeared claiming that Lucas was a fraud who was using – and being used by – unscrupulous police departments looking to clear their backlogs of unsolved murders. At this point, Lucas himself began to recant his confessions. Now he claimed that, apart from his mother, he had only killed Powell and Rich.

Nevertheless, while the claim of six hundred-plus victims seems obviously exaggerated, there are many who still believed the Lucas and Toole may have killed as many as a hundred people. Lucas was tried again for just one murder, that of an unknown female known as 'Orange Socks'. He was found guilty and sentenced to death. However, subsequent investigation proved that this was one murder Lucas could not have committed, as he was working in Florida at the time. Lucas died of heart failure on 13 March 2001.

Lucky LUCIANO

One of the most influential Mafia bosses of the twentieth century, 'Lucky' Luciano almost single-handedly transformed the world of organized crime from a few warring Italian families to a large number of affiliated ethnic groups running criminal activities on a grand scale. A vicious killer who was finally jailed for running one of the biggest prostitution rings of all time in the US, he was also an intelligent, able businessman, and a patriotic American to boot. The contradictions of his life were such that, while serving a prison sentence for his crimes, he also helped the American government in the war effort during the Second World War.

He was born Salvatore Lucania in Lercara Friddi, a village near Corleone in Sicily. When he was ten years old, he moved with his family to the US. He began his career of crime early, demanding that younger children playing on the streets pay him a cent a day to protect them from older ones. Children who refused to pay were given a sound thrashing. One of those who refused protection was the young Meyer Lansky, who put up a good fight when Luciano attacked him. Lansky went on in later years to become a top Mafia boss like Luciano, and the pair became friends.

THROAT CUT

As a young man, Luciano joined a team of thugs known as the Five Points Gang, headed by John Torrio. Members of the gang were suspected by local police of being involved in many crimes, including murder. Luciano specialized in pimping and in protection rackets; he also dealt heroin on the streets. It was not long before his ruthless spirit of enterprise

◀ Jewish mobster Meyer Lansky. Luciano broke with Mafia tradition by openly associating with him and other gangsters from different ethnic groups

▶ *Although given his nickname when quite young, Luciano was indeed lucky – dying of natural causes is a rare way for a Mafia mobster to go*

attracted the attention of the most influential mobsters in New York, such as Vito Genovese and Frank Costello. He began working for them, and soon became a leading member of one of the biggest Mafia families in the US, the Masserias, organizing prostitution, bootlegging, drug trafficking and other criminal activities.

At the end of the 1920s, Joe 'The Boss' Masseria became embroiled in a gang war with Salvatore Maranzano, leader of another important Italian mobster family. During this period, Luciano was captured by Maranzano's men as he waited for a shipment of drugs at the docks in New York. His mouth was taped shut and he was driven out to Staten Island. There, the gangsters cut his throat and threw him in a ditch, thinking that he was dying or dead. Amazingly, he survived, and was known by the nickname of 'Lucky' for the rest of his life.

DEAD MEN'S SHOES

The incident prompted Luciano to become even more ambitious. Already, he had broken with several of the traditional ways of doing business among the Mafia. For example, he associated openly with gangsters from other ethnic groups, an innovation to which his boss Masseria was deeply opposed. Luciano had close links with two major Jewish gangsters,

Meyer Lansky and 'Bugsy' Siegel; later, this threesome was to form the National Crime Syndicate, with Luciano as the originator, Lansky as the brains and Siegel as the brawn.

For now, however, Luciano had to operate within the constraints of the old-time Mafia bosses. The only way to change the situation, he realized, was to kill off the top men. When Maranzano began to gain the upper hand in the turf war, he switched sides and, together with Siegel, arranged for Masseria's murder. Within six months, however, he was plotting against his new boss, Maranzano. Maranzano was duly dispatched with ruthless efficiency. Now, with both the big men out of the way, the field was clear for Luciano and his men to take the lead.

Luciano went on to head the Mafia and to restructure the world of organized crime. Instead of continuing with the old gang wars, he divided up different areas of crime between the major families, including families who were not of Italian origin. He then developed a system where, when problems arose, he could balance the interests of all concerned. Luciano was one of the first Mafia bosses to realize the obvious fact that, at the end of the day, all criminals have one common interest: to make the maximum amount of money in the shortest time possible, whatever the means might be.

Charles MANSON

Charles Manson has gone down in history as the mastermind behind a series of celebrity murders in California that shocked the United States. He and his band of followers, known as 'The Family', revealed a dark side to the hippy ideals of drugs, free love and rebellion against social convention that characterized the youth culture of Los Angeles during the 1960s and early 1970s. The seemingly amoral attitude of Manson and his followers was deeply disturbing, and to this day no simple explanation of the events that took place can be given. In particular, Manson's apparently hypnotic hold on his teenage acolytes remains a mystery. On paper, Manson had nothing to recommend him, but in person he seems to have had a strange charisma that attracted young people – especially women – to him.

Charles Milles Manson was born in 1934 to a mother who did not want him. When he was thirteen, she abandoned him. He was sent to a school for boys in Terre Haute, Indiana, but after a year he ran away and went back to his mother. She rejected him again and he began to live on the streets, scraping a living by stealing. By the time he became an adult, most of his life had been spent in prison for stealing cars, forging cheques, pimping and assault.

HELTER SKELTER

In 1955, he married a seventeen-year-old girl named Rosalie Jean Willis, with whom he had a baby son. Rosalie left him, with the baby, for a truck driver. Manson married again, to a woman named Leona, with whom he had another son, but the pair was soon divorced.

In 1967, after his release from jail, Manson moved to California. A small, mentally unstable man nearing forty, he nevertheless seemed to possess a considerable sexual magnetism and personal charisma. He adopted the pose of a spiritual guru, quoting from the Book of Revelation, and arguing that a race war between black and white was about to begin. He named his Armageddon philosophy 'Helter Skelter' after a Beatles song. According to Manson's tortured logic, in order to spark the race war, from which he and his followers would emerge unscathed, Family members would murder rich white people. The Family moved into an unused ranch that had once been used to make western movies. In this ghost town, he somehow convinced his followers that the normal rules of behaviour towards fellow human beings did not apply to them. Evidently, their subsequent crimes were influenced by large amounts of mind-altering drugs, but this still did not explain why, under Manson's influence, they went on to act with such extraordinary savagery.

'DEATH TO PIGS'

On 9 August 1969, followers Susan Atkins, Charles 'Tex' Watson and Patricia Krenwinkel broke into the home of actress Sharon Tate, who was eight months pregnant at the time. Her husband, film director Roman Polanski, was away. They brutally murdered her, daubing the word 'Pig' with her blood over the door, and killing the other people who happened to be in the house. These were hairdresser Jay Sebring, coffee heiress Abigail Folger and her lover Wojciech Frykowski, and eighteen-year-old Steven Parent, who was visiting the caretaker.

The following day, businessman Leno LaBianco and his wife Rosemary were found murdered in their house. Watson, Krenwinkel and another Family member, Leslie Van Houten, had broken in and brutally strangled, stabbed and murdered them. The word 'War' was carved into Leno LaBianco's stomach with a knife and the words 'Death to

▶ *Small in stature and unhealthy looking, Manson still managed to attract people, manipulating them to do his bidding*

pigs' and 'Helter Skelter' were daubed in blood about the house.

Naturally, the attacks provoked a horrified response, and were widely reported, especially as several of the victims were rich Californian celebrities. When the case came to trial, it emerged that there were other murders connected to these, including that of a music teacher named Gary Hinman. It also emerged that Manson may have had a crazed motive for at least some of the killings.

REVENGE KILLINGS

Manson was an aspiring songwriter and singer who had at one time made friends with Dennis Wilson of the Beach Boys. The Beach Boys had recorded one of Manson's songs, and Wilson had introduced Manson to record producer Terry Melcher. Melcher had auditioned Manson for a contract but turned him down. The prosecutor's theory was that on the night of the murder, Manson had sent his followers to Melcher's house to kill him, not knowing that Melcher was away and had rented the house to Polanski and Tate. When the followers got there, they decided to kill the residents anyway.

During the trial, state-appointed defence attorney Ronald Hughes was murdered. This was widely believed to be another Family killing. Hughes had been planning to defend his client, Leslie Van Houten, by claiming that she was under the evil influence of Manson. It seems that the Family, who viewed their leader as a kind of god, had decided to take revenge on Hughes for daring to criticize Manson.

LACK OF REMORSE

The trial itself was full of bizarre moments, such as when Atkins, Krenwinkel and Van Houten arrived at court singing and wearing party dresses; when Manson, with a large 'X' carved into his forehead, flew into a rage and threatened to cut the judge's head off; and when the women broke into Latin chant. What especially shocked onlookers, and the public at large, was the complete lack of remorse shown by the young women, especially Atkins, who laughed and joked throughout the trial, and seemed not to understand that she had committed an appallingly brutal crime.

On 25 January 1971, Manson was convicted of murder, although he had not been present at the scene of the crimes. He was sentenced to death, but later escaped the death penalty when it was outlawed in the state of California. Also convicted of murder were Krenwinkel, Atkins, Watson and Van Houten. Later, cult members Robert Beausoleil, Bruce Davis and Steve Grogan were convicted of the murders of victims Gary Hinman and Donald Shea.

Edmond Jay MARR

The case of Edmond Jay Marr is one of the most extraordinary in the history of the Los Angeles Police Department (LAPD). Twenty years after committing a murder, for which he was not punished at the time, Marr was finally tracked down. The department's new cold case unit reopened the file on his victim, Elaine Graham, and through advances in DNA technology, which involved taking samples from her daughter – a two-year-old at the time of the murder – this time they were able to gain a profile of the killer.

Thus it was that the brutal murder of a young mother was finally avenged, after decades of being just another statistic in the city's roll of violent crimes. Elaine's family and friends thought the authorities had forgotten about her – but they were wrong: they just had to wait a very long time for justice to come their way.

When Elaine Graham met her death, she had everything to live for. She was a hard-working, twenty-nine-year-old nurse with a husband and a young daughter. She had ambitions to become a writer, and was taking writing classes at university. Every night, she wrote a journal in which she addressed her entries to her baby daughter. The night before she was murdered, she wrote an entry about a dream that she had had, in which she and her daughter were a pair of detectives engaged on a case where they caught a bad man and solved a big case. The dream was to prove prophetic, but only after years had gone by. And little did Elaine Graham think at the time that it was she herself who would be the victim in the case.

A DOUBLE-EDGED DAGGER

On that fatal morning, 17 March 1983, Graham dropped her daughter off with her carer, and set off to attend her writing class on the campus of the California State University Northridge, which was near her home. That was the last time anyone saw her. She never returned to collect her child that day, and no one knew where she had gone. The police were called in, and next day, in the early hours of the morning, her 1971 Volkswagen was found at a parking lot in the Santa Ana Fashion Square Mall (now known as the Main Place Mall). Detectives from the Robbery and Homicide division of the police department were assigned to the case, and began by focusing their attention on a young man who had been near the

Cal State campus on the day that Elaine had disappeared. His name was Edmond Jay Marr.

Marr was twenty-five years old at the time of the investigation. He had just been dishonourably discharged from the army, and was having a difficult time at home, arguing with his parents, especially his father. On the night of the

seventeenth, he had visited his sister, who lived only a few blocks away from the mall where Elaine's car was later found. Marr was found in possession of a double-edged dagger. The dagger was taken in for examination, using the conventional techniques of serology that were available at the time. A tiny patch of blood on the well-cleaned dagger was

▼ It is all too easy for a murderous urge to be expressed by a knife attack, as Elaine Graham found out to her cost

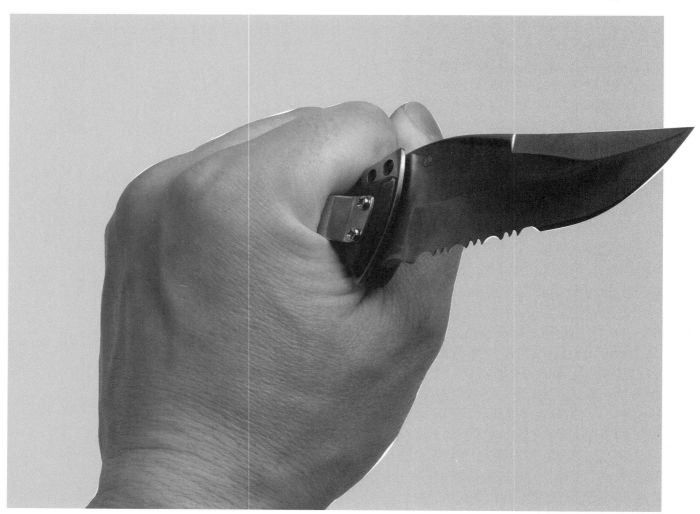

found that was consistent with the blood type of Elaine Graham, but it was impossible to narrow the match down any further. As the investigation proceeded, it was found that Marr had been arrested for violent robbery, and his dishonourable discharge from the army came to light. However, none of this in itself was concrete enough evidence to charge him with the murder.

HUMAN BONES DISCOVERED

Eight months later, human bones were discovered by some hikers in Brown's Canyon, a remote area of the hills above Chatsworth. The bones were examined, and it became clear that the victim had met a violent death. There was a dent in one of the rib bones which suggested that the victim had been stabbed. A woman's blouse was also found in the bushes near the bones, and when it was examined, it was noticed that there were no holes in the fabric. The combination of the dent in the bone and the unpunctured fabric of the blouse suggested that the killer had stripped his victim before stabbing her to death.

For Elaine's family, these meagre but horrifying details were all they knew about her last moments. It was a relief for them to know that she had not simply run away and abandoned her dearly loved husband and daughter, but it was deeply traumatic to learn that she had been murdered in such a brutal, terrifying way.

Detectives on the Graham case brought Marr back in for questioning when it was discovered that, as a young man, he had often hiked in the area of Brown's Canyon. The following year, the detectives brought the case to the Los Angeles District Attorney's office, and the decision was made to keep the evidence in the case, including Marr's knife, until advances in forensic technology could give a clearer result. For the time being, despite the new findings, and much to the disappointment of the police officers concerned, there did not seem to be enough evidence to bring the case to the courts.

Sadly, for the next two decades, there were no new leads on the case, and the file on Elaine Graham lay on a shelf in the LAPD's offices. It was not until November 2001 that the case was reviewed, by which time the leading detectives in the investigation, Paul Tippin and Leroy Orozco, had retired from their jobs. In the new millennium, a new unit had now been formed in the Robbery Homicide Division: the Cold Case Homicide Unit. The aim of the unit was to try to solve old, cold cases on the police's files, using the now much improved techniques for DNA profiling. Two new detectives were assigned to the Elaine Graham case: Rick Jackson and Tim Marcia.

MISSING PIECE IN THE PUZZLE

Going back through the files, Jackson and Marcia discovered that Marr's dagger had been carefully stored as evidence. Jackson and Marcia ordered the dagger to be reanalysed by the police forensic department, who re-found the minute amount of blood that had remained underneath its handle. The next step was to obtain a DNA sample from the victim to match it with, so they went to Graham's daughter, Elise. From Elise's DNA, which was the same as her mother's (DNA works in such a way that although there are minute differences between peoples' DNA, these differences are smaller between blood relatives), they matched the blood on the handle. This was something that could not have been done back in 1983, and it was to prove the crucial missing piece in the puzzle of Elaine Graham's death.

As a result of Jackson and Marcia's investigations, which involved witness interviews, phone tap recordings and forensic analysis, Edmond Jay Marr was arrested and charged with the kidnap and murder of Elaine Graham. He was held on a one million dollar bond. His trial received a great deal of publicity, and the courtroom was packed. Friends and

◀ *The skeleton tells a story: although DNA evidence rarely survives in bone, the bones themselves often retain a good record of how their owner died*

relatives of the deceased were there, including one of the detectives who had worked on the case originally in 1983. Graham's daughter Elise, now aged twenty-four, stood up in court and told Marr exactly what losing her mother at such a young age had meant to her. 'You ask this court for mercy,' she said. 'Where was the mercy for my mother? You've given me a life sentence of a broken heart,' she went on. 'You took from me the most important person in the world.' It became clear that, over the twenty years following Graham's death, while the case had gathered dust in terms of the police investigation, there were many for whom it had never grown cold.

Edmond Jay Marr, now forty-seven, pleaded guilty, and admitted the use of a knife in his crime. As a result, his lawyers were able to cut a deal with the prosecution, which resulted in a verdict of second, rather than first-degree murder. He was sentenced by the judge to a prison term of sixteen years.

It had taken twenty years, but in the end, Elaine Graham's prophetic dream had finally come true. She and her daughter Elise had caught a criminal, and solved a case of murder.

A BAND-AID ON A BULLET HOLE?

The case was a triumph for the newly opened unit in the LAPD, which had been criticized in some quarters as 'putting a band-aid on a bullet hole': journalists had pointed out that there were only six detectives and one supervisor assigned to the unit, yet there were over eight thousand unsolved homicide cases on the files for them to deal with, some of which dated as far back as the 1960s. If one calculated that each detective could solve a cold case a month – which was unlikely, given the complications of most criminal investigations – it would take over a century for the team to get up to date. Many felt that public funds would be better spent on detective teams that would solve current crimes, rather than delving into old cases that were unlikely to be resolved.

However, the solving of the Graham case did much to improve the image of the new cold case unit, and it was pointed out that, even if only a few cases were ever solved, this was of crucial importance, not only to the relatives of the victims, but to the morale of the city as a whole. The fact that the unit had been set up, and that there was some impetus towards finding the perpetrators of homicidal crimes, was of great symbolic – if not always literal – significance to the citizens of Los Angeles, in that it showed that the many victims had not been altogether forgotten, and that justice could still be served for at least some of them.

Timothy McVEIGH

Timothy McVeigh was a terrorist executed by lethal injection for his part in the bombing of the Federal Building of Oklahoma in 1995, which killed 168 people and injured many more. He was the first person to be executed by the state in this way. Although he was portrayed as a mentally unbalanced loner by the media, many believe that he was rational at the time, and that he was acting as part of a wider conspiracy to undermine the government.

McVeigh was born in upstate New York in 1968 and grew up in rural communities near Buffalo, Niagara and Canada. He had two sisters and was the middle child of the family. His father worked in a car factory, and his mother in a travel agency. The marriage was an unhappy one, and the couple separated several times, finally splitting up for good in 1984. As a school pupil, McVeigh was shy and quiet; as a teenager, he kept to himself and did not socialize much with friends or date girls.

GUNS AND SURVIVALISM

After graduating from high school in 1986, McVeigh went to business college for a short while, living at home with his father and working at Burger King. He then found a job as a security guard in Buffalo, receiving a permit to carry pistols. It was at this time that he became obsessed with guns. He was also beginning to show signs of paranoia, according to the testimony of a co-worker, who remembered that he stockpiled guns and food in readiness for the breakdown of 'civilized society', which he believed was just around the corner. In 1988, he bought a ten-acre plot of land with a friend and began to use it as a shooting range. The same year, he enlisted in the army.

McVeigh became a gunner in the army and did well; he was soon promoted to platoon leader. He spent a great deal of time maintaining his collection of guns, and was interested in politics. He spoke highly of a novel, *The Turner Diaries*, to his army colleagues. The novel is generally regarded as racist and anti-semitic, but there is some controversy as to whether McVeigh himself was actually racist. What is clear is that he had by now adopted a survivalist philosophy, in which he regarded the individual's right to have and use guns as paramount, and the authorities – particularly the US government – as corrupt and evil.

▶ *Timothy McVeigh was found guilty of the deaths of 168 men, women and children in Oklahoma City*

COLD-BLOODED KILLING

In 1991, McVeigh's division was sent to the Gulf to take part in the war there. During his time in action, his hatred for the US government increased. He later claimed that he had been ordered to execute surrendering Iraqi prisoners, and that he had witnessed the carnage after the US army had massacred Iraqi soldiers on the road out of Kuwait City. Whatever the truth of these colourful allegations, there is no doubt that McVeigh learned to kill without compassion when he was on active service during the first Gulf War.

TIMOTHY McVEIGH

Returning from the Gulf, McVeigh attempted to get into the Special Forces section of the US army, but failed a physical endurance test. The experience left him disappointed and at a loss as to how to advance his career. In 1991, he took advantage of the offer of early discharge from the army and went back home to his father once more. At first he worked as a security guard, as he had done in the past, but he then began to travel around by car, staying in trailer parks and cheap motels, and occasionally visiting his old army buddies around the country.

THE WACO FIASCO

In 1993, the Waco incident hit the headlines. A cult community known as the Branch Davidians, a religious group that had originated in the Seventh-Day Adventist Church, was targeted by federal agents, who accused the cult members of crimes such as paedophilia. A siege mounted by the authorities ended in the destruction of the cult's compound and the killing of many cult members, including leader David Koresh. Along with others, McVeigh was incensed by the government's handling of the siege, and went to Waco to visit the scene.

At around this period, it appears that McVeigh began making bombs. Along with an old army colleague, Terry Nichols, he made a plan to undermine the state government by planting a bomb at the Alfred P. Murrah Federal Building in Oklahoma City. He drove a truck loaded with explosives up to the offices, ignited a timed fuse on the vehicle and then walked away.

THE OKLAHOMA ATROCITY

The explosives detonated just as the office workers were beginning to open up for business. Children were also arriving at a daycare centre in the building at that time. Having detonated the bomb, McVeigh sped away on the highway out of town, but was arrested for speeding, for driving without a licence and for carrying a concealed weapon. He was nearly released for these minor crimes before being identified as the culprit behind the bombing, after an international manhunt.

In 1997, after a controversial trial, McVeigh was finally convicted of the bombing and sentenced to death. On 11 June 2001, he was executed by lethal injection in Terre Haute Prison, Indiana. His co-conspirator Terry Nichols received a sentence of life imprisonment.

Although McVeigh always assumed sole responsibility for the crime, and the press helped to maintain his image that he was acting alone, many believe that the truth behind the atrocity was somewhat more complex. Some think that McVeigh had other accomplices besides Nichols, including Nichols' brother, James. Others allege that the government itself had a role in the attack, since one report concluded that bombs had been placed within the building itself. According to this far-fetched theory, the government needed grounds for persecuting right-wing groups and thus had a hand in planning the attack in some way.

TERRORIST LINKS

More convincing are the theories that McVeigh was operating as part of a larger group. He may have been connected to a criminal group called the Midwest Bank Robbers, who were active in the US in the early 1990s, and who held white supremacist views. The FBI found that the same type of explosive caps were used by both McVeigh and the Robbers, and there was some evidence to show that he and the Robbers had met in Arkansas a short time before the Oklahoma bombing occurred. Another possibility is that McVeigh had met with Islamic fundamentalist terrorists in the Philippines not long before the attack, and may have been linked to the al-Qaeda network.

Whatever the truth of the matter, Timothy McVeigh will go down in history as the biggest American mass murderer. The Oklahoma City bombing was an atrocity that shocked the nation and the world, not only because of the sheer scale of the attack, but also because it was so random in nature, killing innocent victims, most of them civilians, and some of them children and babies.

Jacques MESRINE

Jacques Mesrine was an infamous French bank robber and kidnapper who became known for his daring prison escapes. During the 1960s and 1970s he became popular in France as a romantic 'Robin Hood' figure, who would rob the rich and, allegedly, give to the poor. He was also admired by the public for his ability to outwit the French police force, who were unable for many years to capture him, and eventually named him 'Public Enemy Number One'. The police finally caught up with him on 2 November 1979, and shot him to death.

Mesrine was born into a middle-class family in Clichy, France, in 1936. As a child, he got into trouble at school for his violent behaviour, and was expelled twice. As a young man, he served in Algeria, and then returned to France, where he embarked on a career of crime. A good-looking man, he charmed those around him – sometimes even those he was robbing. However, his courteous exterior belied his true nature, which was that of a ruthless criminal who would stop at nothing to get what he wanted.

A LOVE OF PUBLICITY

Mesrine liked to live well, enjoying good food and wine at the best restaurants in France. He was extremely attractive to women, and had a succession of beautiful girlfriends, who sometimes accompanied

◀ The changing faces of Jaques Mesrine. He seemed to delight in coming up with different disguises with which to outwit the police

him on his bank robbing sprees. He also dressed well, and often made his raids attired in the height of fashion. All this, of course, together with his love of publicity and his talent for sensational escapades, made him a tremendously popular figure in the national press.

Mesrine's first arrest took place in 1962, when he attempted to rob a bank with three accomplices. He served a sentence in prison and was released the following year. After a short stint working for a design company, he resumed his criminal activities in Spain, and was arrested but set free after only six months. He then opened a restaurant in the Canary Islands, but left to pursue a life of crime once more, first robbing a hotel in Chamonix, France, and then attempting a kidnap in Canada.

Together with his girlfriend, Jeanne Schneider, Mesrine planned to kidnap a Canadian grocery and textile millionaire named Georges Deslauriers. Deslauriers had employed Mesrine and Schneider as domestic servants and then sacked them. The kidnap failed, and Mesrine and Schneider were sentenced to ten years in prison for the attempt. However, they managed to escape in style, capturing a prison

◀ *The legend ends: Mesrine was gunned down at close range while waiting at traffic lights*

warder, stealing his keys, locking him in a cell and fleeing to live in the woods.

SENSATIONAL ESCAPES

Mesrine was soon recaptured, and this time sent to the high-security Saint Vincent de Paul prison outside Montreal. Before long, he had led five inmates in a daring escape that involved using a pair of pliers stolen from a workshop to cut through several fences. After managing this extraordinary feat, the group then flagged down cars on the highway, and got clean away.

Mesrine's next move was audacious in the extreme: he decided to return to the prison and help the remaining inmates of the prison to escape. He robbed a number of banks to raise the money he needed, and then went back, armed with shotguns and wire cutters. However, the complicated plan failed and Mesrine had to make a quick getaway. He was on the run once more.

COURTROOM DRAMA

With his accomplice Jean-Paul Mercier, Mesrine fled to Venezuela. However, before long he was back in France, robbing banks again. In 1973, he was caught and tried. During his trial in court, he caused a sensation by managing to take a judge hostage. An accomplice had hidden a gun for him in one of the toilets of the court, which he stuffed into his belt and pulled out as his charges were being read. Holding on to the judge and using him as a human shield, he ran under a hail of bullets from police, jumped into a getaway car and sped away. He was arrested several months later and imprisoned once more.

Mesrine's next sensational exploit was to escape from his maximum security jail at La Sante de Paris. Using a secret stash of guns, Mesrine and two other prisoners held up guards, stole their uniforms and locked them in the cells. They then commandeered some ladders and climbed over the prison walls, using ropes and grappling irons. They became the first prisoners ever to escape from La Sante. The incident infuriated the French authorities, who were completely humiliated by Mesrine's disappearance from their top-security prison. Mesrine now became the most wanted man in the country.

THE FINAL SHOWDOWN

Free once more, Mesrine continued his criminal career, becoming ever more daring – and ruthless. He used a variety of disguises to evade police during his exploits, including wigs, which he sometimes wore one on top of the other for quick changes. He kidnapped rich individuals, robbed banks and jewellery shops, and smuggled arms. He boasted that he had killed over thirty victims in the process of committing his crimes, although this figure has never been verified. Despite this, sections of the French press continued to view him as a romantic figure, painting him as a kind of Robin Hood, a thorn in the side of authority. Mesrine, too, evidently saw himself as a folk hero, and often attempted in interviews to convince journalists that his crimes were motivated by radical political ideas rather than by self-interest. The fact that he had boasted about cold-bloodedly murdering scores of victims, and that he obviously spent more money than he ever gave away, did not stop the tabloid press from seeing him as something of a hero – perhaps because his escapades made the French authorities look so foolish and inept.

As Mesrine's criminal activities continued, the French government became more and more embarrassed by him, and ordered police departments to intensify their efforts to catch him. On 2 November 1979, police found out where he was living and ambushed his car, surrounding it as he waited at traffic lights in the street. They shot nineteen rounds of bullets through his windscreen, killing him instantly.

Dennis NILSEN

In February 1983 an engineer was called to a house in north London to investigate a blocked drain. He soon found the cause: backed-up human flesh. The owner of one of the apartments in the building – a tall, bespectacled civil servant called Dennis Nilsen – had been flushing the remains of his victims down the lavatory.

But not by any means all of them. For police found in his flat two severed heads and a skull that had been boiled down to the bone, as well as half a male torso and various human parts in the cupboards. They hadn't been kept there for any other reason than Nilsen, living right at the top of the house, had had a problem with disposal. If he hadn't had to move in 1981 from the garden flat he'd previously occupied, where more human bones were later found, he'd probably have gone undetected. For there he'd had options: he'd been able to bury the bones of his dead after crushing their skulls with a garden roller or else burn them on garden fires, with a tyre tossed on top to disguise the smell. At his new address, after dissecting his three victims, he'd had to put out the larger bones for the garbagemen – and use the lavatory for the rest.

Nilsen, a lonely homosexual, confessed all this more or less immediately, and pointed the police to his previous apartment, where they found about 13 kilosworth of human bones, all that remained of his twelve earlier victims. The fifteen dead had all been homosexuals or drifters whom Nilsen had picked up, brought back to his apartment promising food and drink, and then strangled while they were asleep or insensible from drink. He didn't, he said

▼ Dennis Nilsen – claimed he was an 'egg and bacon man'

▲ *Nilsen apparently killed because he was lonely and wanted company*

firmly, have sex with their corpses or eat their flesh —

'I'm an egg-and-bacon man myself.'

he later said indignantly. His motive seems to have been simply that he wanted company. His first victim had been picked up and killed on 30 December 1978, because he had spent a miserable Christmas alone and wanted someone to share New Year's with him —

'even if it was only a body.'

In October 1983, he was convicted on six charges of murder and two of attempted murder and sentenced to life. During the course of the trial, it became clear that the police had earlier failed to charge him when two separate complaints had been made by men he had attacked. They'd also ignored the three carrier-bags full of human flesh found not far from Nilsen's garden apartment.

Anatoly ONOPRIENKO

Anatoly Onoprienko was the second major serial killer to emerge in the former USSR after the collapse of communism, following the Rostov Ripper, Andrei Chikatilo. Onoprienko was a brutal killer with a particularly unusual pathology. Quite simply, Onoprienko liked to kill families — children and all — acting with a ruthlessness that led the newspapers to dub him 'the Terminator'.

Onoprienko was born in the town of Laski in the Ukraine. His mother died when he was just four years old and his father placed him in an orphanage, though he kept his older son at home. This appears to have been the foundation of Onoprienko's rage at humanity and families in particular. He never forgave his father for discarding him, and he took a terrible revenge.

JACK OF ALL TRADES

After he left the orphanage, Onoprienko worked as a forester and as a sailor, and was known to the mental health authorities in the Ukrainian capital of Kiev. The first spate of killings with which he is associated happened in 1989.

With an accomplice, Sergei Rogozin, Onoprienko carried out a series of burglaries. During one of these robberies the pair were interrupted by the house owners. Onoprienko promptly killed them. He followed this up by killing the occupants of a parked car.

Afterwards, Onoprienko split with Rogozin. His movements over the next six years, as communism collapsed and the Ukraine became an independent state, remain mysterious. He is known to have roamed around central Europe for a while and was expelled from both Germany and Austria, but whether he was responsible for any further murders during that time remains unclear.

BLOODIEST SPREE IN HISTORY

What is certain is that he was back in the Ukraine at the end of 1995, for it was then that he began one of the bloodiest murder sprees in history, killing forty-three victims in little more than three months. As before, Onoprienko targeted houses on the edge of small towns and villages across the Ukraine; this time, however, he was not interested in burglary, only in killing.

He began on Christmas Eve 1995 by breaking into the home of the Zaichenko family. He murdered the couple and their two children with a double-barrelled shotgun, took a few souvenirs, then set the house on fire. Six days later in the town of Bratkovichi, a place that was to become a regular hunting ground, he broke into another house and killed the couple who lived there and the wife's twin sisters. Before his next family killing, almost as a side show, he spent 6 January killing motorists, four in all, along the Berdyansk-Dnieprovskaya highway. He later explained: 'To me it was like hunting. Hunting people down.'

Next, on 17 January, he headed back to Bratkovichi. There he broke into the house of the Pilat family, killing the five people who lived there and then setting the house on fire, As he left, two people saw him, so he shot both of them as well.

Later that same month he headed east to the town of Fastova, where he killed four more people, a nurse and her family. He then went west to Olevsk, where, on 19 February, he broke into the home of the Dubchak family. He shot the father and son, and battered the mother and daughter to death with a hammer. He later told investigators that the daughter had seen him murder her parents and was praying when he came up to her. 'Seconds before I smashed her head, I ordered her to show me where they kept their money,' he said. 'She looked at me with an angry, defiant stare and said, "No, I won't." That strength was incredible. But I felt nothing.'

Just over a week later, Onoprienko drove to Malina, where he murdered all four of the Bodnarchuk family, shooting the husband and wife and using an axe to despatch two daughters, aged seven and eight. Once again a passer-by who was unfortunate enough to witness the killer leaving the house was added to the death list.

Just over three weeks passed before Onoprienko struck again on 22 March 1996. He travelled to the small village of Busk, just outside the beleaguered town of Bratkovichi, to slaughter all four members of the Novosad family, shooting them and then burning their house. At this stage, the terrified villagers demanded help from the government, who responded by sending a full National Guard Unit, complete with rocket launchers, to ward off this unknown menace. Meanwhile, two thousand officers became part of a gigantic manhunt.

CACHE OF WEAPONS

In the end, however, it was a relative of Onoprienko who brought about his capture. Onoprienko was staying with a cousin who, on finding a cache of weapons in his room, told him to leave the house and phoned the police. The police tracked Onoprienko to his girlfriend's house, where he was arrested on Easter

Sunday, 16 April 1996. They found him listening to music on a tape deck stolen from the Novosad family. Further investigation revealed weapons used in the murders, plus a collection of souvenirs taken from his victims.

Once in custody Onoprienko demanded to speak to 'a general', and as soon as one was provided he confessed to fifty-two murders. He claimed to have been hearing voices that told him to commit the crimes. He also said that he had been treated for schizophrenia in a Kiev mental hospital. Disturbingly, Kiev's Interior Ministry initially disclosed that Onoprienko was an outpatient whose therapists knew him to be a killer, but they then refused to say any more about the matter.

In 1999, Onoprienko was convicted on fifty-two counts of murder and sentenced to death. This sentence has yet to be carried out, as Ukraine is now a member of the Council of Europe, which has agreed to ban capital punishment. Investigations are continuing as to whether Onoprienko may have committed any more murders, either in the Ukraine or elsewhere between 1989 and 1995.

▲ *Once Onoprienko was in custody, the Ukrainian police tried to piece together an accurate account of his many crimes*

PAPILLON

Henri Charriere was a small-time Parisian crook who achieved lasting fame when he wrote his life story, entitled Papillon. The book told of the many thrilling adventures that befell this highly intelligent, resourceful criminal as he planned escapes from various prisons in South America, where he was sent after being convicted of murder in 1931. Charriere's escapes were carefully planned, but he also learned to take opportunities when they arose, using the skills he had learned as a thief on the streets of his native city. The title of the autobiography, French for 'butterfly', was Charriere's nickname which derived from a tattoo of a butterfly that he had on his chest.

Charriere grew up in Paris and, as a young man, began a criminal career as a thief and safe-breaker. He managed for the most part to evade the law until, in 1931, he was accused of murdering a pimp named Roland le Petit. He maintained that he had been framed for the murder, but no one believed him. When the case came to trial, he was found guilty and sentenced to a term of life imprisonment with hard labour. He was ordered to serve out his sentence at a penal colony in French Guiana, which was infamous at the time for its brutality and tough living conditions.

PRISON CAMP ORDEAL

In the book, Charriere described in detail the horrific conditions for prisoners in the penal colony of French Guiana at that period. He also made it clear that, although he was no angel, and had for many years made his living as a thief, he was innocent of the crime of murder that he had been convicted of. His abiding sense of outrage that he had become the victim of a miscarriage of justice carries the reader's sympathies; it also helps to explain the iron determination that Charriere showed throughout his long career as an escape artist, making every effort to break out of his confinement at every opportunity, whatever the cost.

Once at the penal colony, Papillon effected the first of many bids for freedom. He escaped from hospital on the mainland in the company of two other prisoners, and made his way to Riohacha, Colombia. He sailed along the coast for hundreds of miles in an open boat. After this gruelling ordeal, he finally reached Colombia, only to be caught there and imprisoned once again.

◄ *The lined face of an experienced escape artist – Charriere's adventures made for a lively lifestyle*

ESCAPE AND CAPTURE

Undaunted, Charriere escaped and went on the run again, this time to Guajira, where he lived in a native village and took two wives as his consorts. This episode in his eventful life was a relatively peaceful one, in which he lived in peace and harmony with his wives, Lali and Zoraima. Their relaxed attitude towards sex pleased him greatly, differing entirely as it did from the mores of the French women he had known. Both of his wives eventually became pregnant by him. However, although he could probably have carried on living in the village for the rest of his life, working and raising his children in obscurity, his lust for adventure caused him to move on. When he did so, he was once again captured and imprisoned, this time at Santa Marta.

Charriere was then moved to Barranquilla, where he made various audacious attempts to escape, but these all failed. In 1934, he was sent back to French Guiana, where he was punished for his escape attempts by being put into solitary confinement on the island of St Joseph.

After two years of a miserably lonely existence, he was sent to another island, Royale, where he again attempted to escape. However, on this occasion his attempt was foiled by an informer, whom he murdered.

Once again, Charriere was punished; and once again, he continued to make his escape attempts from wherever he was imprisoned. It seemed that nothing would deter him. His next ruse was to pretend to be mad, so that he was sent to the mental hospital on the island of St Joseph. He attempted to escape from the hospital, but was caught and transferred to Devil's Island.

FREEDOM AT LAST

As its name suggests, Devil's Island was a hellish place, rife with disease, where prisoners lived under a brutal regime in fear of their lives. Legend had it that no prisoner had ever escaped from the island – until Papillon came along, that is. Not surprisingly, soon after arriving, Charriere made his bid for freedom, throwing himself into the shark-infested sea surrounding the island with only a makeshift raft of coconut sacking to keep him afloat in the water.

Against all odds, he succeeded in reaching the mainland, and once there travelled on to Georgetown. In company with five other fugitives, he managed to get to Venezuela, but once there, was soon taken prisoner at El Dorado.

Gordon PARK

One of the longest murder enquiries ever to take place in the United Kingdom was finally resolved when Gordon Park was brought to trial and found guilty of murdering his wife. The crime had happened twenty-nine years earlier, and might never have been discovered had not amateur divers in the beautiful Lake District of the North of England come across a body one summer's day: the body of a woman in a blue baby-doll nightdress.

THE 'MYSTERY LOVER'

Gordon Park and his wife Carol were teachers. They were a successful couple, living what seemed from the outside like a happy, settled life. Gordon had built the family home himself. But all was not as it seemed, and those who knew the couple well realized there were problems in the marriage. According to Gordon, when they first married they were deliriously happy – he described their relationship as 'love's young dream'. However, as his defence lawyer later pointed out when describing the relationship in court, trouble then began to surface as Carol – described as 'vivacious and attractive' – took to having affairs quite openly. On two occasions, she left her husband to live with her lovers. Yet Park was understanding about his wife's behaviour. Although upset by her dalliances, he made a great deal of effort to be open-minded and let his wife have her freedom. The defence stressed that the relationship had not been an abusive one, and that Park had hoped that he and his wife could have a peaceful 'open marriage'. As the lawyer put it, Park had 'put up with a great deal' from his wife, and had behaved in a restrained way as far as was humanly possible.

However, by 1976, the couple's relationship had deteriorated and was unstable. By this time, both Gordon and Carol Park were involved with other partners, and it was not uncommon for them to spend weeks apart.

On the day Carol disappeared, 17 July 1976, the family had planned a trip to the seaside resort of Blackpool, but at the last minute Carol had said she felt ill, and had stayed at home. When the family returned home, Carol was not there. Gordon reported her absence to the police – but only after six weeks. Naturally enough, this caused suspicion, but Gordon told the police of his wife's affairs and said that he thought she had left him, taking off with a 'mystery lover'.

▲ *Gordon Park lived a full life – something he denied his wife when he bludgeoned her to death with an ice axe before dumping her body in a lake*

THE BODY IN THE LAKE

The police conducted an investigation, but it was only a routine operation. Carol Park was filed as a missing person. No one suspected that Gordon had killed his wife, even though he issued no emotional appeals through the media for her to come back to him. He seemed unperturbed about her disappearance, but this was put down to the fact that the couple's relationship had deteriorated in recent years. Speaking later at Park's trial, Detective Chief Inspector Keith Churchman, who took over the investigation in 2001, commented that he and his officers had done everything they could to find Carol, but that the enquiry was conducted as a 'missing persons' incident, not a murder case, and that they had very little to go on as a result.

And there the mystery might have remained, had not the body of Carol Park been found, by pure chance, twenty-one years later. In August 1997, a small group of amateur scuba divers was exploring a part of Coniston Water in the Lake District. This was a part of the lake that people usually avoided swimming in, because the water was so murky there. They swam far out from shore, and dived down eighty feet below the surface of the water. There, they unwittingly discovered a body resting on an underwater shelf. It was that of a woman, still wearing the blue baby-doll nightdress she had been killed in. The body was later identified as that of Carol Park, and when the story hit the headlines, she was dubbed 'the lady of the lake'.

If the body had been thrown in the lake a little further away from the shore, it would have sunk to the bottom of the lake and would almost certainly never have been found. And Gordon Park would have got away with murder. As it was, the divers reported their finding to the police, who went straight round to Park's house. When they called, however, he was away on a cycling holiday in France with his third wife, Jenny. The house and his boat were searched for clues, and when Park returned, he was arrested on a murder charge and taken into custody.

However, the police were thwarted when the legal authorities decided that there was not evidence to bring the case to court. Park was let go, but the case remained open.

BLUDGEONED TO DEATH

Four years later, the case of the 'lady in the lake', as it had now become known, was taken over by Chief Inspector Churchman. Churchman decided to review the investigation, going all the way back to 1976, to see if new clues could be uncovered.

In the process, he managed to turn up new evidence. This time, it was found that the stones that had been attached to Carol Park's body to weigh it down in the water were the same kind used in the building of Gordon Park's house. Not only this, but a fellow prisoner who had spent time with Park while he was in police custody, Michael Wainwright, now contacted the police with new information. He said that while on remand in Preston prison, Park had confessed to him that he had murdered his wife.

There now seemed to be enough evidence to bring charges against Gordon Park, and this time when the police went back to the legal authorities to press for a court case, they were successful. In January 2004, Park was arrested again, and charged with the murder of his wife twenty-nine years before.

The ten-week trial attracted a great deal of attention from the media. As the prosecutor in the case pointed out to the jury, this was not a cut-and-dried case. Park could not be convicted on a single piece of evidence. On the contrary, there were many different pieces of evidence, but when they were all put together, they pointed to Park's guilt. In the context of this new evidence, Park's story about his wife leaving home with a 'mystery lover' looked flimsy, to say the least. Why had she never returned home once the fling was over, as she had before? And why had she never contacted her children, even after decades? These were questions that could not be answered except by one theory: that Park had murdered his wife and tried to cover his tracks.

The prosecution alleged on 17 July 1976 Park had brutally battered his wife to death with an ice axe. He had then wrapped her body in the nightdress she was wearing. Trussed up, he had put her body into several bags and then hauled it to his car. He had driven to Coniston Water, transferred the body to his boat, rowed out far into the lake and thrown the body overboard. As it turned out, of course, he did not row out quite far enough.

A TRANCE-LIKE STATE

The jury believed the prosecution's story and, after a ten-week trial at Manchester Crown Court, Park was found guilty. Evidently, the fact that Park had had 'a lot to put up with' as a result of his wife's infidelities did not, in the jury's eyes, constitute a defence for battering her to death in her nightdress and throwing her body in the lake.

When he heard the verdict, Park looked stunned, and began to blink repeatedly, while a piercing shriek erupted from the public gallery. Park's wife, Jenny, began to sob as he was led away, still dazed and disoriented. It seemed that Park had never expected to be convicted after so long – before the verdict, he had told reporters that he expected to be released, and would be back soon to give interviews about his experience.

The judge sentenced him to life in prison, and told him that he must serve at least fifteen years before being considered for parole. He was not convinced that Park had conducted the murder in a premeditated manner, but he felt the degree of violence he had exhibited, as well as his cold-blooded disposal of the body, and his covering up of the murder for so many years, causing untold grief and anxiety to his wife's family, warranted an extremely long prison sentence.

Park was apparently pole-axed by the verdict. He was led from the court room

◄ A happy family – but Park's wife, Carol, had a string of affairs, leaving her husband and children on two occasions to live with lovers

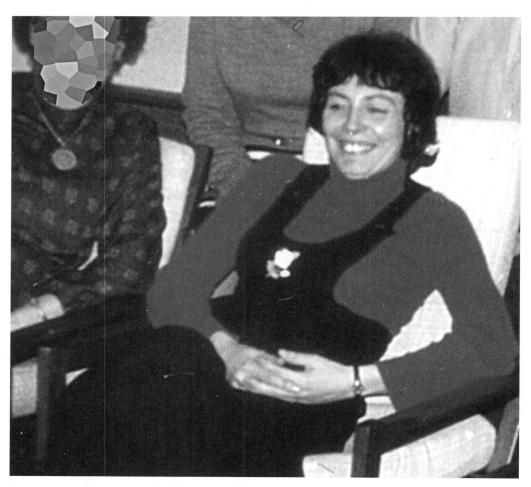

▶Carol Park was described by her husband as 'attractive and vivacious' — qualities that would prove to be her downfall

in a trance-like state, holding out his hands in front of him and grasping a handrail for support. It was as though he could not believe that, after all this time, his crime had been discovered and that he would now have to pay the penalty for it. Today, he still maintains that he is innocent.

The body of the 'lady in the lake' tells a different story, however. Gordon Park thought that he had committed the perfect murder, and had managed to keep his secret safe for twenty-one years. But, by an extraordinary twist of fate, the body of his wife was dredged up from the depths of the lake where he had tried to hide it decades before.

Thus it was that 'the lady in the lake' returned to haunt her husband, and Gordon Park, apparently merely a quiet, retired school master, was finally brought to justice.

BONNIE and CLYDE

The relationship between Bonnie Parker and farmer's boy Clyde Barrow didn't get off to a good start. The first time twenty-one-year-old Clyde came calling at her house in Cement City, Texas, he was arrested for burglary and car theft – he later got two years in jail. Nineteen-year-old Bonnie, though, was no stranger to this kind of trouble – the man she'd married three years before had been sent down for ninety-nine years for murder. So she knew just what to do. She smuggled a gun into Clyde as he languished behind bars, and he duly made his escape. Trouble was, he was recaptured in a matter of days after holding up a railroad office. This time he got fourteen years.

True love, though – as it's said – conquers all; and Clyde was soon out, though this time on crutches: He'd persuaded a fellow prisoner to cut off two of his toes with an axe. To please Bonnie's devout Baptist mother, he then tried to go straight. He took a job in Massachusetts, but it didn't last long – he pined too much for home. He returned to West Dallas; and three days later they were both gone, off to gather material for the poem Bonnie later wrote, *The Story of Bonnie and Clyde*.

With three men along for the ride, Bonnie and Clyde robbed and hijacked their way across Texas. Bonnie was picked up on suspicion of car theft, so the first three murders the gang was responsible for were committed without her. First, in April 1932, they shot a jeweller in Hillsboro, Texas for just $40; and then, just for kicks, a sheriff and his deputy as they stood minding their business outside a dance-hall.

They never took big money: the biggest haul they ever came up with was $3,500 from a filling-station in Grand Prairie – and it didn't take them long to blow that on tour of the best hotels and restaurants they could find. The rest was penny-ante stuff; and increasingly they killed for it. Bonnie gunned down a Texas butcher for small change; and even sixteen-year-old William James got in on the act: He shot to death the owner of a car he was caught stealing.

By now they were notorious; and in March 1935 in Missouri, joined by Clyde's brother Buck and sister-in-law Blanche, they had to shoot their way out of the apartment building they were staying in, killing two policemen in the process. Later, after a car accident in which Bonnie was badly burned, the farmer who took them in became suspicious and called the

▶Bonnie and Clyde are probably the most famous criminal couple in history

police; and again they had to come out firing. Finally, in July, while resting up in a tourist-camp in Missouri – and once again surrounded – they fought yet another running battle in which Buck was killed and Blanche taken. Only Bonnie and Clyde got away.

In her poem, Bonnie predicted that she and Clyde would die; and after another three months of running they did. Their V-8 sedan was ambushed by six heavily armed policemen who pumped eighty-seven bullets into it. They hadn't stood a chance.

When the remains of twenty-one-year-old Bonnie and twenty-three-year-old Clyde were buried in Dallas, huge crowds flocked to their funeral. The flowers were snatched from the top of their coffins and taken as souvenirs. Long before Arthur Penn's rosy-eyed film version of the brief career of the two young killers, they were already stars.

Dr. Marcel PÉTIOT

Dr. Marcel Pétiot's crimes, among the most grisly in European history, were motivated by nothing but greed. As he walked to the guillotine in Paris on 26 May 1946, he is said to have remarked,

'When one sets out on a voyage, one takes all one's luggage with one.'

This was not a privilege given to any of his more than sixty victims. For at his trial two months before, the jury had been shown forty-seven suitcases that belonged to the men and women he'd murdered – containing over 1500 items of their clothing. All had been found at his death house on the rue Lesueur.

Pétiot, born in 1897 in Auxerre, was, it later transpired, a childhood sadist who stole from his schoolmates, and while serving at a casualty clearing-station in World War I, started out on another career: selling drugs. He qualified as a doctor in 1921, and soon set up shop in the village of Villeneuve-sur-Yonne, where he made a reputation for himself as a drugs-supplier and provider of illegal abortions. As a result of dogged canvassing on his part, he was elected

mayor in 1928, by which time he'd married. But question-marks began to gather about the doctor. He was caught stealing twice – and there was worse. Screams were heard coming from his surgery late at night. His housekeeper became pregnant and then disappeared. Later a woman patient was robbed and killed; and another patient, who persisted in accusing the doctor of being responsible, suddenly died – of 'natural

◄ *Dr Marcel Pétiot went to the guillotine in 1946*

causes,' wrote the doctor on the death certificate.

All this persuaded Pétiot to up sticks to Paris, where he took up what came to be a successful practice in the rue Caumartin. Outwardly, again, he was respectability itself, with a wife and child; and no doubt it was this that enabled him to survive charges, once more, of shoplifting and drug-dealing, for which he received only fines. He was popular with his patients, and no one seemed to pay any attention when, after the German occupation of Paris, he bought another house on the Rue Lesueur and started having it rebuilt to his own specifications.

The rebuilt house contained a new furnace in the basement beneath the garage, and an airtight triangular room with peepholes let into the door, 'for my mental patients,' said Dr. Pétiot. It was, in fact, for something a lot more sinister. For once the house had been finished, he put out word that he was in touch with the French Resistance, and could smuggle people out of Paris.

He immediately had customers, among the first a rich Jewish businessman and his family, who paid him two million francs for his help. He treated them exactly the same as all the others who were to follow – Jews, Resistance fighters, those on the run from the Gestapo: he gave them an injection of poison – the injection was to protect them against typhus, he said – and watched them die behind the peepholes in the airtight room. He then treated their bodies in quicklime, bought in bulk from his brother in Auxerre, and burned what was left of them in the furnace below. In each case – and there were sixty-three of them – he kept scrupulous records, including of the furs, cash, jewellery and precious metals his 'clients' had brought with them to take into exile.

It was the furnace which in the end proved Pétiot's undoing. For in March 1944, a neighbour complained about the smoke that was billowing from it and called the police and the fire brigade. The police went off to find the doctor at his house on the Rue Caumartin. But the firemen broke in, and soon found the furnace surrounded by dismembered corpses. The doctor, though, when he arrived at the scene, had a plausible and patriotic explanation: they were the bodies, he confided, of Nazi soldiers and of collaborators condemned to death by the Resistance, for which he was working.

The French gendarmes, half convinced, returned to their headquarters without him; and he, his wife and seventeen-year-old son immediately fled before senior officers demanded – as they later did – a proper search of the premises. Once Paris

▲ *Pétiot gave people hope before brutally murdering them*

was liberated a few weeks later, Pétiot became France's most wanted man. But instead of leaving the country, he belatedly joined the Free French forces and hand-wrote a letter to a newspaper saying as much, adding that he'd been framed by the Gestapo. A handwriting check soon established who he'd become, a Captain Valéry serving in Reuilly. He was arrested and after seventeen months in captivity he came to trial, charged with murdering the twenty-seven people whose remains the firemen had found.

One intriguing suggestion is that Pétiot at one time himself aroused the suspicions of the Gestapo – who arrested him as what he proclaimed himself to be: a member of the Resistance involved in smuggling people out of Paris. He was freed on the grounds that, in murdering Jews and people on the run, he'd simply been doing their work for them. . .

Dennis RABBITT

It was years before police even realized what was happening, but then rape is perhaps the most under-reported of crimes. According to a 1996 survey, only thirty-nine per cent of such crimes are ever reported to law enforcement officials. Even so, there are some women in St Louis, Missouri, who would claim bitterly that the police would rather the figure was even less.

Nevertheless, the following modus operandi of the person concerned began to emerge: between 1988 and 1997 an individual was breaking into women's houses at night, after they had gone to bed, usually through an unlocked door or open window. He wore a ski-mask and gloves to protect his identity. After the rape, he would usually force the victim to bathe, presumably to destroy any forensic evidence of his crime. The rapes took place in the better neighbourhoods of St Louis, towards the south of the city, areas that had always been relatively safe and crime-free, and for this anomaly the unknown criminal was dubbed the Southside Rapist. When

DNA evidence finally brought his reign of terror to an end, the head of the city police department was compelled to open a new, dedicated crime lab, so no other criminal should escape this newer, longer arm of the law.

THE MAN BEHIND THE MASK

Dennis Nathaniel Rabbitt was born in St Louis in 1957, to a middle-class family. His father was blind, and he was brought up mostly by his stepfather and his mother. During his adolescence, Rabbitt claims his mother drilled a hole in the bathroom door so she could watch him masturbate. Later in his teenage years he returned home one day to find his mother unconscious near the living room, and his stepfather upstairs in their bedroom, dead, with a gun in his hand and blood on the walls.

Rabbitt later said he knew something was wrong with him from an early age. By seventeen, his criminal record had begun, and he had become a known burglar. This did not stop him from leading the semblance of a normal life, however, and Rabbitt eventually married, and became the father of two. During this time he ran a bar and restaurant in downtown St Louis, and those that knew him described him as a typical married father. He was to describe the break-up of his marriage as one of the worst events in his life, although it was he who filed for divorce, in 1987. Observers who watched the case unfold were quick to point out that the first rape of which he was suspected occurred the following year.

THE NIGHTMARE BEGINS

As the police found out, while his *modus operandi* remained fairly consistent, there was no link between the victims of the Southside Rapist, other than that they were women, and they were vulnerable. He had no physical type, or racial preference. The age varied hugely too, starting in the mid-teens and ending in the early eighties. There were no other causative factors that linked them, none of the women knew each other, their daily movements were all different, and they worked and shopped in different areas. Yet each one would awake sometime in the night with a masked man sitting on their chest or legs, holding a knife at their throat, or pointing a gun at their head. Other than the rape itself he inflicted no other harm upon them, which would tend to categorize him as a power-assurance rapist, sometimes described by police as a 'gentleman rapist'. Rabbitt fits the profile reasonably well, being a man of average intelligence, who was rarely physically aggressive, who worried about his social status and may have been insecure about his masculinity, and who had failed at maintaining a strong romantic relationship. He also fantasized that the rape was consensual sex; desired and enjoyed by his female victim. It was anything but; even Jennifer Jewer, a woman of strong Baptist faith, who famously forgave him in court, eventually slid into a paralysing depression that cost her her job.

'TO SERVE AND PROTECT'?

For over a decade, the St Louis Metropolitan Police were at a loss, while the rapes continued. 'He terrorized the city', Police Chief Joe Mokwa confessed. 'We didn't know who he was or where he was going to strike next. We had no solid eyewitnesses to identify him.' In an attempt to narrow down the rapist's area of operations, they contacted James LeBeau, an administration of justice professor at the Southern Illinois University, in 1996. LeBeau was a pioneer of crime mapping (LeBeau: '[Crime mapping] is a generic term for taking locations of crimes and putting them on a map, putting spatial information in a geographical format'). But while crime mapping went on to

prove itself useful for the purposes of trend-spotting and expending resources, it brought St Louis police no closer to the fleet-footed Southside Rapist.

Despite their best efforts, however, many remain critical of the Metropolitan Police's handling of the case, and their handling of rape cases in general. Statistically, St Louis officially had fewer rapes than most American cities, even while the Southside Rapist was at his busiest. As the St Louis Post-Dispatch has reported, this was largely because for decades huge numbers of rapes were never even filed on system, but simply kept as 'memos' for a period of months before being shredded. As late as 2005 the department had to increase its annual rape figure by fifty-three per cent. Physical evidence from rape kits was frequently destroyed too, often without ever having been analysed. In such a culture, critics argue, it is no wonder Dennis Rabbitt got away with so much for so long. There are also allegations that before Rabbitt was identified as the Southside Rapist he was found by police drunkenly passed out only a few houses away from where a rape had occurred the night before.

MANHUNT

Frustrated, the police returned to their crime mapping. Could this new

◄ *Under heavy police protection, including a bullet-proof vest and riot helmet, Dennis Rabbitt is transferred across state. So prolific was the range of his attacks, authorities in St Louis had to discuss which municipality would prosecute him first*

technique be honed and refined to produce a better result? The case had been cold for three years when they extended their search outside the Southside area and begun to look further afield, at rapes in less affluent parts of the city, even in other counties. With these extra cases taken into account, the profile of the perpetrator became clearer, and the list of suspects drastically shorter. Dennis Rabbitt, who had by now been arrested twice for attempted burglaries (failed rapes, he later confessed), was on the list. Crime mapping had worked after all: the officers had just needed to take in all of St Louis.

Under the guise of a peeping-tom investigation, they obtained a saliva sample from Rabbitt and analysed his DNA. It was a perfect match for the Southside Rapist, but when the tests were finished they found Rabbitt had left his new job in waste disposal and fled the city, almost immediately after giving the sample.

The manhunt lasted for months. After an appearance on America's Most Wanted, a woman tipped off his whereabouts for a twenty-five thousand dollar reward. The FBI caught up with him in a motel in Albuquerque, New Mexico, with a fifteen-year-old girl in tow. He initially claimed to be Nathan Babbitt, but this modest alias could not hide his tattoos, which matched the description on record.

BEHIND BARS

Dennis Rabbitt was tried not once but several times, in different counties, until he had been tried for each of the twenty rapes his DNA linked him to, and was found guilty on each count. He was sentenced to five life sentences in Missouri and an additional sixty years in Illinois. There are numerous but inconsistent reports that he has confessed to many more rapes than the twenty he was convicted of, from a total of twenty nine up to a hundred. 'It's only logical that there are many more rapes than we know about', St Louis Detective Mark Kennedy once said. 'Even if he averaged only four a year, that's more than one hundred rapes.'

In April 2005 Rabbitt was stabbed, repeatedly but not fatally, in the exercise grounds of the South Central Correctional Center, and moved elsewhere. Outside prison walls, St Louis police were so impressed by the efficacy of DNA evidence that they opened a new crime lab on Clarke Avenue that now oversees a hundred thousand cases a year. And in and around the Gateway City, a number of traumatized but relieved women are trying to get on with their lives.

Dennis RADER

BTK, which stands for 'bind, torture and kill', was the name by which Dennis Rader, one of America's most notorious serial killers, used to refer to himself. His career of crime spanned a period of thirty years, until the case was finally cracked open.

At the beginning of his killing spree, Rader wrote letters to newspapers and to the police bragging about the murders, often describing macabre details of the crimes. Then the letters stopped, and after a long period of silence, resumed again. In this way, Rader taunted the authorities for years, terrorizing the public in the process. Today, many believe that, had forensic evidence and other clues been followed up more systematically, Rader could have been brought to justice many years earlier, and several of his victims spared their horrifying deaths.

Dennis Lynn Rader was born on 9 March 1945, the son of William and Dorothea Rader. The eldest of four brothers, he grew up in Wichita, Kansas, where he attended high school and college. As a young man, he joined the air force, and travelled abroad, returning home in 1970. A year later he married, and the couple went on to have two children. During this time, he worked in a series of jobs, including a company that sold alarm systems for offices. He also studied at university, gaining a degree. He attended church regularly, becoming a church leader, and also became a Cub Scouts leader.

HANGING IN THE BASEMENT

His first known murder took place on 15 January 1974, when he broke into the home of the Otero family. The Otero parents' bodies, bound and gagged, were found by the couple's eldest son, Charlie, when he returned from school. When police searched the house, the bodies of his brother and sister were found: nine-year-old Joseph junior in a bedroom, his face covered by a hood, and eleven-year-old Josephine, partially undressed, hanging from a pipe in the basement. There were traces of semen at the scene of the crimes.

Nine months later, the local newspapers began to receive mystery calls. The killer directed reporters to a letter hidden in a book in the public library, in which he explained that he killed to satisfy a sexual perversion, referring to 'a monster' within him that he could not stop, and calling himself

'BTK': bind, torture, kill. The letter was badly written and spelt, but it was thought that that was just a ruse; many believed that the killer was actually quite well educated and intelligent.

Meanwhile, the murders continued. On 4 April 1974, Kathryn Bright and her brother Kevin were attacked in broad daylight by an intruder who was lying in wait at their home. Kevin was shot but managed to escape; his sister was stabbed in the abdomen and later died in hospital. Police did not, at the time, connect this killing with the BTK murders, even though there was evidence to show that the killer had tried to strangle Kathryn Bright.

ATTENTION-SEEKING KILLER

The next killing did not come until three years later, when on 17 March 1977, Shirley Vian was found dead in her home, her neck bound with the same type of cord as the other BTK victims. As in the other incidents, the phone line was cut. Her three children thankfully escaped unharmed, although the killer locked them in the closet.

By this time, as the murders began to follow a pattern, the citizens of Wichita were beginning to panic. And sure enough, on 8 December 1977, there was another murder. This time, the killer alerted police to the scene of the crime, telling them the address where the murder had taken place. When police reached the scene, they found that, once again, the victim was a young woman, and once again she had been strangled, this time with a nylon stocking. However, this victim, Nancy Jo Fox, remained fully clothed.

FORENSIC EVIDENCE COLLECTED

For a while, the police heard no more news of BTK. Then more letters from him began to come in to the local papers. It seemed that the murderer was upset at the lack of attention he had received. He wanted the notoriety of Jack the Ripper or the Son of Sam, and he did not seem to be getting it.

Despite all his efforts to attract publicity, police were still unable to track down BTK. During the 1980s, a task force known informally as 'The Ghostbusters' was set up to sift through the evidence. Investigators found that all the killings had taken place within a three and a half mile radius and began to search the records of all white males within the area. The BTK letters were analysed, and the photocopying

▶ *Convicted serial killer Dennis Rader walks into the El Dorado Correctional Facility, Kansas. He admitted killing ten people in a thirty-year span, and was sentenced to ten consecutive life terms*

machine used to copy them was tracked down to the public library. The content of the letters was also studied, and leads followed up. DNA and semen samples were also taken for laboratory analysis. None of this led to the killer's arrest, however.

On 31 October 1987, another murder took place that many believed to be the work of BTK. The body of Shannon Olson, aged fifteen, was found partially naked in a wasteland area. She had been stabbed to death. Exactly two months later, Mary Fager returned to her home to find her husband Phillip shot dead and daughters Kelli and Sherri strangled in the basement. Soon afterwards, Mary received a letter from a person claiming to be BTK. Despite this evidence, the police arrested a builder who was doing some work on the house and charged him with the murders. The builder was later acquitted.

THE 'HIT KIT'

Once again, the BTK case grew cold, and it was not until 2004 that another letter arrived, claiming responsibility for a murder committed in 1986. The

◄ *A mask found by Delores Davis' body in 1991. After Davis was dead, Rader tossed her under a bridge where the body decomposed*

letter contained the missing driving licence of a woman named Vicki Wegerle, who had been murdered at her home.

The following year the police finally made their arrest. They took Dennis Rader into custody, and he immediately confessed to the crimes, giving a detailed account of all of them. Two more crimes were added to the list, the killing of Marine Hedge in 1985, and Delores Davis in 1991. In court, Rader continued to paint a lurid picture of the murders, describing the 'hit kit' he took with him on his grisly missions: guns, ropes, handcuffs, and tape.

A TRAIL OF CLUES

To this day, no one knows what drove Rader to commit his hideous crimes, but what is clear is that over a period of three decades, he purposely left a trail of clues to taunt the police, clues that in retrospect could have led to his arrest many years earlier. For example, DNA analysis of Rader's semen matches that of the BTK semen left at the scene of several of the murders. Also, despite his college education, Rader was a poor writer and speller, and his mistakes matched up exactly with those of the BTK letters. It also transpired that there

◄ *White-collared killer:*
it must have taken a cool
head and some intelligence
to have remained unde-
tected for so long while
committing such appalling
crimes

▲ *Even the guilty deserve a fair trial: Rader's hand is shaken by his attorney after a hearing in El Dorado Correctional Facility. The judge recommended that he should receive treatment as a sexual offender while he spends the rest of his life in prison*

were links between Rader and some of the victims: Joseph Otero had worked in the Air Force at the same time as Rader was there; Julie Otero and Kathryn Bright had worked for the same company as Rader. In addition, the payphones that BTK had used to report his crimes were, in some cases, very near his places of work; and the photocopiers he used could be traced to places where he had studied, including the university. Finally, there was the obvious clue that almost all his victims lived near his home; Marine Hedge even lived on the same street.

Eventually, of course, the net closed in, and Rader was arrested. But had forensic and other evidence been collected more systematically and the results analysed with more care, it seems that BTK could have been caught many years earlier, and the lives of several innocent victims spared.

Richard RAMIREZ

The problem with Richard Ramirez was the pattern of his crimes – or rather the absence of pattern. For almost all serial murderers fixate on a particular type of prey: prostitutes, say; young women; children; adolescents – but Ramirez was an equal-opportunity killer.

His thirteen victims included men and women, whites and blacks; they ranged in age from 30 to 83. All they had in common was that they died in their homes at the hands of the so-called 'Night Stalker.'

Ramirez, a high-school dropout and loner, was 22 by the time he got to California from his native Texas in 1982, and by then he'd already had two arrests for drug possession. In Texas, it had been mostly marijuana and glue-sniffing, but

▼ *Richard Ramirez became known as the 'Night Stalker'*

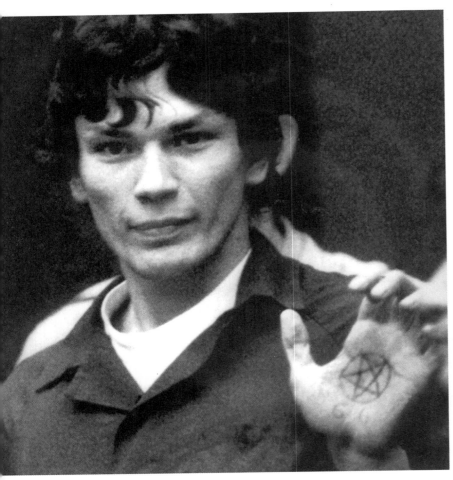

▲ *There seemed to be no pattern to the victims Ramirez singled out*

would never live to finger him. He raped and almost decapitated her; and once he'd done that, he seemed to get a taste for murder. He slipped at night into people's houses and variously ripped off, raped or killed whoever he happened to find there, depending, it seemed, on his mood. In addition to the thirteen murders and thirty felonies he was eventually charged with, he's thought to have racked up at least three more murders and any number of sexual assaults, some of them on young children.

He was caught, almost prosaically, by technology in the end. For three minutes after a new state-wide computerised fingerprint system was set up in Sacramento, Los Angeles police sent through a print found in a stolen car linked to 'the Night Stalker.'

The system quickly came up with a match: Richard Ramirez. He was arrested two days later.

His trial dragged on for four years, largely because of Ramirez's disruptive behaviour. In continual court outbursts and long tirades, he kept referring to his worship of the devil. On at least one occasion he appeared in court with a so-called satanic pentagram drawn on his palm. The jury was unimpressed: in November 1989, he was sentenced to death, and sent to San Quentin Prison's Death Row.

in Los Angeles, he began shooting up cocaine and stealing from cars and houses to feed his habit. He slept wherever he found himself; he lived out of a back-pack; and ate junk food to stay alive. Pretty soon his teeth were rotting.

He did one stint in jail; and it may have been this that in 1984 pushed him over the edge into murder, into making sure that seventy-nine-year-old Jennie Vincow, whose house he'd broken into,

Gary RIDGWAY

The trial of Gary Leon Ridgway, The Green River Killer, was one of the most sensational ever to take place in America. Ridgway confessed to forty-eight confirmed murders, which makes him officially the most prolific serial killer in American history to date. The total count of his victims, who were mostly prostitutes, is thought to be much higher. For many years, he escaped detection, even though he was considered a suspect.

A series of police task forces were mounted to solve the case, but time and time again, the trail went cold. In the end, it was DNA technology that finally enabled the police to nail this brutal killer, who is now serving a total of forty-eight life sentences in jail.

TEENAGE PROSTITUTES

On 15 July 1982 a group of children discovered the body of sixteen-year-old Wendy Lee Coffield, in the Green River, Kent County, Washington State. She had drifted up against a piling near the Meeker Street Bridge, naked save for her tennis shoes, strangled by her own blue jeans. On 13 August that same year, a slaughterhouse worker came across the body of Deborah Bonner, and only two days after that, a man rafting the same stretch of river saw in the shallows what turned out to be seventeen-year-old Cynthia Hinds. Next to her was another body, that of 31-year-old Marcia Chapman. All had been strangled. When police searched the area they found the body of another girl, Opal Mills, sixteen, on the nearby bank, dead by no more than twenty-four hours. The King County Sheriff's Department were hot on the heels of a serial killer, but it was as close as they would get for some time.

The victims of the Green River Killer belonged to a very specific demographic. All of them were women. All of them were believed to be prostitutes. And only a handful of them were older than twenty-one; almost half were eighteen or younger. Unfortunately, there was no shortage of these extremely vulnerable young women in the Washington area. Street prostitution in and around Seattle during the years of the Green River Killer was rife, and changes in state legislature had meant that young runaways could no longer be forcibly detained. As a result, there was an abundance of isolated, inexperienced and defenceless teenage girls who were prepared to climb into a car with a strange man as a way of making a living. When the act of running away had been decriminalized, police no longer even kept records on missing teenagers. Had they continued to do so, the monstrous scale of these murders might have been apparent much earlier.

THE KILLING GROUND

The area in which the prostitutes plied their trade straddled the city limits: when the Sheriff's Department were cracking down on the strip, these women went north to the city, and when the Seattle Police Department did the same, the women came back to the strip. The two forces never combined their efforts, and this problem in dealing with street prostitution made Seattle a rich killing ground for a serial killer.

Furthermore, vice officers for King County did not work weekends, when trade was busiest, and some even freelanced as security in local strip clubs, ensuring prostitutes were kept out of the lounges, forcing them out onto the streets, where they were most at risk. Similarly, in the city itself, police conducted a series of raids on brothels, although none of the girls that worked in them had ever fallen prey to the killer. When arrests were made in the red light district it was invariably the prostitute that was arrested, rather than her customer. There was no effort being made to keep a systematic record of these 'johns', not

◀ *Finger-tip search: investigators search for the remains of one of Gary Leon Ridgway's victims at an unknown location*

▶Jose Malvar Jr, brother of Marie Malvar, on the witness stand at Gary Ridgway's trial. He and his father and Maria's boyfriend searched the streets for the pickup Maria was last seen getting in to

even of the licence plates on their cars. Inadvertently, the Green River Killer was being given a free hand.

On 16 August 1982, King County assembled its Green River Task Force. It was headed by Police Major Richard Kraske, and comprised twenty-five officers, the biggest task force since the Ted Bundy murders seven years earlier — although, as it transpired, these officers were far less experienced. The day after Kraske's appointment, the task force staked out the river, and an overhead news helicopter broadcast their position to anyone with a television.

The first suspect emerged that September; a cab driver and ex-con named Melvin Wayne Foster, who had approached police to inform on other cabbies he considered suspicious. A psychological profile of the Green River Killer had already been performed by FBI agent John Douglas, and police considered Foster to fit perfectly. He was put under surveillance. After searches of his house, he was given a lie detector test, which he failed. Foster attributed his failure to a nervous condition. However, despite constant police observation, young women continued to disappear. Eventually, the task force had to admit they had been looking at the wrong man.

Meanwhile, the death toll had risen to sixteen. The killer was disposing of the bodies faster than the Sheriff's Department could discover them.

The first task force was disbanded when Sheriff Bernard Winckoski left his position in January 1983, to be replaced three months later by Sheriff Vern Thomas. Thomas began campaigning immediately for a new, larger task force. It took the rest of the year to organize, and to overcome his colleagues' concerns of the strain it would put on resources. By January 1984, a task force of forty officers was ready to look again at the Green River Killer, and every one of them must have felt the pressure: the killer was operating seemingly unhindered in a small area that was routinely patrolled by uniformed and plain clothes officers. Furthermore, while Sheriff Thomas had been planning and politicking, these murders had showed no sign of stopping.

CLOSING IN ON THE KILLER

In a change of tactics, Thomas' task force began to arrest the prostitutes' clients instead of the prostitutes. Prior to this, arrests of women prostitutes were three times greater than the number of men arrested for trying to buy sex. Soon, the ratio was almost reversed, and the killings seemed to tail off. Progress was being made at last.

The killer had been scared away, or so it appeared. Police began to speculate that the culprit had moved, or was operating elsewhere. Although much good work had been done, the killer remained free, and morale in the task force began to plummet. Bodies continued to be discovered, but leads were few and far between. There were no physical descriptions of the killer, for the simple reason that no victim ever escaped.

When the sixth victim, Marie Malvar, got into a green pickup with a dark-haired man on 30 April 1983, her boyfriend was there to see it. He followed in his own car, noticing that the two seemed to be arguing, and then lost them at a traffic light near Des Moines.

He reported her missing four days later. He returned to the area with her brother and father, and searched the streets, looking for the pickup, which they found in a driveway. The Des Moines police sent a detective, but she was not inside the house.

It was three months before Des Moines police informed King County homicide of the incident. It was three years before King County factored it into their investigations. It turned out that another victim, Kimi Kai Pitsor, had also been seen getting into a similar vehicle, but the two events were never connected.

A STRANGE LONER

Gary Ridgway was not unknown to police. He was a strange man that people described as friendly but odd, who had been raised in Seattle. His mother was a domineering woman, and he wet the bed as a child, but there was nothing in his childhood to suggest the burning rage that led him, as an adult, to become a serial killer. As a young man, he joined the Pentecostal church, and often collected for the church door to door. However, at the same period, he began visiting prostitutes for sex, and developed an intense hatred for these mostly young, inexperienced women.

In 1980, he was accused of choking a prostitute, but police let him go. In 1982 he was interviewed in a car with prostitute Kelli McGinness (an eighteen-year-old who disappeared the following year), and the same year pleaded guilty to soliciting a decoy female police officer. In 1984, he approached Thomas' Green River Task Force to offer information, and was given a lie detector test, which he passed. Later that year, when police ascertained that he had contact with at least three of the victims, Ridgway finally became chief suspect.

However, a house search provided no clues. In 1986, he passed another polygraph test ('I was too relaxed,' he later said). The following year, bodily

◄ *Ridgway confessed to killing 48 women over a period of fifteen years. He was sentenced to life imprisonment, commuted from the death sentence in return for helping police find the bodies*

samples were taken. Yet, despite the fact that he had been in the area, and had had contact with the women who were killed, Ridgway was not arrested.

THE VITAL CLUE

After this period, the killings tailed off dramatically, and by 1991 the Green River Task Force was staffed by a single officer. But there were many who had not forgotten the victims of the Green River Killer, and who were determined to seek justice for their murders. In 2001 King County gained a new sheriff, Dave Reichert, who formed a new team to solve the case, largely consisting of forensics and DNA experts. All viable evidence the county had collected was sent to the laboratory for investigation.

It was this initiative that was finally to yield results. The experts started with three of the earliest victims, killed in 1982 and 1983; Mills, Chapman, and Carol Christensen. Semen from the bodies was tested using new DNA technology and the match with Gary Ridgway's sample was positive. The Green River Killer had been found.

JUSTICE AT LAST

Ridgway was fifty-two years old when he was arrested on 30 November 2001 on four counts of murder. At first the killer maintained his innocence, but as testing continued on further remains, the evidence become incontrovertible. Two years later, he pleaded guilty to forty-eight counts of murder, mostly in 1982 and 1983, but one in 1990, and one as late as 1998.

In July 2003 Ridgway was moved from the county jail to an undisclosed location amid reports that he was prepared to co-operate if he could escape the death penalty. The plea bargain was defended by the prosecution as 'an avenue to the truth' for the victims and their families. While not all the families were happy with this, forty-one victims were named in court who would never otherwise have been mentioned, and as a result, some of the bodies were located and given proper burial.

It is generally thought that Gary Ridgway killed many more than forty-eight women. Chillingly, he himself has admitted he cannot remember all of the women he put to death. However, through a combination of police work and forensic technology, the case was finally solved, and he was made to pay for at least some of his hideous crimes. Today, with forty-eight life sentences to serve, there is absolutely no doubt that he will remain in jail for the rest of his life. After years of being hunted down, the Green River Killer is finally behind bars – for good.

Issei SAGAWA

The story of Issei Sagawa, a small, shy man who became a celebrity in his native country, is like the plot-line of a perverse Japanese movie. For Issei was a cannibal.

On the evening of June 11th 1981, while studying in Paris, he invited a fellow-student called Renée Hartevelt to his flat to help him with some translation. At some point during the evening, he asked her to have sex with him and when she refused, he calmly shot her in the back of the neck with a .22 rifle, undressed her and had sex with her corpse instead.

Then, in what he called 'an expression of love,' he began to eat her. He cut slices of flesh from her buttocks and consumed them raw, shuddering with delight. Later he cut her body into pieces, taking photographs and reserving choice cuts of meat along the way, and finally stuffed what remained into two suitcases, which he set off by taxi to dump into a lake in the Bois de Boulogne.

At the last minute, though, scared off by passers-by, he abandoned the suitcases and fled. The police were called; and Issei was arrested. His confession was ready enough. But he never came to trial.

◀ *Issei Sagawa's cannibalism shocked the Japanese public*

Instead he was declared insane and held in a mental asylum in Paris until May 1984, when he was returned to Japan under an agreement between the two countries – an agreement which happened to coincide with the signing of a contract between a Japanese company of which Issei's father was president and a French conglomerate.

In Japan, where a book of his letters about the murder had been published, Issei quickly became a star; and after little more than a year, he was released from the Tokyo mental hospital to which he'd been confined. In a magazine interview shortly after his release, he confessed that he still dreamed of eating another woman's flesh – though this time with her consent. He went on to have a career as a journalist and television personality.

Gerard SCHAEFER

Gerard John Schaefer was a vicious serial killer convicted for the murders of two teenage girls but probably responsible for the slaughter of many more. While serving life imprisonment, he wrote disturbing fiction about rape, murder and his experience of living on death row. Whether his work was autobiographical or merely described the violent sexual fantasies of a demented imagination remains unclear; Schaefer himself oscillated between boasting about the body count of girls he had murdered and denying that he was a serial killer. Today, we will never know the exact truth about how many young women he murdered, for he was stabbed to death in his cell by a fellow prison inmate in 1995. At the time, the mother of one of Schaefer's victims commented: 'I'd like to send a present to the guy who killed him… I just wish it would have been sooner rather than later.'

G.J. Schaefer, as he was known, was born in 1946 in Wisconsin. Family life for the three Schaefer children, of which G.J. was the eldest, was by all accounts a misery. His father was an alcoholic and a womanizer. His parents later divorced. The young Schaefer felt that his parents, especially his father, preferred his sister to him, and showed early signs of mental disturbance, tying himself to trees to gain sexual thrills, wearing women's underclothes and fantasizing about dying.

As a young man, Schaefer had tried various vocational jobs, but was unable to find work. He attempted to join the Roman Catholic Church as a priest, and then tried to become a teacher, but was unsuccessful in both fields because of his unbalanced personality.

DIVORCED DUE TO CRUELTY

Schaefer married in 1968, but two years later his wife divorced him, citing cruelty as the reason. He resolved to become a policeman and managed to find a job, even though he had failed a psychological test when he applied. He started well, but was then fired for obtaining personal information on women traffic offenders, and asking them out for dates. He relocated and found police work in Martin County, Florida, where he was soon in much more serious trouble again.

Schaefer picked up two teenage hitchhikers, Pamela Wells and Nancy Trotter, and told them that it was illegal to

◀ The crimes of Gerard Schaefer will forever remain mysterious as he himself was never clear about what he had done.

hitchhike in the county, which it was not. He then drove them home and said that he would drive them to the beach the next day. The following day, he drove the girls out to a swamp, drew a gun on them and bound them to tree roots with nooses around their necks. They managed to escape and contacted the police. This time, he was sentenced to a year in prison.

While awaiting trial, he picked up two more teenage hitchhikers, Georgia Jessup and Susan Place. He took them to the swamp, tied them to trees and savagely attacked them. By the time their mutilated bodies were found, Schaefer was already in jail. When police searched his mother's home, they found items belonging to several more young women and girls who had disappeared from the area: teenage hitchhikers Barbara Wilcox and Collette Goodenough; waitress Carmen Hallock; neighbour Leigh Bonadies; and schoolgirls Elsie Farmer and Mary Briscolina.

Despite the mounting evidence that Schaefer was a maniacal serial killer, he

▲ *Despite the heavy security in jail, Schaefer was murdered by fellow inmate, Vincent Rivera*

was only charged with two murders: those of Susan Place and Georgia Jessup. He was convicted in 1973, and ordered to serve two life sentences, which was more than enough to make sure that he would no longer be a threat to the public. For this reason, no other charges were brought.

CULT FICTION

For almost two decades, Schaefer languished in jail, more or less forgotten by the rest of the world. It was only when a collection of his stories was published under the title *Killer Fiction* that his heinous crimes were remembered. Schaefer described the stories as 'art'; however, many saw them as fictionalized descriptions of actual crimes he had committed. In addition to his tales of rape and murder, there were stories that were evidently products of his demented imagination, including one about copulating with dead bodies recently killed in the electric chair.

Not surprisingly, G.J. Schaefer was not a popular man among his fellow inmates. In 1995, prisoner Vincent Rivera, who was serving a life sentence for murder, rushed into Schaefer's cell and stabbed him in the throat and the eyes, killing him. Very few mourned his passing. However, his fiction continues to have a cult following to this day.

Arthur SHAWCROSS

Arthur Shawcross was born in Watertown, New York on 6 June 1945, the first anniversary of D-Day. He had a less than happy childhood, but it seems that his parents – unlike the Kempers and Heidniks – were relatively blame-free. When Shawcross was finally put away for life he claimed his mother had abused him, setting in motion an eager search for corroborative evidence. None has ever been found. He was a late talker, a chronic bed-wetter, and the butt of schoolmates' teasing, but it seems unlikely that he was physically abused.

Having struck out on 'nurture' – or the lack of it being a reason for Shawcross' behaviour – the researchers moved on to 'nature'. Here they struck gold, not once but three times. Shawcross had suffered several head injuries, with consequences for his frontal lobe. He was born with an extra Y chromosome, a condition said to generate violent antisocial behaviour. And his body contained ten times the normal load of kryptopyrrole chemicals, which are associated with extreme mood swings and violent rages.

Shawcross himself blamed his troubles – and those of his unfortunate victims – on the Vietnam War. Drafted in 1964, he certainly witnessed many incidents of atrocious brutality and sadism, but there is little sense that he was shocked by any of them. On the contrary, he seems to have revelled in the blood and cruelty. He described one encounter with two Vietnamese women – in which he killed and ate the roasted flesh of one before raping and killing the other – with the sort of deadpan relish

▼ *Shawcross on his first arrest. Prison proved no deterrent*

that sent a shiver down the spines of those hearing his testimony.

Life must have seemed tame when he came back home. He took to beating his Christian Scientist second wife, who went to consult a psychiatrist about him. The psychiatrist recommended commital and therapy, but she thought he was exaggerating the problem, and refused to sign the papers. Two years later her husband killed two children, eight-year-old Karen Hill and ten-year-old Jack Blake. Arrested and convicted for raping and killing the girl, he was given a twenty-five year sentence. In prison he confessed to the boy's murder, but not, apparently, until the body had decomposed, because he later claimed to have eaten the heart and genitals.

He was released after only fifteen years. Two communities refused to have him before he settled, unnoticed, in Rochester, New York. He found a third wife and a mistress, and soon started killing again. Between February 1988 and January 1990 Shawcross murdered eleven women, nine of them prostitutes. After strangling or beating them to death, he mutilated their bodies, a process which gave him great sexual satisfaction. In two cases he cut up their bodies and ate parts.

He pretended to take a great interest in his own case. Like Peter Kurten, he warned his wife – in Shawcross' case, his mistress as well – to take precautions against himself. Like Fritz Haarmann and Ed Kemper he hung around in coffee bars, talking to the police whenever he could.

The police were at a complete loss. No one, it seems, went to the trouble of checking out which convicted sex-murderers were on parole in the area. In the event, it was only a ludicrous piece of luck which led to Shawcross' capture – he was spotting by a police helicopter urinating off a bridge, with a body visible in the river below.

His first arrest proved abortive, however, – he did not fit the police profile. It was only when they found one of the dead women's earrings in his car that he was arrested again, and questioned until he broke. Shawcross confessed to eleven killings, including two the police were unaware of. He told them about his cannibalism, and how he had often returned to the decomposing bodies for a sexual recharge. Most of the physical evidence was inconclusive, and a few of the psychiatrists were unconvinced, but most believed Shawcross was what he claimed to be – a cannibal-killer.

The real arguments came later, over why. Shawcross, meanwhile, was serving the first of ten consecutive twenty-five year sentences. He seems likely to die in prison in due course.

◄ *The face of an incorrigible killer: Shawcross was in and out of prison for a string of horrific crimes*

Dr. Harold SHIPMAN

Harold Shipman is almost certainly the most prolific serial killer in British history. A public enquiry in 2002 reported that over his career he had probably killed 215 people, mostly women, all of whom had been his patients. For Shipman was a doctor who killed, apparently, simply because he could. His victims were mostly elderly or infirm – they would die sometime, so why not when he dictated? He was caring, after all: a trouble-taker, a pillar of the community always ready to go out of his way to help. So why on earth would anyone suspect him of using the home visits he made to inject his victims with enough heroin or morphine to stop them breathing? No one ever thought to doubt his word; and covering his tracks was simplicity itself: all he had to do was doctor his victims' medical records, if that was necessary, and write a fake cause of death, as their personal GP, on the death certificate. There was no need at all, he'd announce, for a post mortem.

Occasionally Dr. Shipman would be mentioned in his patients' wills, of course, but that seemed only natural. They mostly didn't have a great deal of money in the first place; sometimes they had no living family; and the doctor, who always worked alone at his surgery in Hyde, Greater Manchester, was the personification of kindness. Then, though, in 1998, he got greedy. For one of his patients, Kathleen Grandy, a woman in her eighties, left him over £380,000. Questions were asked, and the will turned out to have been forged by none other than Shipman himself. He was sentenced to four years in prison.

It was this that triggered a full-scale enquiry. For unlike a great many of his patients – who'd been cremated, along with the evidence in their bones and blood – Kathleen Grandy had been buried. So her body was disinterred; and it was found to contain enough heroin to have killed her. Shipman's records were then seized and searched; relatives of dead patients were interviewed; and police began the grisly business of recovering and testing as many corpses as they could locate. The list of those murdered via injections began to rise; and so, to the horror of relatives, friends and patients alike, did the roster of probables.

Shipman, who turned out to have a history of drug addiction, was tried on fifteen counts of murder, all of which he denied; and in January 2000, he was

◀ *Dr. Harold Shipman, the most prolific serial killer in British history*

sentenced to life on each count, with the judge adding that, in his case,

'life would mean life.'

When the subsequent enquiry reported that he had probably been guilty of another 199 murders, he had nothing to say except, again, that he was innocent; and at the beginning of 2003, he launched an appeal against his sentence, on the grounds that his legal team hadn't been allowed to conduct their own post-mortems and that the jury had been wrongly instructed. It seems oddly apt that one of the solicitors involved in his appeal also acted for Slobodan Milosevic.

Bugsy SIEGEL

One of the most contradictory of criminals, Bugsy Siegel was, on the one hand a notoriously violent gangster, always ready to shoot first and think later (his nickname 'Bugsy' came from his apparent tendency to go 'bugs' with rage) whilst on the other, he was a smooth charmer who became the Mafia's front man, first in Hollywood and later in Las Vegas.

OUT OF THE GHETTO

Bugsy Siegel was born Benjamin Siegelbaum in 1905. His parents were Russian Jewish immigrants who lived in Williamsburg, Brooklyn, one of several city neighbourhoods to be dubbed 'Hell's Kitchen'. Benjamin soon saw crime as the most likely way out of this teeming ghetto. By the age of twelve, he was running a protection racket along with his friend Moey Sedway. Not long after, he met another young would-be gangster, and this time the meeting changed his life. The youth in question was named Meyer Lansky and the two formed a natural partnership. Lansky was the brains, Siegel the brawn. Both were utterly ruthless.

Lansky and Siegel formed a gang and gained a local reputation. Lansky then became friendly with another local gang leader, Charlie 'Lucky' Luciano. This was unusual, as generally the Italian gangs refused to have anything to do with the Jewish gangs. Luciano, however, clearly recognized true criminal talent when he saw it and refused to break his relationship with Lansky and Siegel. The friendship was confirmed when Luciano was sent to jail on drugs charges, after a policeman's son had given evidence against him. On Luciano's release from prison, Lansky and Siegel told him to leave town for the night and make sure he had an alibi. Sure enough, that night the policeman's son disappeared, never to be seen again.

MURDER AND MAYHEM

By now Prohibition had come into force, following the Volstead Act of 1919, and organized crime was developing as a result. Suddenly, the general public wanted something – alcohol – that they could only get from criminals. Siegel and Lansky took to bootlegging with relish, both manufacturing rotgut whisky themselves and hijacking lorry loads of booze from other gangsters. These activities brought them to the attention of the Mafia's overall leader, Joe 'The Boss' Masseria. A power struggle ensued.

Charlie Luciano decided to make a deal with Masseria's great rival, Sal Maranzano, and enlisted a team of hit men, including Siegel, to kill Joe Masseria as he had lunch in a Coney Island restaurant. Soon afterwards, Luciano killed Maranzano in turn, and became the top Mafia boss on the east coast.

Unimpressed by this, yet another rival Mafia chief, Waxey Gordon, took out a contract on Siegel and Lansky during 1932. Two of his men, Andy and Louis Frabrazzo, planted a bomb in Siegel's house. However, just before it exploded, Siegel discovered the bomb and threw it out of the window. Slightly injured by the blast, he was taken to hospital where he remained for several days, leaving only to track down another Frabrazzo brother, Tony, whom he murdered in front of his elderly parents. Siegel was then driven back to the hospital, where he climbed back through the window unnoticed.

HIGH SOCIETY

This escapade brought serious police attention down on Siegel, forcing him to lay low for a while. Meanwhile, he was beginning to get impatient with his role as Lansky's number two. Lansky clearly sensed this and, rather than test the limits of their friendship, or end up as yet

▲ *Bugsy Siegel with movie heart-throb George Raft at a Hollywood court house, where Siegel was charged with bookmaking*

gangsters stemmed from his own experience of growing up among them. Raft was Siegel's entry into Hollywood high society, and he soon became the archetypal player, with a string of mistresses. Six foot tall and good looking, Siegel was perfect for Hollywood: a real gangster who looked like a movie star.

By the mid-1940s, just after the Second World War, Siegel was getting restless, so Lansky had another idea. Why didn't the mob set up a casino in Nevada, a state that had legalized gambling? Siegel was not sure at first: after all, at the time Nevada was little more than an expanse of scrubby desert. However, after going out there to investigate further, Siegel discovered that there were already some gambling operations in a town called Las Vegas. Soon he had a plan.

THE BIGGEST CASINO IN THE WORLD

Siegel decided to build the biggest, smartest hotel and casino operation there had ever been in Las Vegas. It was to be called the Flamingo. He raised a million dollars from a mixture of fellow mobsters and Hollywood contacts. The costs spiralled to six million dollars and Siegel's investors grew worried. The Flamingo finally opened just before Christmas 1946. It was a disaster: the initial earnings were pitiful. A meeting of mobsters was

▲ *Bugsy's death was, fittingly, like a scene from the Hollywood movies; a world that had opened its arms to the debonair mobster*

another victim of Siegel's deadly temper, sent him out west in 1936 to run the California branch of the mob.

The only problem was that the west coast mob already had a leader, Jack Dragna, notionally the head of the Italian Protective League. After initial friction, Dragna kept on running the gambling rackets, while Siegel concentrated on running the corrupt unions that controlled much of what went on in Hollywood. Siegel's arrival in Hollywood allowed him to see his old friend George Raft, an actor whose expertise at playing

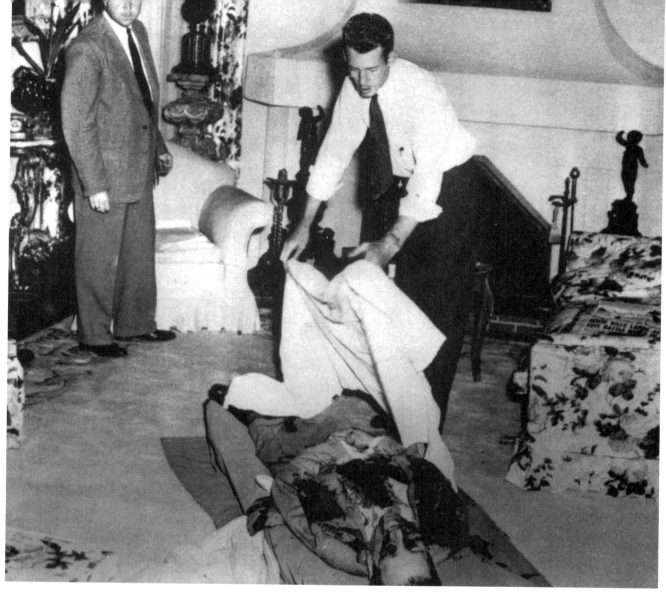

convened, all of them ready to demand Siegel's head. Lansky persuaded them to wait six months. Remarkably enough, Siegel managed to turn things around. By the end of May the casino was making a profit. Perhaps it was not enough, or perhaps his fellow mobsters simply thought that Siegel needed to be taught a lesson. Either way, in June 1947 Bugsy Siegel, veteran of dozens of hits, was finally the victim of one. Two men burst into his Hollywood apartment and shot him dead.

Tellingly, none of his former associates came to his funeral, not even Meyer Lansky.

▲ Used to clearing up the mess Bugsy caused in life, the police had the grisly task of clearing up the gangster himself in death

Charles SOBHRAJ

It is a fact that, while most crimes are committed for financial gain, serial murder very rarely has money as its primary object. Serial murderers often rob their victims, but this is usually a secondary motivation, the main purpose being sexual gratification of some kind. Charles Sobhraj, nicknamed 'the serpent', is a definite exception to the serial killer rule. He stands accused of around twenty murders. All his victims were backpackers travelling around south-east Asia. In all cases, he murdered them for money. As he himself told a journalist at the time of his 1976 murder trial: 'If I have ever killed, or have ordered killings, then it was purely for reasons of business – just a job, like a general in the army.'

Charles Sobhraj was born in 1944 to an Indian tailor and his Vietnamese girlfriend, Song. His father refused to marry his mother or to take much responsibility for his son. Song later married a French soldier, Lieutenant Alphonse Darreau, and the family eventually moved to Marseilles, France. Charles was an unruly child, who did not feel part of his mother's new life; several times he stowed away on ships leaving Marseilles, in an effort to return to his natural father, but each time he was discovered. As he got older, he acquired a reputation for dishonesty. A slight, small boy, he became adept at manipulating people, especially his half-brother Andre, into carrying out his plans for him.

PRISON

In his late teens, Sobhraj left home and went to Paris, where he was arrested for burglary in 1963 and sentenced to three years in prison. This could have been a nightmare experience, but Sobhraj's talents for manipulating people – plus his martial arts skills – came into their own in the prison milieu. One of the people he charmed there was a rich young prison visitor called Felix d'Escogne.

On his release from prison, Charles went to live with Felix and was introduced into a world of glamour and money. Sobhraj felt in his element, and married an elegant young woman, Chantal. However, in order to keep up in this world he had to have money, and the only way he knew of getting money was to steal it. He began to burgle his wealthy friends' houses and write bad cheques. Finally, with his wife, he fled France. The couple spent the remainder of the 1960s scamming their way across eastern

Europe and the Middle East before settling down in Bombay, India. Chantal gave birth to their son during this time.

MURDER

In 1971, the family had to flee India following a botched jewel robbery. They went to Kabul, Afghanistan, for a while. Here Charles specialized in robbing hippies who were passing through. However, by now Chantal had had enough and she returned to Paris with their son. Charles went back to his wanderings, accompanied for a while by his brother Andre. Their partnership ended in a Greek jail from which Charles managed to escape, leaving his brother behind. Soon Charles found a new partner, Marie Leclerc, who fell madly in love with him. They moved to Thailand and set up home in the beach resort of Pattaya. Gradually Sobhraj built up an entourage around him, reminiscent of the 'Family' set up by Charles Manson.

It was at this time that Sobhraj started to add murder to robbery. His first victim was an American called Jennie Bollivar. She was found dead in a tide pool in the warm waters of the Gulf of Thailand, wearing a bikini.

At first it looked like an accident, but the autopsy revealed that she must have died by being held under the water. The next victim was a young Sephardic Jew,

Vitali Hakim, who was robbed, beaten and set on fire.

A pair of Dutch students, Henk Bintanja and his fiancée, Cornelia 'Cocky' Hemker, were next, both strangled and their bodies burnt. At that point, a friend of Hakim's, Charmaine Carrou, came looking for him. Like Bollivar, she was drowned in her bikini, causing the murderer to be branded the 'bikini killer'.

▲ *Nicknamed 'The Serpent', Sobhraj killed for profit*

▲ *During his trial Sobhraj was always careful to cover his face in some way as presumably he assumed that one day he would be released: an eventuality that is unlikely*

DISCOVERY

After reports of the murders in the Thai press, Sobhraj decided to lie low for a while. He flew to Nepal, where he met and murdered another couple, Laddie Duparr and Annabella Tremont, then left the country using the dead man's passport.

Back in Bangkok, some of Sobhraj's erstwhile followers had found a stash of passports in his office and suspected him of murder. Sobhraj fled back to Nepal using Henk Bintanja's passport, then fled again to Calcutta, India, where he carried out another murder, that of an Israeli called Avoni Jacob. A bewildering series of moves followed, until he eventually returned to Thailand. By now the fuss had died down, and Sobhraj was able to bribe his way out of trouble. He soon went back to robbing and killing tourists,

until the heat built up again and he returned to India in 1976, where he was finally arrested for the murder of a Frenchman.

When he was brought to trial, two of his associates testified against him. However, he was sentenced to only twelve years in prison. Once there, he began to live a life of luxury: special food, drugs and books were brought in to him, and he was free to spend his time more or less as he pleased. In 1986 he contrived a daring escape, but soon afterwards gave himself up to police in Goa. He realized that he needed to go back to prison in order to avoid being extradited to Thailand, where he would have faced the death penalty.

Finally, after twenty-one years in captivity (by which time, under Thai law, he could no longer be charged for his crimes), he was released from prison and deported to France. There he sold the rights to his story and enjoyed living off his notoriety. For a while, it looked as though he had actually managed to get away with murder.

However, in 2003, for reasons that remain inexplicable, Sobhraj returned to Nepal, where he was arrested. He was charged with the murders of Duparr and Tremont, and sentenced to life imprisonment – a sentence that he is currently appealing against.

Richard SPECK

In a nurses' hostel in Chicago in the early hours of 14 July 1966, Richard Speck was responsible for what was later called 'the most bestial rampage in the city's history.' If he hadn't been so bad at counting and so expert at tying knots, the good-looking 24-year-old sailor might never have been caught.

Just before midnight on July 13th, a twenty-three-year-old nurse called Corazon Amurao opened her door to find a strange man wearing a dark jacket and trousers and smelling of alcohol pointing a gun at her. He forced her at gunpoint into another room where three other nurses were sleeping. Soon nine nurses were gathered together and herded into a bedroom, where the unknown man cut bed sheets into strips with a knife as they lay on the floor, and then bound and gagged them. He said that he wouldn't harm them, he only wanted money, but when that had all been collected, he sat on the bed looking at them, fingering his knife.

Then, one by one, he took seven of them out of the room to various parts of the building and knifed or strangled them to death. For the last one – or so he thought – he reserved special treatment: he raped and sodomised her where she lay for twenty-five minutes before killing her.

He'd forgotten, however, about Corazon Amurao, who'd hidden herself during one of his absences under a bunk bed. After he'd left and when she thought it finally safe to move, she managed to get outside to a balcony and scream for help.

When the police arrived, they found mutilated corpses, mayhem, bedrooms awash with blood. But they also had a witness who could give them a description. The killer, she said, was pock-marked; had a tattoo on his arm with the words 'Born to raise hell;' and had talked about needing money to get to New Orleans. This – together with the square knots he'd used to tie up his

◀ *Richard Speck went on a 'bestial rampage'*

▲ *Speck on trial – he was found guilty of first-degree murder*

victims – immediately suggested to the police that he might be a seaman. And half a block away was the hiring hall of the National Maritime Union.

They soon discovered that a man answering to Ms. Amurao's description had visited the hiring hall enquiring about a ship to New Orleans, and had filled out an application form in the name of Richard E. Speck. There was a photograph and a contact number, which turned out to belong to Speck's sister. With a positive ID from Corazon Amurao in hand, they called Speck's sister with the offer of a job. But though Speck himself called back within half an hour, he never turned up for the 'interview.' So

detectives started scouring sailors' haunts – hotels, flophouses and bars – across the city.

They quickly came across Speck's tracks: a hotel where he'd picked up two prostitutes on the night after the murders; another he'd checked out from half an hour before they came. He was finally arrested only after they'd named him as their chief suspect and released his description and photograph to the media. For a surgeon at Cook County Hospital, examining an emergency patient who'd been admitted after slashing his wrists, remembered a tattoo he'd read about in his newspaper that day.

Richard Speck was tried and sentenced – first to death, then after commutation to several centuries in prison – for first-degree murder. The seaman – who had regularly worked the ore-barges in the Great Lakes – had a record of violence towards women and may have killed several times before the attack on the hostel. There had been a rash of unsolved murders in Benton Harbor, Michigan earlier that year when Speck was in the area, and another in Monmouth, Illinois, where he'd gone to stay with his brother. And on July 2nd 1966, twelve days before the massacre of the nurses, three girls who'd been swimming in Indiana Harbour had disappeared. Their likely killer had been found.

STARKWEATHER and FUGATE

The case of Charles Starkweather and Caril Fugate is a fascinating if shocking one. Charles Starkweather, a rebellious nineteen-year-old, modelled himself on James Dean. Caril Fugate was his underage girlfriend. Together, they went on an unprecedented killing spree, murdering family members, friends, strangers and anyone else who got in their way. Eventually, the law caught up with them and they were found guilty of a string of murders. Starkweather was sentenced to death; being only fourteen at the time of her conviction, Caril Fugate's sentence was commuted to life imprisonment. Just why the pair suddenly showed such unbelievable brutality to a series of innocent victims, leaving a trail of bloodshed behind them wherever they went, remains to this day something of a mystery.

REPUTATION FOR VIOLENCE

Charles Starkweather hailed from Nebraska, and was one of seven children. His family was poor but seemingly settled. However, when he went to school he was teased and became oversensitive, often getting into fights with other boys in his class. The frenzied nature of his attacks was remarkable, and by the time he was a teenager, he had developed a reputation for violence. He and his close friend Bob Von Busch idolized the film star James Dean, imitating their hero down to the last detail, a pose that impressed Barbara Fugate, Bob's girlfriend, and her younger sister Caril.

Charles was not a very intelligent young man, but this did not bother the young, impressionable Caril, who was herself none too bright. The pair started going out together, despite the fact that Caril was only thirteen. Soon it became clear that Charles was besotted with his new girlfriend, boasting that he was going to marry her and that she was pregnant with his child – a claim that, even though untrue, did not endear him greatly to Caril's parents.

FATAL ROBBERY

Starkweather left school aged sixteen and began work at a newspaper warehouse. However, he soon gave up the job, and took on work as a garbage man, mainly so that he could see more of Caril after she came out of school. He had moved out of his family home into a rooming house, but now found he could not pay the rent. He became increasingly frustrated by his life of poverty, and felt trapped in a

▲ *Charles Starkweather and Caril Fugate caught in a family snap before they began their murderous career of mayhem*

situation that seemed to hold no future for him or his girlfriend. Finally, his patience snapped when he was refused credit to buy Caril a stuffed toy animal at a gas station, and he decided to take matters into his own hands.

At 3am on a freezing cold night in December 1957, Starkweather returned to the gas station. There he robbed the attendant who had previously refused him credit, Robert Colville, took him out to a deserted area and shot him.

His next crime was even more unbelievable. He drove to Caril's house

and, after a violent altercation, shot her mother Velda Bartlett, her stepfather Marion Bartlett and stabbed her baby half-sister Betty Jean to death. Then he dragged Velda's body to the toilet outside, put Marion's in the chicken coop and stuffed the baby's into a garbage box. When Caril returned home from school, the pair cleaned up the blood and spent several days in the family home doing as they pleased. Visitors to the house were told to go away because everyone 'had the flu'. By the time the police investigated, the couple were on the run. The first victim they killed together was August Meyer, a bachelor of seventy-two who had been a family friend of the Starkweathers for many years. They shot him, hid his body in an outhouse and made off with his guns. They then hitched a ride with teenagers Robert Jensen and Carol King. They shot Jensen repeatedly in the head, while King was stabbed to death and left naked from the waist down.

HOSTAGE OR ACCOMPLICE?

The couple's next stop was a wealthy part of town where Starkweather had once collected garbage. They called on Clara Ward and her maid Lillian Fencl. Starkweather ordered Mrs Ward to make breakfast for them before stabbing her to death. When her husband came home, a fight ensued and he was killed.

Finally, the maid was tied to a bed and stabbed to death. The pair then made off in the Wards' black Packard. On their journey, just for good measure, they shot a travelling shoe salesman, Merle Collison.

Finally, after a car chase, police arrested Starkweather and Fugate in Wyoming. To protect herself, Fugate alleged that she had been taken hostage by Starkweather. In response, Starkweather claimed that some of the murders were her doing. No one believed their stories; both were tried

for murder and both were found guilty.

Starkweather was sentenced to death and Fugate, because of her age, received a life sentence. Their extraordinary story, which seemed motivated not just by extreme violence but also by a curiously child-like lack of intelligence, inspired several successful Hollywood movies.

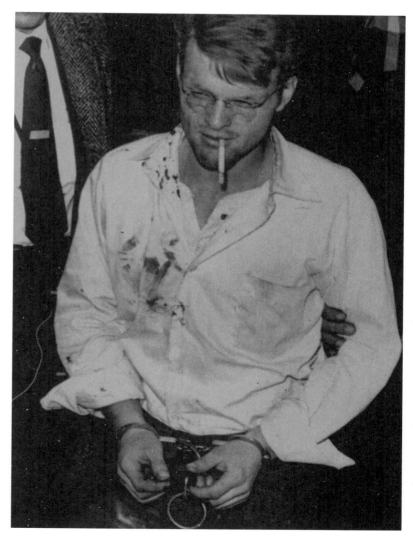

▼ *James Dean to the end – Starkweather did not give up the pose even in custody*

Peter SUTCLIFFE

No one could quite believe that the softly spoken, scrupulously polite Peter Sutcliffe was the 'Yorkshire Ripper', responsible for the brutal murders of at least thirteen women, plus seven others left hideously wounded. His wife Sonia could not, nor his parents, John and Kathleen. Nor, for a long time, could the police. After all, they had interviewed him no less than nine times in connection with the case before he was finally caught.

There was little in Peter Sutcliffe's childhood to point to his subsequent evil career as Britain's most notorious serial killer since Jack the Ripper. He was born in Bingley, Yorkshire, on 2 June 1946. He was much closer to his mother than his father, and was an effeminate child with little interest in sports. There was also a tension between his parents, his father suspecting his mother of having an affair. Conceivably, this may have inclined Sutcliffe to be suspicious of women.

SHY OF WOMEN

Certainly, Sutcliffe was shy of women and did not have a girlfriend until he was nineteen and met Sonia, the daughter of Czech immigrants. They began to go out together and eventually married eight years later. Meanwhile, Peter worked at a series of jobs. For a while he was a gravedigger. He liked to steal trophies from the bodies he buried, and horrified his workmates with his persistent references to necrophilia. Evidently there was already something seriously disturbed about Peter Sutcliffe's fantasy life. This was also hinted at by his fondness for visiting a wax museum that specialized in macabre displays of dead bodies.

Peter and Sonia married on 10 August 1974. Shortly afterwards, in June 1975, he qualified as a long-distance lorry driver. Then he learnt that, following a miscarriage, Sonia would not be able to have children. The following month, he carried out his first attack on a woman. He assaulted Anna Rogulskyj, hitting her over the head with a hammer and then slashing her body with a knife. She survived the attack, as did Sutcliffe's second victim, Olive Smelt. Both women were severely injured and utterly traumatized.

TRADEMARK INJURIES

Sutcliffe's next victim was unluckier. Wilma McCann, a Leeds prostitute he attacked in October 1975, was his first victim to die, killed by his trademark combination of hammer blows and knife wounds. However, police did not link this crime with the two previous attacks. Murders of prostitutes have traditionally been treated by both police and public with a lack of urgency. Thus, when Sutcliffe's next three victims, killed over an eighteen-month period, all turned out to be Leeds-based prostitutes, the general public was scandalized, but not yet terrified.

All that changed on 16 June 1977. This time, the victim was a sixteen-year-old schoolgirl named Jayne MacDonald. Distastefully, the papers referred to her as the first 'innocent' victim, but, by this time, the whole of the north of England was now on alert that the Yorkshire Ripper was a menace to all women.

Over the next three years, Sutcliffe killed eight more women and severely injured several more. Some were prostitutes and some were not. The crimes were carried out at various locations around the north of England. As the death toll increased, the Yorkshire Ripper, as he was now known, became the target of one of the biggest police investigations ever mounted in Britain.

Various clues were found. The Ripper had size seven or eight shoes; he drove a certain kind of car; he had type B blood; he left a new banknote at one crime scene

▲ *Sutcliffe came close to being arrested more than once, but police were misled by what turned out to be false clues*

that could be traced to the payroll of his employer. All this information pointed to Sutcliffe, which is why he was repeatedly interviewed by the police. Each time, however, he was so pleasant, and so plausible in his excuses, that the police let him go. The situation was not helped by numerous pieces of false information that were circulating about the Ripper. The voice on a tape believed to be from him had a north-east accent that did not tally with Sutcliffe's way of speaking.

FINALLY CAUGHT

Finally, however, the law caught up with Sutcliffe. On 2 January 1981, he was apprehended while sitting in a car with a prostitute in the south Yorkshire city of Sheffield.

The policeman checked his car registration and found that the car had false number plates. He arrested Sutcliffe, though not before Sutcliffe had hidden a hammer and knife he had been carrying.

While in custody, Sutcliffe's history as a Ripper suspect surfaced. The arresting officer decided to go back to the crime scene, and found the weapons Sutcliffe had hidden. At this point, Sutcliffe realized the game was up and began to confess. His five-year reign of terror was at an end.

Sutcliffe was sentenced to life imprisonment on thirteen counts of murder. Soon afterwards, psychiatrists pronounced him insane and he was transferred to Broadmoor. While in prison he has been attacked several times, culminating in a 1997 assault in which he lost the sight in one eye.

▶ *Some of Sutcliffe's victims. Top row, left to right: Vera Millward, Jayne MacDonald, Josephine Whittaker. Bottom row, left to right: Jean Royle, Helga Rytka and Barbara Leach*

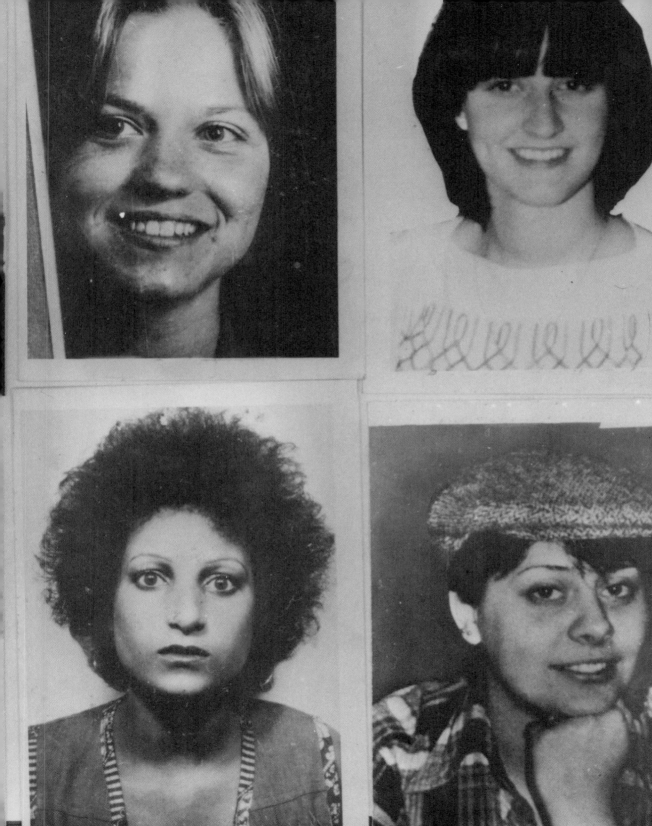

Chester TURNER

For such a large and crime-ridden city, Los Angeles has not perhaps seen quite as many serial killers as other American cities. For years its most prolific serial killers were Michael Player, the 'Skid Row Slayer', convicted of killing ten transients in the downtown area in 1986, and Douglas Clark, the 'Sunset Strip Killer', found guilty of half a dozen murders in 1980.

During the 1980s' crime wave, annual homicide figures sometimes topped a thousand a year. Perhaps this stark statistic acted as a smokescreen, which hindered police from apprehending, or even suspecting, that from 1987 onwards there was a killer at work who would eventually become one of the most prolific serial killers in the history of the city. All this changed when in 2001 the Los Angeles Police Department (LAPD) Cold Case Unit began looking at a single unsolved homicide, thanks in no small part to the use of a DNA record system and testing. In fact, the technology not only led officers to a prime suspect, it also freed an innocent man.

THE FIGUEROA STREET STRANGLER

Chester Dewayne Turner was not a native Californian, having been born in Warren, Arkansas, in 1968. When he was five his parents separated and his mother moved out west to live with her own father, taking her son with her. She worked hard to provide for him, holding down two jobs for much of his childhood. Turner was a pupil at 97th Street Elementary School and Gompers Middle School before dropping out of Locke High in his mid-teens. By this point he had grown to six foot two, and had a naturally heavy-set physique. His appearance was, by all accounts, intimidating and very noticeable.

After school, Turner went on to work for Domino's Pizza, where he began to carve out a promising career for himself, first as a delivery boy, then as a cook, and finally as a trainee manager. He then appears to have turned, quite suddenly, to a life of crime. From that point on, he spent the rest of his life in and out of jail, for a series of offences ranging from drug possession to theft. As time went on, Turner's life became more and more chaotic, as his drug use spiralled and his law-breaking became more frequent. He flitted from place to place, but always staying within the same small area, living in homeless shelters, at the apartments of women friends and at his mother's house. When Turner's mother moved to Salt Lake City, Utah, in 1991, he went to live with her there on several occasions despite the fact that by this stage he was spending an increasing amount of time in prison.

After his first felony conviction for car theft in 1995, Turner returned to prison seven times, and these periods always coincided with a lull in murders taking place in and around the area where he lived. When he got out, they would start up again within a few weeks but at the time, however, nobody noticed.

In 2002, Turner was convicted of rape, the first violent crime on his record, and sentenced to eight years. After that, the killings stopped entirely. Again, nobody noticed, but it was this conviction that required him to give a DNA sample, and so began his journey on the long road to justice.

THE KILLING YEARS

Beginning in the late 1980s, a series of murders occurred in the same small area where Turner lived, within a couple of blocks either side of Figueroa Street, between Gage Avenue and 108th Street, a stretch itself of no more than a few dozen blocks. The thirteen murders began in 1987 and ended in 1998, most of them involving women who were involved in prostitution or were homeless, although some were just passers-by with the terrible luck to have been in the wrong place at the wrong time. The roll call of the dead is a long one.

In March 1987, the body of a twenty-one-year-old woman named Diane Johnson was spotted on the road by passing motorists. She was found strangled, and partially nude. In October that same year, Annette Ernest, twenty-six, met the same fate. Two years later, police received a call about a dead body in an alleyway. It turned out to be Anita Fishman, aged thirty-one. Again, she was found strangled and partially nude. In September the same year, the body of 27-year-old Regina Washington was discovered in the garage of an empty house. She was six months pregnant at the time. She had been asphyxiated.

In 1992 there were three murders in the area: Debra Williams, Mary Edwards, and Tammie Christmas, were found in September, November and December respectively. In early April the following year, the body of Andrea Tripplett, twenty-nine, was found by a builder. Only a month later, Desarae Jones, also twenty-nine, was killed. In 1995, there was Natalie Price, thirty-one; in 1996, Mildred Beasley, forty-five; and in 1997, Brenda Bries, thirty-seven. All were found strangled and in a state of undress.

The final victim was Paula Vance, forty-one, who was murdered in February 1998. It was this killing that put police on Turner's trail. It was recorded by no less than five different security cameras, each capturing various stages of the crime, but in each case, the camera panned away before the killer could be fully revealed; frustratingly, another second and the man's face would have come into view. As it was, all the police had to go on was a bulky silhouette.

CODIS AND THE COLD CASE UNIT

In 2001 LAPD detective Cliff Shephard became a member of the city's Cold Case Unit. He had over nine thousand unsolved homicides to choose from, but a specific brief to focus on those which were sexually motivated, and it was perhaps that tantalising silhouette that attracted him to the Vance murder. He had worked that part of town earlier in his career, and had always believed there were several serial killers in the area, although his hunch had never developed into a full-scale investigation.

Shephard's first step was to have the semen recovered from Vance's body sent to the laboratory for testing. The Serology Section of the LAPD's Scientific Investigation Division

◄ Turner's mother worked hard to provide for her son, and he appeared to start off well in life. However, he then turned to crime, and never looked back

performed the extractions and made sure the resulting profiles were uploaded to the FBI-administered Combined DNA Identification System (CODIS) that is being compiled across the country. Then Shephard and his partner walked the streets again, as he had done before, as a beat cop, looking for registered sex offenders in the neighbourhood and handing out flyers. He spread the news that the Vance investigation was open again, in public and throughout the department, and made sure to consult other parts of the LAPD that might help him, like the Robbery-Homicide Division's special rape section. He even took the security camera footage to Paramount Studios where they enlarged it on a massive screen.

However, all this got him nowhere, at least initially. In deep frustration, he had almost decided to move on to another case when a call came back from the lab. The DNA from Vance matched that of a man already serving an eight-year sentence in California State Prison: Chester Dewayne Turner. As the suspect was already off the streets he posed no further immediate threat to the public, so Shephard was able to take the time to investigate the matter thoroughly. More samples from countless other homicides were fed into the computer, and CODIS crunched the numbers. Soon, another match came back

(this one for Mildred Beasley); and then another; and then another.

'The number kept on growing,' Shephard said. 'We hit five, and thought, "Where are we going to end?"' All in all, this further testing took almost another year, as the detectives looked on in amazement. Eventually it peaked at thirteen. In October 2004, the police pressed charges against Turner.

ANOTHER VICTIM?

Cliff Shephard had been with the LAPD for thirty years by the time he was investigating Turner. Unofficially, some colleagues might say this made him a bit set in his ways. Certainly, there were not many officers who would have checked Turner's DNA not just against unsolved murders but also against solved ones. Yet had he not, Dave Allen Jones would never have been exonerated of the murders of Debra Williams, Mary Edwards and Tammie Christmas.

Jones was a retarded part-time janitor with low IQ and a mental age of eight, who had incriminated himself while being interviewed (people like Jones frequently incriminate themselves under police questioning; the University of Chicago Law Review found that ninety-eight per cent of people with a low IQ or some form of mental disability believed they would be penalized in some way if they did not talk). His low IQ was further confirmed by the fact that when Jones signed his first letter for appeal, which was written for him by a fellow inmate, he misspelt his own first name.

However, thanks to DNA testing, it became clear that Jones was wrongly convicted of the murders. 'What's unusual here,' said Jones' lawyer, 'is that after he had his man and after he had found crimes that Mr Jones could not have done, he took that extra step. He suspended his own disbelief that such a mistake could happen and pursued it. And for that, Mr Jones and I have nothing but gratitude,' Gordon said.

Chester Dewayne Turner was charged with the murder of ten women in Los Angeles. On 30 April 2007, he was convicted on every charge and he was also found guilty of causing the death of one of his victim's unborn foetus. He was sentenced to death on 15 May 2007.

As for Jones, after investigations showed that his blood did not match the blood types found at the scenes of crimes for which he had served 11 years behind bars, he was exonerated as a murderer and released from prison. He has also filed a law suit against the City of Los Angeles which has still not been resolved at the time of writing.

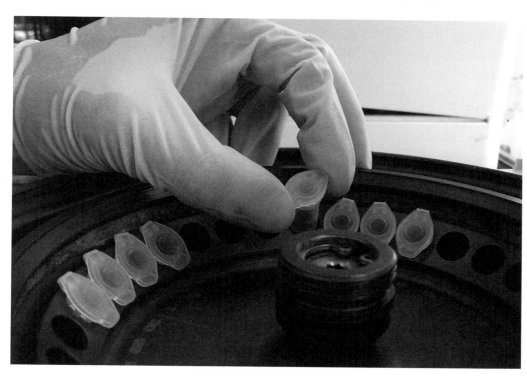

◄ *Thanks to DNA testing, Jones was eventually cleared*

Jack Unterweger was an Austrian serial killer who achieved notoriety not only as a murderer but also as a literary celebrity. While he was committing a string of murders both in Austria and in the US, he was also enjoying fame and fortune as a writer, and even took to posing as an investigative journalist, publishing articles about the serial killer at large. Convicted of murder as a young man, and imprisoned for life, Unterweger somehow persuaded the authorities that he was a reformed character and was let out of jail, only to murder again and again until he was finally brought to justice. What had impressed the parole board was that he had worked so hard to educate himself in prison; however, his education was shown to have meant nothing in terms of improving his criminal behaviour, as was all too sadly revealed after his release.

Unterweger was born in 1952 in Austria. His mother, Theresia, was a prostitute, and he never knew his father. Theresia did not want to look after her son, and left him in the care of his grandfather, an alcoholic. The circumstances of Jack's childhood left him with a violent temper and an abiding hatred of women, especially prostitutes. As a young adult, he began to steal cars, break into houses and offices and to act as a pimp. In 1974, he raped and killed an eighteen-year-old girl called Margaret Schaefer, beating her to death and strangling her with her bra. He claimed that the victim was a prostitute, but there was little evidence to show that this was the case. Questioned by police, Unterweger confessed what had happened, adding that as he beat Schaefer, he had imagined that it was his mother he was attacking. He was brought to trial, convicted of murder and given a life sentence.

STRANGLED WITH UNDERWEAR

While in prison, Unterweger transformed himself from an ignorant, illiterate thug into an educated young man. He learned to read and write, edited a prison newspaper and read highbrow literature. He also began to write poems, plays and short stories, and in 1984 completed an autobiography called *Purgatory* about his life in prison. The book became a bestseller and, together with some of his other writings, helped make a name for him in the literary world. His newfound career also helped him to gain credibility as a reformed character. In 1990, after a

press campaign to set him free, he was released from prison.

In the months after his release, Austria found itself in the grip of panic. A serial killer was on the loose. The killings began in 1990, when a woman named Blanka Bockova was found beaten and strangled by a river. She was not a prostitute but worked at a butcher shop in Prague, Czechoslovakia, and had last been seen in a bar, talking to a man who none of her friends knew. A few weeks later, a prostitute identified as Brunhilde Masser disappeared from her home in

Graz. Not long afterwards, Heidemarie Hammerer, also a prostitute, vanished from where she lived in Bregenz. Both Masser's and Hammerer's bodies were later found; like Bockova's, the women appeared to have been strangled with their own underwear, and their bodies covered with leaves.

A BLAST FROM THE PAST

The next victims were prostitute Elfriede Schrempf, whose body was discovered in a forest outside Graz, and four prostitutes from Vienna: Silvia Zangler, Sabine Moitzi, Regina Prem and Karin Eroglu. All the corpses were left naked, wearing only their jewellery, and all had been strangled or suffocated with their underwear. Despite mounting evidence that the murders were linked, police were reluctant to admit that a serial killer was at large, until the man who had brought Unterweger to justice for his first murder intervened.

August Schenner had by now retired, but he told the police the circumstances of Unterweger's initial conviction, and also expressed his fears that, at around the same time, Unterweger had murdered another prostitute called Marcia Horveth, whose strangled body had been discovered near Salzburg. This was a crime that Unterweger had never been charged with because he was already in jail, supposedly for life, for the murder of Schaefer.

By the time Schenner caught up with him, Unterweger had become something of a celebrity in Austria. He was making good money as a media pundit; in particular, he liked to cover stories on the Austrian serial killer, now known as 'The Courier'. He drove flashy cars, dressed snappily in white suits and was tremendously popular with women.

THE EDUCATED PSYCHOPATH

As the investigation began, Unterweger made a trip to Los Angeles, where shortly after his arrival three prostitutes were found strangled with their bras. American and Austrian police began to liaise, building up a powerful case against him. Aware that police were now on his trail, Unterweger and his girlfriend, eighteen-year-old Bianca Mrak, fled to Miami, where the police eventually caught up with them.

Unterweger was arrested there and later tried in Graz, Austria. In a sensational trial, he was convicted of nine murders and sentenced to life imprisonment. Shortly afterwards, he hanged himself in his cell. Thus ended the career of a psychopath all the more deadly for being intelligent, educated and self-motivated.

Faryion WARDRIP

Terry Sims was found dead in her apartment in Wichita Falls, Texas, in the December of 1984. The next spring, the naked body of Toni Gibbs was found lying in a scrub-brush field by an electrician checking a malfunctioning transformer, and in the late summer of that same year, the naked corpse of Ellen Blau was discovered in a ditch by a county employee mowing the verges of a country road.

Sims' murder was investigated by the Wichita Falls City Police. Gibbs' body was discovered a stone's throw over the county line, and was investigated by the Archer County Sheriff's Department. Blau was found outside the city limits, and the murder was investigated by the local sheriff.

Three dead bodies and three different law enforcement agencies. None of them shared notes or other information, nor did they pool resources and work collectively. The murders were not seen as being related and each agency had their own suspect. The city police thought Sims' killer was a co-worker; in Archer County they believed that Gibbs was

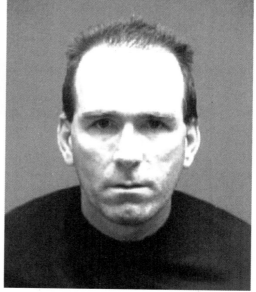

◀ *Faryion Wardrip, a non-descript looking man: a fact that helped protect him as people found him to be likeable and trustworthy*

murdered by her admirer Danny Laughlin. The Wichita Falls sheriff focused his attentions on Blau's former boyfriend. Of the three suspects, only Laughlin was ever charged, and a jury acquitted him eleven to one. The three cases went cold. It was years later before anyone realized that they might have been connected.

BRICKLAYER TURNS SLEUTH

John Little had always wanted to be a policeman, but he failed the medical due to poor eyesight. Instead he went into construction, and gained a reputation as an adept and reliable bricklayer – although his heart was never in it. After several attempts he succeeded in realizing his dream in 1993, and became part of the District Attorney's investigative team.

It was December 1998, almost fourteen years to the day after Terry Sims was murdered, when DA Barry Macha admitted to Little that he had come to see the three unsolved murders as a stain on his career. He asked Little to look into it. Perhaps something had been missed.

For John Little, it was not just a regular investigation. He could remember the night he found out Toni Gibbs had gone missing. He remembered telling his wife, who had been friends with Gibbs at college. When the police asked for volunteers to help the search parties he had stepped forward, and brought his brother with him. They had spent the whole day on foot, a silent group of solemn strangers, their eyes peeled to the ground, braced for the worst. But they had found nothing. Eventually, several weeks later an electrician had stumbled upon Gibbs' corpse in the course of a routine repair.

Although Little never told Bracha this, the murders had never been far from his mind. Over the years he had found himself taking solitary drives to sites that were connected with them, hoping something might jog his memory, or get him thinking. Now that he was on the case, it was plain old diligence that got him on the right track. Little went through the three files and made lists of every name that came up or could come up in each one, and then compared lists to see if any of them reappeared. One name

came up three times, and after a brief records check, the former bricklayer knew he was onto something.

THE PREACHER WITH A PAST

Faryion Wardrip was living in Olney, Texas, when John Little made the connection. He had gained a reputation as a conscientious worker and taught Sunday school at his local chapel. A well-known figure in the parish, he hoped to begin training as a Baptist preacher. But Wardrip was a preacher with a past. If you looked closely, you could see an electronic monitoring bracelet around his ankle. Clearly, Wardrip was on parole for a serious crime. If parishioners asked, he usually told them he had been serving a manslaughter sentence for killing his girlfriend in a drink-driving accident. Sometimes he would say he got into a bar-room brawl and ended up killing a man. As his family would later put it, 'Faryion is one of those people who would climb a tree to tell a lie when it was just as easy to stand on the ground and tell the truth.' Even in his youth in Marion, Indiana, where he was a school dropout, Wardrip had lied extensively. Later, he would boast about the glory of his military days, although the truth was that he had been discharged from the army for drug use.

But as it turned out, Wardrip really did have something to hide. He had been

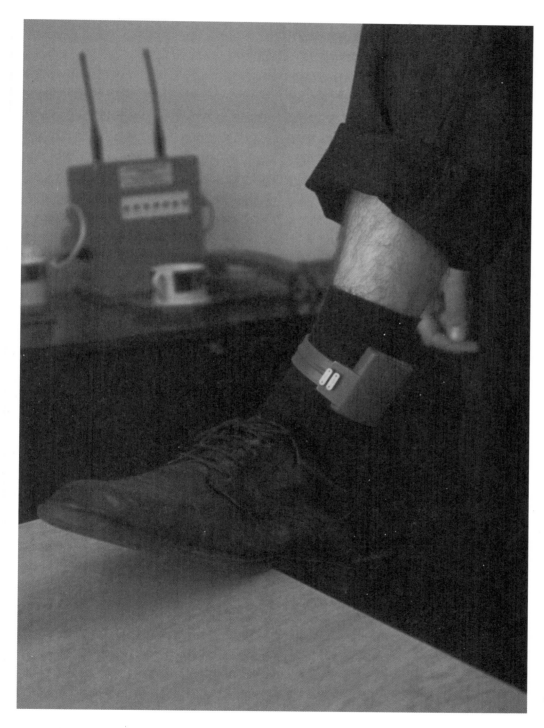

◀ *Tagged but unrepentent: by apparently turning to God, Wardrop literally talked his way out of jail — allowing him to rape and murder again*

convicted in 1986 of murdering a female friend, Tina Kimbrew, and sentenced to thirty-five years.

Kimbrew's parents had campaigned to secure a life sentence, but the Texas Department of Criminal Justice had launched a new Victim Offender Dialogue programme, and the family was asked if they wanted to participate. The idea was to give a victim's family an opportunity to question the criminal who had killed their loved one, about their reasons; about the crime; about anything. Wardrip, who claimed to have found God while he was behind bars, was keen to get talking.

After a five-hour session, Robert Kimbrew was so convinced that Wardrip was full of remorse, that his opinions changed. 'When you get out of here,' he said to the supposedly penitent Wardrip, 'if you find yourself headed for trouble again, and you run out of other people to turn to for help, you can call me.' Thanks in no small part to the results of this new dialogue programme, Wardrip was paroled in 1993. Tina's father had expressed admirable Christian sentiments, but he was wrong about Wardrip. Wardrip had not told him the full story, by any means.

A STOLEN COFFEE CUP
Semen samples had been collected from the bodies of Terry Sims and Toni Gibbs when their bodies had been autopsied; Ellen Blau's body had been in such a severe state of decomposition when it was found that it offered practically no physical evidence. In a police laboratory archive the samples were kept carefully, until such time as forensic technology would develop to a level where it might become useful. In 1996, DNA profiling became part of the law enforcement programme in Texas. It showed that Gibbs and Sims had been raped (and almost certainly killed) by the same man.

It seemed obvious that a DNA sample from the suspect was the lynchpin upon which a successful prosecution would depend, but for legal reasons the district attorney argued that simply asking for a sample would be a waste of time.

Then again, if the sample had been obtained without the suspect's consent, this might give the defence lawyer a shot at throwing the case out of court. So the detectives had to come up with another plan.

Little trailed Wardrip for weeks, in plain clothes, in a borrowed car. Being careful not to draw attention to himself, he learnt the details of Wardrip's daily routine, even the habits of his second wife. He found out what day the Wardrips did their laundry on, and spent the whole day in the launderette they frequented, washing the same clothes over and over again. That was when he got his chance. The suspect arrived in his car and parked outside, and Little saw that he was finishing a cup of takeaway coffee. Wardrip was about to throw it away. Thinking quickly, the investigator filled his mouth with a wad of chewing tobacco and approached the suspect:

'Do you mind if I have your cup?'
'My cup?'
'Yeah, for a spit cup.'
'Help yourself.'

Their little verbal exchange was a piece of legal chicanery that meant under an 'abandoned interest' law, any samples taken from the cup would be entirely admissible in court. Back in the lab, working on a trace of Wardrip's saliva, everyone awaited the results with some eagerness. Everyone apart from John Little; he was already convinced.

A FIFTH VICTIM

Armed with a positive DNA match from the saliva, Little collected Wardrip and brought him to the DA's office. It was the day before Wardrip was due to read at church. Wardrip was hopeful at first that the meeting might be about the removal of his surveillance anklet, and he was right, in a sense. He would not need one where he was going.

The police confronted him with the incontrovertible evidence that Little had collected. Within minutes, Wardrip had confessed. While he was not forthcoming on the details, and made a string of excuses for himself, he admitted to the murder of Terry Lee Sims, a twenty-one-year-old student; Toni Gibbs, a twenty-three-year-old general nurse at the hospital where he had once worked; and Ellen Blau, another student, a year older than Sims. Then came a shock: Wardrip added that he would like to confess to the murder of housewife Debra Taylor in Fort Worth in March 1985, a twenty-six-year-old mother of two. The police had never considered him a suspect for this murder.

As the interview concluded, Wardrip was asked for the record, as is routine, if he had been promised anything in return for making his statement.

'Eternal life with God,' was his answer. 'I was promised I wouldn't burn in hell.'

In November 1999 Faryion Wardrip was sentenced to death by lethal injection. Whoever promised him he would not burn in hell is a matter of speculation, but the promise that he was about to meet his maker cannot have been of much comfort to him, for within months, and perhaps unsurprisingly, he was trying to bring an appeal against the court's decision.

Fred and Rosemary WEST

The crimes of Fred and Rosemary West utterly shocked the people of Britain when they emerged in 1994. It was not simply that nine bodies were found buried under the couple's house in Gloucester. It was not that one of the bodies belonged to their own daughter, Heather. It was not even the discovery of other bodies belonging to Fred West's first wife and child. What was almost unbearable for people to accept was that this bloody carnage had taken place in an apparently normal family home, a place full of children and visitors, presided over by a happily married couple.

VIRTUALLY ILLITERATE

To understand the crimes of the Wests one has, as so often in such cases, to go back to their early childhoods. Fred West was one of six children born to Walter and Daisy West in 1941, in Much Marcle on the edge of the Forest of Dean. At the time, the village was a very poor rural backwater. Fred was very close to his mother. He claimed that his father sexually abused his sisters, though whether this was actually the case is not known. He did badly at school and was virtually illiterate when he left, aged fifteen. He worked, like his father and grandfather before him, as a farmhand. At the age of seventeen he had a serious motorbike accident in which he sustained a head injury – a common factor in the backgrounds of a large number of serial killers. Two years later, he was arrested for having sex with a thirteen-year-old girl. He managed to avoid going to prison after his lawyer told the judge that Fred suffered from epileptic fits, but his parents threw him out of the family home for a while.

A DIFFERENT STORY?

In 1962, Fred met Catherine 'Rena' Costello, a young woman with a record of delinquency and prostitution. They fell in love, moved to her native Scotland and got married, despite the fact that she was already pregnant by an Asian bus driver. The child, Charmaine, was born in 1963. The following year they had their own child, Anna Marie. They then moved back to Gloucester, where they split up. Fred took up with a friend of Rena, Anne McFall. By 1967 McFall was pregnant with Fred's child, and demanded that he divorce Rena and marry her. This provoked Fred's first murder: he killed McFall, dismembered her body and that

◀ *Fred West is taken into custody by police*

of their unborn baby, and buried them near the trailer park in which they had been living. Curiously, he cut off the tops of McFall's finger and toes before burying her. This was to become a Fred West trademark.

Following McFall's murder, Rena moved back in with Fred. During this period, he is thought to have murdered fifteen-year-old Mary Bastholm, whom he abducted from a bus stop in Gloucester. Later the couple split up again, and it was then that Fred met a young girl who turned out to be as vicious and depraved as he was.

Rosemary Letts was born in November 1953 in Devon. Her mother, Daisy Letts, suffered from severe depression. Her father, Bill Letts, was a schizophrenic who had sexually abused her. A pretty, rather

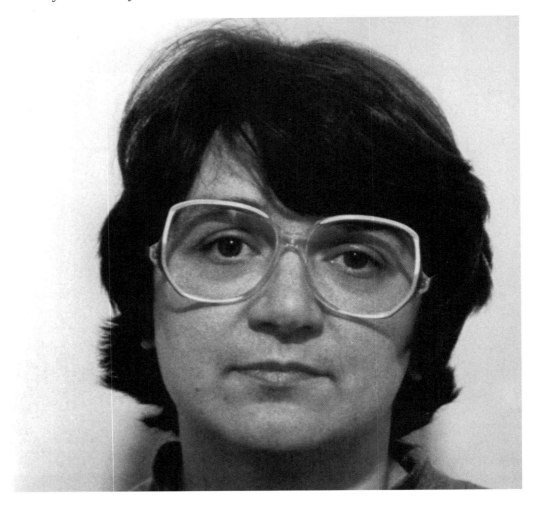

▶ *Rosemary West at first denied involvement, but the evidence was against her*

slow child, she became fat and sexually precocious as a teenager. When she met Fred West, twelve years her senior, he seemed to be the man of her dreams. Soon afterwards, however, Fred was sent to prison for non-payment of fines. By then Rose, not yet sixteen, was pregnant with his child.

When Fred came out of jail, Rose went to live with him, Charmaine and Anna Marie, and in 1970 gave birth to Heather. The following year, while Fred was once again in prison, Charmaine went missing. Rose told people that Charmaine's mother Rena had come to take her back. In fact Rose herself had murdered Charmaine while in the grip of one of the ferocious tempers her other children would become all too familiar with.

When Fred was released from prison, he buried the body of the child under the house. Not long after, Rena did indeed come looking for Charmaine. Fred killed her too, and buried her in the countryside.

In 1972, Fred and Rose married and had a second child, Mae. They moved to a house in Cromwell Street, Gloucester. There, they began to indulge in deviant sex, using the cellar of the house as a perverse sexual playpen. They even raped their own eight-year-old daughter Anna Marie there. Later that year, they employed seventeen-year-old Caroline

Owens as a nanny. Owens rejected their sexual advances – Rose by now was having sex with both men and women – so they raped her. She escaped and told the police, but when the matter came to trial in January 1973 the magistrate, appallingly, believed Fred's word over that of Owens' and let the Wests off with a fine.

At least Owens escaped with her life. Their next nanny, Lynda Gough, ended up dismembered and buried under the cellar. The following year, in which Rose gave birth to another child, Stephen, the couple murdered fifteen-year-old Carol Ann Cooper. In late December, they abducted university student Lucy Partington, tortured her for a week and then murdered, dismembered and buried her.

The Wests' perversions became ever more extreme. Over the next eighteen months they killed three more women: Therese Siegenthaler, Shirley Hubbard and Juanita Mott. Hubbard and Mott had been subjected to almost unimaginable tortures: their bodies, when exhumed, were trussed in elaborate bondage costumes. Hubbard's head had been wrapped entirely with tape, with only a plastic tube inserted in her nose to allow her to breathe.

In 1977, Rose, who was also by now working as a prostitute, became pregnant

by one of her clients. However, at around the same time, their latest lodger Shirley Robinson, an eighteen-year-old ex-prostitute, became pregnant with Fred's child. Rose was angry about this, and decided the girl had to go. In December 1977, she was murdered and, as the cellar was now full, she was buried in the back garden, along with her unborn baby.

In May 1979 the Wests killed once again. The victim this time was teenager Alison Chambers – another body for the back garden. Then, as far as is known, the Wests stopped killing for pleasure. It may be that they carried on killing and that the bodies of their victims have never been found; or it may be that they found other sources of sexual excitement.

Exactly what happened at this time is still not known for certain.

During the 1980s, Rose had three more children, two by another client, one more with Fred. She continued to work as a prostitute, specializing in ever more extreme bondage. Fred found a new interest in making videotapes of Rose having sex, and continued to abuse his daughters, until Heather told a friend about her home life. Her friend's parents told the Wests about Heather's allegation and Fred responded by killing her, the last of his known victims.

It was not until 1992 that a young girl whom the Wests had raped went to the police. On 6 August that year, police arrived at Cromwell Street with a search warrant to look for pornography and evidence of child abuse: they found plenty, and so arrested Rose for assisting in the rape of a minor. Fred was arrested for rape and sodomy of a minor. Anna Marie made a statement supporting the allegation, as did their oldest son Stephen, but following threats from the Wests they withdrew them and the case collapsed. Meanwhile, the younger children had been taken into care. While there, care assistants heard the children joke about their older sister Heather being buried under the patio. A day's digging revealed human bones – and not just Heather's. A total of nine bodies were found in the garden, and others were found elsewhere.

On 13 December 1994, Fred and Rosemary West were charged with murder. A week later, Fred hanged himself in prison with strips of bed sheet. Rose's defence tried to put the blame for the murders on Fred, but she was duly sentenced to life imprisonment.

Wayne WILLIAMS

In the early hours of May 22nd 1981, police on watch near a bridge over the Chattahoochee River in Atlanta, Georgia heard a sudden splash, and later saw a young black man driving away from the scene in a station-wagon. When they stopped the car, the driver identified himself as twenty-three-year-old Wayne Williams, a music-promoter and freelance photographer; and he was allowed to go. The police, though, remained suspicious and put Williams under surveillance; and when a body was discovered in the river two days later, they pulled him in.

The body was that of a twenty-seven-year-old black man, whom a witness later said he'd seen together with Williams, holding hands coming out of a cinema. Dog-hairs found on the corpse were found to match samples of those found in Williams' house and in his car. It was, it seemed, an open-and-shut case. But was Wayne Williams a serial killer? Had he killed twenty-six young blacks, teenagers and children in Atlanta over the past two years?

The first disappearances and discoveries had caused little fuss, given the city's high crime-rate. Two teenagers had been found dead by a lake in July 1979; another had disappeared two months later. The fourth case, it was true, had caused some to-do, since the missing nine-year-old boy was the son of a locally well-known ex-civil rights worker. But it wasn't until the number of disappearances had mounted and the bodies had begun to pile up that the police started to take serious notice.

By the time a year was over, seven young blacks had been murdered – one of them a twelve-year-old girl tied to a tree and raped – and three more were still missing. The police were by now being accused of protecting a white racist killer. A number of bereaved parents formed a group and held a press conference to say that, even if the killer was black, the police were still not doing enough, simply because none of the victims was white. The police argued back that a white person, picking up kids in black neighbourhoods, would have stood out a mile; and that the killer was probably a black teenager, someone who could get his victims' trust.

None of this, though, made any difference, for the killings went on. Within a month, two more black children had disappeared; and the body count

◀ *Was Wayne Williams a serial killer?*

kept rising. One boy went missing that September; another in the following month. Civic groups offered a reward of $100,000; special programmes were offered to keep black kids off the streets; a curfew was even imposed. But the disappearances and the number of bodies discovered continued to rise. By May 1981, there were twenty-six dead, with one black kid still missing. The police had

▲ Many felt Williams was used as a scape-goat, as much of the evidence against him was circumstantial

who said they'd seen Williams with both the men found in the river. Others came forward to say that he'd tried to have sex with them; and one of these linked him to yet another victim. The police then re-examined a number of the dead and found on eight others not only dog-hairs, but also fabric and carpet fibres that matched those in Williams's bedroom.

Williams was tried only for the murders of the two men found in the river. The evidence against him was entirely circumstantial, but it was reinforced when the judge reluctantly allowed evidence from the other murders to be admitted.

Gradually a picture of Williams was formed: the son of two schoolteachers who had grown up gifted and indulged, he had turned into a man obsessed with the idea of success – he worked on the fringes of show business. He also seemed to hate blacks, even though he regularly handed out leaflets offering blacks between the ages of eleven and twenty-one help with their musical careers.

no leads at all. They were only watching the river that night because that's where the latest victim had been found.

With Wayne Williams in custody, though, they did at least have a suspect; and, quite suddenly, they had witnesses

Wayne Williams was found guilty on both counts of murder and sentenced to two consecutive life terms. Though many believed he was a scapegoat – and had been railroaded by the police – the murders of young blacks in Atlanta stopped with his imprisonment.

Aileen WUORNOS

Aileen Wuornos has become one of the most famous of all serial killers, not because she killed a huge number of victims, nor because she killed them in an exceptionally brutal way, but because of the simple fact that she was a woman. Before her arrest, the received wisdom was that there was no such thing as a female serial killer.

This was not true. There had been many female serial killers before Wuornos, but they had mostly committed domestic murders, such as poisoning husbands or killing elderly invalids.

SEVERE BURNS

She was born Aileen Pittman in Rochester, Michigan, on 29 February 1956. Her teenage parents had split up before she was born. Her father, Leo, later became a convicted child molester. Her mother, Diane, proved unable to cope alone and, in 1960, Aileen and her brother Keith were legally adopted by Diane's parents, Lauri and Britta Wuornos. This failed to improve matters. Aged six, Aileen suffered severe burns to her face after she and her brother had been setting fires. Aged fifteen, she gave birth to a child, who was adopted.

SCHOOL DROP-OUT

Aileen dropped out of school early, left home and hit the streets. It was not long before she started to work as a prostitute. She had regular run-ins with the law,

▼ *Wuornos began talks on selling her story to Hollywood almost as soon as she was arrested*

mostly for drink-related offences. In 1986, she met lesbian Tyria Moore, who became the love of her life. Aileen and Tyria set up home together. Aileen became a notoriously belligerent individual, often in fights and always carrying a gun in her purse. In her efforts to keep Tyria happy, she supplemented her income with theft. Some time in November 1989, Aileen Wuornos went one giant step further – into murder.

Her first victim was Richard Mallory, a 51-year-old electrician whose main interests were commercial sex and drinking. Wuornos would later claim that she killed Mallory to defend herself against rape. While she went on to make this claim in regard to all her murders, in this case there may have been some truth to it, as it later emerged that Mallory had a conviction for rape.

In June 1990, the body of David Spears was found in Florida woodlands, once again shot with a .22 and this time naked. By then another victim had been found, Charles Carskaddon. The next victim was Peter Siems, who had last been seen on 7 June, heading off to visit relatives. His car was dumped by two women.

Victims five, six and seven followed in August, September and November of 1990. All of them were shot with a .22. The police were reluctant to admit that a serial killer was at large but they finally agreed to release the sketches of the women who had dumped Siems' car.

Very soon reports came in that the two women might be Aileen Wuornos and Tyria Moore. The police arrested Wuornos in a biker bar in Florida on 9 January 1991. They then found Moore at her sister's house in Philadelphia. In the interests of saving her own skin, Moore helped the police to extract a confession from Wuornos. The ploy worked. Rather than see Moore charged with murder, Wuornos confessed to six of the murders; however, she did not confess to the killing of Peter Siems, whose body has never been found to this day.

MEDIA CIRCUS

At that point, the media furore began. Film-makers and journalists vied for the rights to Wuornos' story. Some portrayed her as a monster, others as a victim. The truth of the matter seems to be that Wuornos was a woman brutalized by a miserable life, but that the murders she committed were motivated by rage.

Certainly that was the verdict of the jury that sentenced her to death on 27 January 1992. She spent ten years on death row while campaigners attempted to have the death penalty rescinded. However, Wuornos demanded that the penalty be carried out. She was executed by lethal injection on 9 October 2002.